D0815934

Index to
Best American Short Stories
and
O. Henry Prize Stories

A
Reference
Publication
in
Literature

Ron Gottesman
Editor

Index to
Best American Short Stories
and
O. Henry Prize Stories

RAY LEWIS WHITE

G.K. HALL & CO.
70 LINCOLN STREET, BOSTON, MASS.

Library of Congress Cataloging-in-Publication Data

White, Ray Lewis.
  Index to Best American short stories and O. Henry prize stories /
Ray Lewis White.
      p.   cm.—(A Reference publication in literature)
  ISBN 0-8161-8955-2
  1. Short stories, American—Bibliography.   2. Short stories,
American—Indexes.   3. Best American short stories—Indexes.
4. Prize stories—Indexes.   I. Title.   II. Series.
Z1231.F4W52   1988
[PS374.S5]
016.813'01'08—dc19   87-28112

In Honor Of
Joseph Blotner

Contents

Preface   1

Index to *Best American Short Stories*   3

     Introduction   5

     Volumes   17

     Author Index   23

Index to *Prize Stories: The O. Henry Award*s   61

     Introduction   63

     Volumes   75

     Prize-Winning Stories by Year   81

     Author Index   89

Index of Titles   117

Collections from the Volumes   183

Preface

The American short story remains the generally unrecognized glory of American literature. Just why writers should ever apologize for choosing to compose and publish stories instead of novels, plays, and poems remains to me a matter of mystery. Perhaps, after all, the old hierarchies endure: the ranking of epic poetry over lyric poetry, of tragedy over comedy, and of all possible literary genres over fiction. With poetic epics dead, with lyric poetry admired by precious few, and with drama becoming divorced from literary studies, lowly fiction has gained the top position in the rankings of the genres; and the longer the fiction, it must be thought, the more worthy the writer. Or perhaps the explanation is that with palpable bulk in the literary marketplace comes apparent bargain—hence the low official status of the American short story.

Whatever, American authors—from Washington Irving to Cynthia Ozick, from 1820 to today, from pastoral romanticicists to postmodern expressionists, from the genteel to the naturalistic, from mimesis to fantasy—have achieved greatness in writing the short story; and it is the short story form that has continually provided the field for the narrative exploration and experimentation that are needful in extending the boundary of the feasible in fiction writing. In America, story has preceded novel in all ways—in stylistic experimentation, in subject exploration—except in the most important way—in critical acceptance and just evaluation.

In demonstration and in celebration of the achievement of American writers of the short story, I have provided histories and indexes for the two premier anthology series that have so strongly and beneficently encouraged and rewarded twentieth-century American short story writers. *The Best American Short Stories* since 1915 and *Prize Stories: The O. Henry Awards* since 1919 have dependably bestowed the professional recognition and the substantive tribute due to the writers of the nation's most vital form of literature.

This volume provides the first historical account of the origin, the development, and the accomplishment of these two long-running short story anthologies; and it provides separate author indexes to the hundreds of writers whose thousands of stories have appeared in the volumes of the two series. Following the author index appears a title index to the combined volumes of the two series.

I apologize in advance for any errata that may remain among these many data; thanks to the excellent aid of Gary Summers, the remaining errors are many fewer than they otherwise would be. I acknowledge also my continuing debts to two constant friends—Charles B. Harris, Chairperson of the Department of English, and

1

Preface

William C. Woodson, Director of Graduate Studies in English, Illinois State University. Equally sincere is my gratitude to Helga Whitcomb, Joan Winters, and Destiny Robertson of Milner Library, Illinois State University.

RLW

Index to

Best American Short Stories

Introduction

*Some men are like the twang of a bow-string. Hardy was like
that—short, lithe, sunburned, vivid. Into the lives of Jarrick, Hill,
and myself, old classmates of his, he came and went in the fashion of
one of those queer winds that on a sultry day in summer blow
unexpectedly up a city street out of nowhere.*

With these words there began in 1915 the publication of an annual
volume of short stories that would come to exert enormous influence
on the development and achievement of American literature. For
with these words—the first sentences of "The Water-Hole" by Maxwell
Struthers Burt—Edward J. O'Brien opened *The Best Short Stories of
1915 and the Yearbook of the American Short Story,* first of the annual
volumes of *Best Short Stories* that O'Brien would continue to edit
through 1941. Seldom does the editor of a literary anthology achieve
such influence—especially such beneficent and long-term influence
—on the course of a nation's literature. From the first of his annual
volumes, O'Brien knew what he admired in short fiction, he knew
how seldom he found contemporary short fiction to be admired, and
he knew how difficult would be the development of a large audience
for the best short fiction that American authors were capable of
writing.

And the contents of *The Best Short Fiction of 1915 and the
Yearbook of the American Short Story* were not, in retrospect, very
promising. O'Brien had selected from the American periodicals of
1915 twenty stories that came somewhat close to meeting his criteria
for good short fiction. These twenty stories—by such now-forgotten
authors as Will Levington Comfort, W. A. Dwiggins, Frances Gregg,
Arthur Johnson, Virgil Jordan, Mary Boyle O'Reilly, and Mary Synon—may indeed have been the best stories published in America in
1915; but, of these authors of 1915, only the name of Wilbur Daniel
Steele is occasionally still to be found in discussions of American
literature.

The idea for publishing an annual volume of the best American
short stories had come to Edward J. O'Brien in 1914, the previous
year, when he had been asked by Hiram M. Greene, editor of *Illus-
trated Sunday Magazine,* to choose twenty-one American short stories
for republication in issues of this Sunday newspaper supplement, a
periodical distributed with weekend editions of many of the nation's
newspapers. So favorable had been the public response to these
twenty-one stories in 1914 that O'Brien—Harvard graduate, dramatist
and poet, employee of the *Boston Evening Transcript*—sought and
found a book publisher—Small, Maynard & Company of Boston—

willing to bring out in hard covers a collection of the best stories of 1915 and willing to guarantee for several years the continued publication of such an annual volume, each volume to be edited by O'Brien.

In the introduction to his first volume, O'Brien set as his goal publication of an annual "study of the American short story from year to year as it is represented in the American periodicals which care most to develop its art and its audiences, and to appraise so far as may be the relative achievement of author and magazine in the successful fulfilment of this aim." Instead of the then general lamentation for "the pitiful gray shabbiness of American fiction," O'Brien proposed that Americans "affirm our faith anyhow in our own spiritual substance. Let us believe in our materials and shape them passionately to a creative purpose. Let us be enthusiastic about life around us and the work that is being done, and in much less than twelve years from now a jury of novelists and critics will pronounce a very different verdict on American fiction from their verdict of to-day."

Thus wishing to reform the domestic and foreign opinion of American short fiction in and after 1915, O'Brien set forth to "study" and reward the American authors and publishers of the short story by collecting and introducing annually the best stories and listing the other most worthy stories along with the names and addresses of the periodicals in which they appeared. For a short story to come up to O'Brien's standards and appear on his lists, that story would have to meet firm criteria: it must be tested "by the double standard of substance and form."

"Substance" for O'Brien was "something achieved by the artist in every act of creation, rather than something already present, and accordingly a fact or group of facts in a story only obtain substantial embodiment when the artist's power of compelling imaginative persuasion transforms them into a living truth. I assume that such a living truth is the artist's essential object. The first test of a short story, therefore, in any qualitative analysis is to report upon how vitally compelling the writer makes his selected facts or incidents."

With the test of "substance"—defined also as "imaginative life"—primary to judging successful short fiction, Edward O'Brien put forth his second test, that of "form." To O'Brien, "form" comes from the effort of the creative artist to "shape this living substance into the most beautiful and satisfying form, by skilful selection and arrangement of his material, and by the most direct and appealing presentation of it in portrayal and characterization."

Claiming to have read in the last twelve months over 2,200 short stories published in many American periodicals, O'Brien classified for the "yearbook" section of his 1915 volume the worthy stories that he had read by establishing four groupings. The worst—those stories completely without substance or form—received his attention but not his comment. A second grouping of stories satisfied either the requirement of substance or the requirement of form but not both

criteria; these stories received in his lists one asterisk. The third grouping of stories—those with satisfactory substance and satisfactory form—received from O'Brien a second reading and two asterisks. And the fourth grouping of stories—ninety-three stories from 1915—received three asterisks and separate listing in a "Roll of Honor." These stories, O'Brien claimed, possessed "the distinction of uniting genuine substance and artistic form in a closely woven pattern with a spiritual sincerity so earnest, and a creative belief so strong, that each of these stories may fairly claim, in my opinion, a position of some permanence in our literature as a criticism of life." An asterisk awarded to stories listed in the "Roll of Honor" indicated stories worthy of being published in *The Best Short Stories of 1915.*

To his short list of the most worthy stories of 1915, O'Brien added further considerations used in forming his first anthology: he would not republish a British story, he would not republish more than one story by a single author, and he would not republish any story "whose immediate publishing in book form elsewhere seem[ed] likely."

And O'Brien, having surveyed the entire production of American writers in the short story form, found in the stories of 1915 a foundation for his belief that, with proper encouragement and recognition, American writers and periodical publishers could appeal through superior short fiction to the average American reader, the common reader who would "respond heartily and make higher standards possible by his support." For, concluded O'Brien, "we have scarcely begun to build our democracy of letters."

In the twelve years that followed publication of the first *Best Short Stories* in 1915—the period that O'Brien had allowed to American writers to earn and receive the approval of those critics so disappointed with the American short story in 1915—there occurred a revolution in American literary taste and achievement; and the existence of *Best Short Stories,* with its annual recognition of the best twenty or so short stories, deserves considerable credit for the growing achievement of American short fiction. Further, the existence, sometimes brief, of the "little magazines" that sought and published unconventional fiction deserves much credit; indeed, the post-war reformation of national values exerted enormous influence over the directions that American writers followed; and, finally, the mere explosion of demand for publishable material to fill the huge number of periodicals that entertained and informed America in the 1920s played a part in the improvement of the American short story. But *Best Short Stories,* appearing annually, with its contents ordered strictly by alphabet according to the authors' last names, provided a means of awarding distinction to the highest creative efforts of American story writers.

And the appearance of remembered authors in the O'Brien volumes in the twelve years after 1915 demonstrates the innovation and achievement that the editor encourged: in 1916, Gertrude Atherton and Theodore Dreiser; in 1917, Susan Glaspell and Edna Ferber;

7

in 1918, Sinclair Lewis and Mary Heaton Vorse; in 1919, Sherwood Anderson, Djuna Barnes, James Branch Cabell, and Joseph Hergesheimer; in 1920, James Oppenheim; in 1921, Waldo Frank, Ellen Glasgow, and Manuel Komroff; in 1922, Conrad Aiken, F. Scott Fitzgerald, Ben Hecht, and Ring Lardner; in 1923, Ernest Hemingway, Ruth Suckow, and Jean Toomer; in 1924, Floyd Dell, Zona Gale, and Glenway Wescott; in 1925, Eleanor Wylie; in 1926, Robert E. Sherwood; in 1927, DuBose Heyward and J. P. Marquand. In greeting and accepting new directions in storytelling since 1915, O'Brien had already—against odds—been successful.

Not only did O'Brien prove charitable and wise in recognizing traditional and innovative authors' attempts at short fiction, but through the introductions to his annual volumes he provided annual "lectures," the reading of which surely influenced the noted improvement in the American short story since 1915. Each year O'Brien explained by repeating, usually verbatim, his criteria for story selection—the test of substance and the test of form, the exclusion of British material and material to come forth soon in hard-cover format, and the inclusion of only one story per author each year; and each year he briefly undertook to educate authors and readers in one particular aspect of worthy short fiction.

In 1916, O'Brien wrote of his attempt to turn the short story away from deadly formulas and toward organic, life-like form: "No substance is of importance in fiction, unless it is organic substance. Inorganic fiction has been our curse in the past, and we are still surrounded by it in almost all of our magazines. The new impulse must find its own substance freshly, and interpret it naturally in new forms, rather than in the stereotyped utterances to which we have been so long accustomed." In 1917, O'Brien responded to complaints from a European critic that America was seized by such a mania and market for short stories that writers could virtually avoid firm judgment of substance and form in their productions.

In 1917, O'Brien complained that "there has been a marked ebb this year in the quality of the American short story," a decline due probably to the understandable absorption of Americans with the world war. Further, the editor did not think that superior fiction about the war itself would emerge until at least a decade after hostilities ended—a prediction that proved prescient. Further, O'Brien believed that special curses upon American short story writers allowed their indulgence in sentimentality and commercialism and the avoidance of any unpleasant facts of life. His subject for the introduction to the 1918 volume became the general adolescence of American society—the immaturity of intellect (and of imaginative literature) as compared with the overall maturity of the nation's commerce and industry.

In his volume of stories for 1920, O'Brien warned against repetitiveness by authors and arrogance by owners and editors of commercially successful magazines; in 1921, he lamented the short-

ness of American history, the absence of a "racial memory" common to all Americans. In 1922, the editor warned against American adoption of the "dadaist," studiously nonrealistic style of such European writers as James Joyce and Dorothy Richardson. O'Brien's advice in 1923 and 1924 was, it now seems, seriously off-target, when he gratuitously wondered why American short fiction of great merit was invariably sad or tragic. In 1925, his topic was the theory that the short fiction form fits the hustle of American life—a life without time for extended fictionalizing by writer or reader. O'Brien's topic in 1926 concerned whether American story writers were ranging too far from the elements of the folk-tale.

And in 1927, Edward O'Brien finally came out and named the baleful influence against which he had been crusading since 1915—namely, the "O. Henry short story" with its emphasis on the surface of life, with its trick ending, and with its stultifying, mechanical structure. For, by 1927, through leading American writers by example and by stricture, Edward O'Brien had met his own challenge twelve years earlier: American short fiction had indeed come far toward the cultural sophistication and imaginative maturity that had seemed to him so seriously lacking back in 1915.

Edward J. O'Brien had achieved much literary good in the first twelve years of his editorship of *Best Short Stories*, and this beneficence was continued and amplified by this editor through the 1941 volume. In the 1930s, O'Brien discovered and reprinted fiction by such new writers as Louis Bromfield, Morley Callaghan, Dorothy Parker, and Elizabeth Madox Roberts (1928); Willa Cather and William Carlos Williams (1929); William March and Katherine Anne Porter (1930); Kay Boyle, Erskine Caldwell, and William Faulkner (1931); Laurence Stallings (1932); John Peale Bishop, Robert Cantwell, James T. Farrell, and Nancy Hale (1933); Caroline Gordon, Langston Hughes, Allen Tate, and Leane Zugsmith (1934); William Saroyan and Thomas Wolfe (1935); Albert Maltz (1936); Jesse Stuart (1937); Stephen Vincent Bénet, John Cheever, Frederick Prokosch, Mark Schorer, John Steinbeck, Robert Penn Warren, and Eudora Welty (1938); Richard Wright (1939); Irwin Shaw (1940); and Wallace Stegner (1941).

O'Brien was always fortunate that reputable and important American publishers were willing to commit their resources to the publication of his *Best Short Stories*. Small, Maynard and Company had assumed publication of the volumes from 1915 through 1925; Dodd, Mead and Company brought out the annual volumes from 1926 through 1932; and Houghton Mifflin Company became the annual publisher in 1933—a commitment that this company would generously honor for decades thereafter.

In his introductions to the annual *Best Short Stories,* O'Brien kept addressing current problems faced by the writer and publisher of the best American short stories. In 1928, he encourged writers to avoid in their writing the socialistic and communistic doctrines brought to the

United States from Europe. In 1929, he argued against the influence of creative-writing teachers. In 1930, he paid credit again to innovative "small" magazines of limited circulation, particularly those published in the Midwest. In 1931, he lamented the influence of behavioristic psychology on American fiction. In 1932, he declared that the time had come for consolidation of past achievement. In 1933, with a new publisher and in the midst of a great depression, O'Brien reintroduced his 1915 program and criteria for creating and judging the best short fiction—fiction since 1915 clearly exemplified by the achievements of Sherwood Anderson and Ernest Hemingway. In 1934, O'Brien was optimistic about the future of American writing; in 1935 he argued against the strong political pressures being brought wrongly to bear on writers and editors by partisans of the right and of the left.

And, finally, in his introductory remarks for the 1936 volume of *Best Short Stories,* O'Brien surprised his readers by responding openly to the negative criticism that he and his anthologies had drawn from some quarters for many years. Along with the offer of a ten-cent pamphlet analyzing the chosen stories of that year's collection (an offer seemingly at odds with O'Brien's dislike of creative-writing classes and teachers) and along with a published summary of the fine points of each included story, the editor defended himself against several serious charges: that he was acting too obviously as a Communist or as a Fascist; that he was an aging critic in service to past interests and moribund media; that he suffered from pompous humorlessness; that he profited financially from choosing stories from certain periodicals; that he hated stories with traditional plots; and that he would willingly kill off certain small magazines (certainly those that too readily accepted other small magazines' rejected manuscripts). These defensive statements in 1936, coming from an editor who had effaced himself in the annual volumes since 1915, still appear strange to the reader unacquainted with the feuding of political and intellectual partisans in the 1930s. (One particular aspect of O'Brien's life apparently never publicly held against him was his long-time residence in England while serving as a valiant American editor, for he had lived in England since 1919.)

Fortunately, O'Brien could in 1937 return from self-defense to his accustomed role as editor and commentator on short fiction, this time with a plea for the recognition and the encouragement in America of the novella form so long respected in Europe. In 1938, O'Brien published a fanciful introduction to *Best Short Stories* by Manuel Komroff, after which in 1939 he returned forcefully and eloquently to warn America in his introductory comments about the Nazi destruction of esteemed old cultures in Europe, a warning made more desperate in 1940, when English culture was falling and when only American culture remained free and able to defend civilization against the forces of the new barbarism destroying Europe.

Finally, in 1941, in the last volume of *Best Short Stories* that he would edit, O'Brien commissioned the American writer to recognize the importance of the moment: "It is now the American writer's urgent job at this historic moment in time, where eternity must cross time if any spiritual life is to survive on this planet, to keep his head. While England holds the bridge, he must use such intellectual integrity as he possesses to maintain truth as a point of reference in this mad world. England's integrity in crisis frees the American brain for clear thinking. The American writer may therefore thank God, or whatever he believes in, for the chance which is still left to him to carry on the torch, a chance which would not be left to him if England failed."

The 1941 *Best Short Stories* volume was prefaced with an encomium written by Martha Foley—words of praise for the American editor who had died at fifty-one while defending England from Nazi bombings and who had since 1915 significantly informed and formed the modern short story of his nation; who had read sometimes 8,000 short stories a year in his search for the best few; who had never changed his short-story criteria of "substance" and "form"; and who had unselfishly encouraged other writers to succeed in their creative work far beyond his own personal literary ambitions and creative accomplishments.

No one at the time of Edward O'Brien's death in 1941 could have predicted that his annual short story anthology would continue to appear for many decades, much less that an editor of even more longevity would succeed O'Brien in the annual publication of the influential volumes; but, in 1942, Martha Foley became editor of the volumes, renamed, in time of war, *The Best American Short Stories and the Yearbook of the American Short Story*.

Foley had begun her career as an American correspondent in Europe. In 1931, with her husband, Whit Burnett, she founded the periodical *Story*, first published in Vienna. After moving the prestigious *Story* to New York City in 1933, Foley continued to coedit the monthly issues through 1937 and the bimonthly issues through World War II. As founder and editor of this well-known magazine of short stories, Foley would in almost every one of her volumes of *Best American Short Stories* rightly praise the efforts and achievements of "small" or "literary" magazines in the field of the short story. And, from serving as a teacher of creative writing at Columbia University for several years after World War II, Foley in her editorial forewords to the *Best American Short Stories* volumes that she edited provided less theoretical, less abstract statements about short fiction than had O'Brien in his many annual introductions; instead, the new editor's forewords were informal, personal, and casual in mood and content.

During the war years, Foley told readers of the anthology that the best war fiction would come not during the struggle but instead several years after the fighting had ended, as had happened with fic-

tion following World War I. She oversaw the changing of the name of the anthology to include "American" and commented in 1942: "Since America is defending today what is her own, the short story has a right to be considered as among the cultural institutions the country is now fighting to save." The stories that Foley admired from 1942 through 1945 were nonpropagandistic and contained fictional defenses of the values on which America had been founded, the defense of which now occupied the nation's emotional and financial energies.

From her earliest forewords, Foley praised (often by name) the literary magazines in which she continually found the best contemporary story writing; and she criticized (often by name) the mass-circulation magazines that sought a cheapened, happy-ending, unintellectual fiction to fill their pages. Foley wished to see more general magazines that depended on actual subscription income rather than on advertising income, for the emphasis on advertising matter over reading matter became a concern of almost annual comment from her. Thus would she write in 1959: "There used to be a place called Hell. The name seems to have been changed to Madison Avenue. From there issues a modern Mephistopheles to corrupt magazines with richly paying advertisements, the kind that cause their readers to lose all sense of balance [for,] like Faust, the readers are required to pay, finally, too high a price."

In other ways Foley stated what reforms she would like in the *Best American Short Stories* volumes. She wisely expanded the scope of the collections to include Canadian authors, and she wished that the name of the series could drop the word "best"—that word forming an impossible stricture that forced exclusion of much that was fine in current story writing and, at the same time, sounded exclusivist in a democracy of letters. In one further way would Foley have liked to change the series: to include authors from all parts of the world, not just from the United States of America and from Canada. Finally, Foley did modify the format of the volumes in one other way: she shortened the "yearbook" appendixes from the extensive (often 100-page or more) lists that O'Brien had maintained to a modest list (often twenty pages long, sometimes shorter) of distinctive short stories published during the year and the addresses of the magazines worthy of the readers' notice; in some years she published no yearbook at all.

As O'Brien had tried to identify and comment on trends in short-story subjectmatter, so did Foley discover that in some years certain topics seemed to dominate the published short fiction. In the war years she found that the subject of anticipated postwar peace interested most writers. In the early 1950s, she noted the surprisingly large number of stories that dealt with children and old people, as well as with ghosts. In the later 1950s, she deplored the change to writing about characters—especially minority and immigrant characters—in terms of economic class rather than in terms of individuality. She noted the growing and then lessening interest of writers in creating fiction based on dreams, psychiatry, childhood,

adolescence/initiation, explicit sexuality, and overt drug use. Occasionally, she noted a lack of humor and a dearth of adventure or detective themes. Several of the emerging new areas of experience—especially sex and drugs—discomfited the usually selfpossessed editor.

But Foley's taste in short stories was wide-ranging, and her criteria for selecting the best annual stories remained constant as she published volumes from 1942 through 1977. To please her taste, a story had to be nonmoralistic but æsthetically pleasing; a story must begin in reality even if it moved into fantasy; a story had to be an adventure in reading, an adventure from which the reader returned somewhat startled, somewhat exhilarated, somewhat changed; and a story had to reveal the artistic integrity of the author, an integrity uncompromised by commercialism, propaganda, distorted views of life, or forced jollity. She wrote in 1964: "Good short stories must have a springboard of reality, no matter how high the authors' imaginations may afterwards soar, and at their end they must leave the reader in one way or another revitalized, even if it be only with anger." Good short fiction, she stated, must provide more than a cameraview of life; it must provide art, it must "have something *more*—such as music or poetry have." The best fiction had to provide feeling as well as thought.

Given her criteria for choosing each year's best short stories and given the thousands of stories that she must have read over her forty-six years as editor of *Story* and of *Best American Short Stories,* Foley (occasionally aided by her son, David Burnett) could not have failed to make discoveries of new writers to please her and to delight her readers. Seldom did she publish a volume that did not include a writer whose name became a constant in the developing literary canon. In the 1940s, she discovered and reprinted stories by Nelson Algren, Peter Taylor, James Thurber, Shirley Jackson, James Still, Truman Capote, Joseph Heller, and J. D. Salinger. In the 1950s she admired and reprinted stories by Bernard Malamud, James Agee, Randall Jarrell, Flannery O'Connor, Philip Roth, Tillie Olsen, William Gass, and John Updike. In the 1960s, perhaps occasionally against her most private taste, Foley admitted to her anthologies works by Thomas Pynchon, Joyce Carol Oates, Reynolds Price, Sylvia Plath, Stanley Elkin, William Maxwell, Arthur Miller, and Donald Hall. And in the 1970s volumes that Foley published before her death in 1977, there appeared with her commendation stories by the emerging and puzzling but still important writers Cynthia Ozick, Robert Coover, Larry Woiwode, Richard Brautigan, Donald Barthelme, Maxine Cumin, Alice Walker, Rosellen Brown, Evan Hunter, and Tom Robbins.

Had O'Brien been able in 1941 to choose the editor to succeed him in directing the annual anthologies that he had begun in 1915, it is possible that he would have chosen Martha Foley, a friend and a periodical editor whom he had admired. Houghton Mifflin recogniz-

ed Foley's work with *Story* magazine and wisely named her to continue the tradition of editorial wisdom, evolving taste, and critical generosity that O'Brien had begun and maintained. Whether a third editor could be found in 1978 to continue the long-lived tradition of the only two editors who had served from 1915 through 1977 must have worried the executives at Houghton Mifflin. They solved their dilemma both cleverly and admirably: instead of hiring one editor, they chose several of the most elegible potential editors to continue *Best American Short Stories.*

The idea of inviting a different guest editor for each annual volume of *Best American Short Stories* came from Ted Solotaroff, an editor of *American Review* associated with Bantam Books. When invited by the executives at Houghton Mifflin to replace Martha Foley as series editor, Solotaroff "wisely suggested," wrote the publishers, "that perhaps the time had come to modify the arrangements by inviting a different writer or critic to edit each new annual volume. A variety of fresh points of view should add liveliness to the series and provide a new dimension to the title. 'Best' thereby becomes a sequence of informed opinions that gains reliability from its very diversity."

But the idea of having a different editor for each annual anthology was not totally innovative, for Shannon Ravenel of Houghton Mifflin, who had worked with Martha Foley on some of that editor's volumes, would alone read the hundreds of short stories published annually in America; then, from a list of approximately 120 stories chosen by Ravenel, the guest editor would select approximately twenty stories for the planned volume. Ravenel, of course, saw each volume through the press after deferring in last judgments to the prestigious editor's taste.

Houghton Mifflin chose well-known contemporary writers and critics for guest editing the volumes of *Best American Short Stories* published after 1977: Ted Solotaroff in 1978, Joyce Carol Oates in 1979, Stanley Elkin in 1980, Hortense Calisher in 1981, John Gardner in 1982, Anne Tyler in 1983, John Updike in 1984, Gail Godwin in 1985, and Raymond Carver in 1986. In these volumes, the "yearbook" aspect of the annual was reduced to short biographical notes about the authors included, along with Shannon Ravenel's list of one hundred outstanding stories and the names and addresses of American and Canadian periodicals that dependably published worthy short fiction.

While there existed the opportunity for disparate critical standards and criteria among the various guest editors, personal circumstances determined the degree of cooperation between Ravenel and her co-editors. Some of the contributors faithfully chose their selections from the 120 stories picked annually by Ravenel; some guests selected stories from their own lists of the year's best stories. Some editors attempted a balance of stories from "little" or literary magazines and from mass, general magazines, some wishing that more superb stories could appear elsewhere than in the weekly *New Yorker.* Some editors sought a balance between male and female story writers;

others chose established and newly arriving authors; some arranged the order of the chosen stories to form a theme, while most maintained the long-traditional ordering of the contents by authors' last names.

All of the guest editors of *Best American Short Stories* felt compelled to state—clearly or otherwise—their selection criteria, these criteria being invariably the acceptance or rejection of the traditional story (the story with plot, characters, and beginnings, middles, and endings) and the innovative story (one with perhaps little plot, little discernible characterization, and little noticeable organization).

All of the editors took care to defend their catholic tastes in short fiction and their willingness to include fiction written against their own creative tastes while they all acknowledged the difficulty in narrowing their individual choices to twenty stories. All of the editors admitted their surprise at the impressive number and overall high quality of the short stories written and published in America and Canada; and all finally proclaimed *The Best American Short Stories* a monument to developing literary taste and tradition, an institution well worth continuing for as long as possible.

Edward O'Brien and Martha Foley—as well as the hundreds of American authors of the short stories anthologized by the two since 1915—could rest assured that their lifework has been both continued and appreciated. Over seventy years after *The Best American Short Stories* series was established, America may proudly claim first place among the nations of the world that have aspired to produce distinguished short fiction.

Volumes

The Best Short Stories Of 1915 and the Yearbook Of the American Short Story. Edited By Edward J. O'Brien. Boston: Small, Maynard & Company, 1916.

The Best Short Stories Of 1916 and the Yearbook Of the American Short Story. Edited By Edward J. O'Brien. Boston: Small, Maynard & Company, 1917.

The Best Short Stories Of 1917 and the Yearbook Of the American Short Story. Edited By Edward J. O'Brien. Boston: Small, Maynard & Company, 1918.

The Best Short Stories Of 1918 and the Yearbook Of the American Short Story. Edited By Edward J. O'Brien. Boston: Small, Maynard & Company, 1919.

The Best Short Stories Of 1919 and the Yearbook Of the American Short Story. Edited By Edward J. O'Brien. Boston: Small, Maynard & Company, 1920.

The Best Short Stories Of 1920 and the Yearbook Of the American Short Story. Edited By Edward J. O'Brien. Boston: Small, Maynard & Company, 1921.

The Best Short Stories Of 1921 and the Yearbook Of the American Short Story. Edited By Edward J. O'Brien. Boston: Small, Maynard & Company, 1922.

The Best Short Stories Of 1922 and the Yearbook Of the American Short Story. Edited By Edward J. O'Brien. Boston: Small, Maynard & Company, 1923.

The Best Short Stories Of 1923 and the Yearbook Of the American Short Story. Edited By Edward J. O'Brien. Boston: Small, Maynard & Company, 1924.

The Best Short Stories Of 1924 and the Yearbook Of the American Short Story. Edited By Edward J. O'Brien. Boston: Small, Maynard & Company, 1925.

The Best Short Stories Of 1925 and the Yearbook Of the American Short Story. Edited By Edward J. O'Brien. Boston: Small, Maynard & Company, 1926.

The Best Short Stories Of 1926 and the Yearbook Of the American Short Story. Edited By Edward J. O'Brien. New York: Dodd, Mead and Company, 1927.

The Best Short Stories Of 1927 and the Yearbook Of the American Short Story. Edited By Edward J. O'Brien. New York: Dodd, Mead and Company, 1928.

The Best Short Stories Of 1928 and the Yearbook Of the American Short Story. Edited By Edward J. O'Brien. New York: Dodd, Mead

and Company, 1928.

The Best Short Stories Of 1929 and the Yearbook Of the American Short Story. Edited By Edward J. O'Brien. New York: Dodd, Mead and Company, 1929.

The Best Short Stories Of 1930 and the Yearbook Of the American Short Story. Edited By Edward J. O'Brien. New York: Dodd, Mead and Company, 1930.

The Best Short Stories Of 1931 and the Yearbook Of the American Short Story. Edited By Edward J. O'Brien. New York: Dodd, Mead and Company, 1932.

The Best Short Stories Of 1932 and the Yearbook Of the American Short Story. Edited By Edward J. O'Brien. New York: Dodd, Mead and Company, 1932.

The Best Short Stories 1933 and the Yearbook Of the American Short Story. Edited By Edward J. O'Brien. Boston: Houghton Mifflin Company, 1933.

The Best Short Stories 1934 and the Yearbook Of the American Short Story. Edited By Edward J. O'Brien. Boston: Houghton Mifflin Company, 1934.

The Best Short Stories 1935 and the Yearbook Of the American Short Story. Edited By Edward J. O'Brien. Boston: Houghton Mifflin Company, 1935.

The Best Short Stories 1936 and the Yearbook Of the American Short Story. Edited By Edward J. O'Brien. Boston: Houghton Mifflin Company, 1936.

The Best Short Stories 1937 and the Yearbook Of the American Short Story. Edited By Edward J. O'Brien. Boston: Houghton Mifflin Company, 1937.

The Best Short Stories 1938 and the Yearbook Of the American Short Story. Edited By Edward J. O'Brien. Boston: Houghton Mifflin Company, 1938.

The Best Short Stories 1939 and the Yearbook Of the American Short Story. Edited By Edward J. O'Brien. Boston: Houghton Mifflin Company, 1939.

The Best Short Stories 1940 and the Yearbook Of the American Short Story. Edited By Edward J. O'Brien. Boston: Houghton Mifflin Company, 1940.

The Best Short Stories 1941 and the Yearbook Of the American Short Story. Edited By Edward J. O'Brien. Boston: Houghton Mifflin Company, 1941.

The Best American Short Stories 1942 and the Yearbook Of the American Short Story. Edited By Martha Foley. Boston: Houghton Mifflin Company, 1942.

The Best American Short Stories 1943 and the Yearbook Of the American Short Story. Edited By Martha Foley. New York: Literary Classics; [distributed—Boston: Houghton Mifflin Company], 1943.

The Best American Short Stories 1944 and the Yearbook Of the

American Short Story. Edited By Martha Foley. Boston: Houghton Mifflin Company, 1944.

The Best American Short Stories 1945 and the Yearbook Of the American Short Story. Edited By Martha Foley. Boston: Houghton Mifflin Company, 1945.

The Best American Short Stories 1946 and the Yearbook Of the American Short Story. Edited By Martha Foley. Boston: Houghton Mifflin Company, 1946.

The Best American Short Stories 1947 and the Yearbook Of the American Short Story. Edited By Martha Foley. Boston: Houghton Mifflin Company, 1947.

The Best American Short Stories 1948 and the Yearbook Of the American Short Story. Edited By Martha Foley. Boston: Houghton Mifflin Company, 1948.

The Best American Short Stories 1949 and the Yearbook Of the American Short Story. Edited By Martha Foley. Boston: Houghton Mifflin Company, 1949.

The Best American Short Stories 1950 and the Yearbook Of the American Short Story. Edited By Martha Foley. Boston: Houghton Mifflin Company, 1950.

The Best American Short Stories 1951 and the Yearbook Of the American Short Story. Edited By Martha Foley and Joyce F. Hartman. Boston: Houghton Mifflin Company, 1951.

The Best American Short Stories 1952 and the Yearbook Of the American Short Story. Edited By Martha Foley and Joyce F. Hartman. Boston: Houghton Mifflin Company, 1952.

The Best American Short Stories 1953 and the Yearbook Of the American Short Story. Edited By Martha Foley and Joyce F. Hartman. Boston: Houghton Mifflin Company, 1953.

The Best American Short Stories 1954 and the Yearbook Of the American Short Story. Edited By Martha Foley. Boston: Houghton Mifflin Company, 1954.

The Best American Short Stories 1955 and the Yearbook Of the American Short Story. Edited By Martha Foley. Boston: Houghton Mifflin Company, 1955.

The Best American Short Stories 1956 and the Yearbook Of the American Short Story. Edited By Martha Foley. Boston: Houghton Mifflin Company, 1956.

The Best American Short Stories 1957. Edited By Martha Foley. Boston: Houghton Mifflin Company, 1957.

The Best American Short Stories 1958 and the Yearbook Of the American Short Story. Edited By Martha Foley and David Burnett. Boston: Houghton Mifflin Company, 1958.

The Best American Short Stories 1959 and the Yearbook Of the American Short Story. Edited By Martha Foley and David Burnett. Boston: Houghton Mifflin Company, 1959.

The Best American Short Stories 1960 and the Yearbook Of the American Short Story. Edited By Martha Foley and David Burnett.

Boston: Houghton Mifflin Company, 1960.

The Best American Short Stories 1961 and the Yearbook Of the American Short Story. Edited By Martha Foley and David Burnett. Boston: Houghton Mifflin Company, 1961.

The Best American Short Stories 1962 and the Yearbook Of the American Short Story. Edited By Martha Foley and David Burnett. Boston: Houghton Mifflin Company, 1962.

The Best American Short Stories 1963 and the Yearbook Of the American Short Story. Edited By Martha Foley and David Burnett. Boston: Houghton Mifflin Company, 1963.

The Best American Short Stories 1964 and the Yearbook Of the American Short Story. Edited By Martha Foley and David Burnett. Boston: Houghton Mifflin Company, 1964.

The Best American Short Stories 1965 and the Yearbook Of the American Short Story. Edited By Martha Foley. Boston: Houghton Mifflin Company, 1965.

The Best American Short Stories 1966 and the Yearbook Of the American Short Story. Edited By Martha Foley and David Burnett. Boston: Houghton Mifflin Company, 1966.

The Best American Short Stories 1967 & the Yearbook Of the American Short Story. Edited By Martha Foley and David Burnett. Boston: Houghton Mifflin Company, 1967.

The Best American Short Stories 1968 & the Yearbook Of the American Short Story. Edited By Martha Foley and David Burnett. Boston: Houghton Mifflin Company, 1968.

The Best American Short Stories 1969 & the Yearbook Of the American Short Story. Edited By Martha Foley and David Burnett. Boston: Houghton Mifflin Company, 1969.

The Best American Short Stories 1970 & the Yearbook Of the American Short Story. Edited By Martha Foley and David Burnett. Boston: Houghton Mifflin Company, 1970.

The Best American Short Stories 1971 & the Yearbook Of the American Short Story. Edited By Martha Foley and David Burnett. Boston: Houghton Mifflin Company, 1971.

The Best American Short Stories 1972 & the Yearbook Of the American Short Story. Edited By Martha Foley. Boston: Houghton Mifflin Company, 1972.

The Best American Short Stories 1973 & the Yearbook Of the American Short Story. Edited By Martha Foley. Boston: Houghton Mifflin Company, 1973.

The Best American Short Stories 1974 & the Yearbook Of the American Short Story. Edited By Martha Foley. Boston: Houghton Mifflin Company, 1974.

The Best American Short Stories 1975 and the Yearbook Of the American Short Story. Edited By Martha Foley. Boston: Houghton Mifflin Company, 1975.

The Best American Short Stories 1976 and the Yearbook Of the American Short Story. Edited By Martha Foley. Boston: Houghton

Best American Short Stories

Mifflin Company, 1976.

The Best American Short Stories 1977 and the Yearbook Of the American Short Story. Edited By Martha Foley. Boston: Houghton Mifflin Company, 1977.

The Best American Short Stories 1978: Selected From U.S. and Canadian Magazines By Ted Solotaroff and Shannon Ravenel. With an Introduction By Ted Solotaroff. *Including the Yearbook Of the American Short Story.* Boston: Houghton Mifflin Company, 1978.

The Best American Short Stories 1979: Selected From U.S. and Canadian Magazines By Joyce Carol Oates and Shannon Ravenel. With an Introduction By Joyce Carol Oates. *Including The Yearbook Of the American Short Story.* Boston: Houghton Mifflin Company, 1979.

The Best American Short Stories 1980: Selected From U.S. and Canadian Magazines By Stanley Elkin and Shannon Ravenel. With an Introduction By Stanley Elkin. *Including The Yearbook Of the American Short Story.* Boston: Houghton Mifflin Company, 1980.

The Best American Short Stories 1981: Selected From U.S. and Canadian Magazines By Hortense Calisher and Shannon Ravenel. With an Introduction By Hortense Calisher. Boston: Houghton Mifflin Company, 1981.

The Best American Short Stories 1982: Selected From U.S. and Canadian Magazines By John Gardner and Shannon Ravenel. With an Introduction By John Gardner. Boston: Houghton Mifflin Company, 1982.

The Best American Short Stories 1983: Selected From U.S. and Canadian Magazines By Anne Tyler and Shannon Ravenel. With an Introduction By Anne Tyler. Boston: Houghton Mifflin Company, 1983.

The Best American Short Stories 1984: Selected From U.S. and Canadian Magazines By John Updike and Shannon Ravenel. With an Introduction By John Updike. Boston: Houghton Mifflin Company, 1984.

The Best American Short Stories 1985: Selected From U.S. and Canadian Magazines By Gail Godwin and Shannon Ravenel. With an Introduction By Gail Godwin. Boston: Houghton Mifflin Company, 1985.

The Best American Short Stories 1986: Selected From U.S. and Canadian Magazines By Raymond Carver and Shannon Ravenel. With an Introduction By Raymond Carver. Boston: Houghton Mifflin Company, 1986.

Author Index

Abbott, Lee K. "The Final Proof Of Fate and Circumstance." 1984: 1-12.
Abdullah, Achmed. "A Simple Act Of Piety." 1918: 3-23.
Abish, Walter. "The Idea Of Switzerland." 1981: 1-28.
Adamic, Louis. "The Enigma." 1931: 3-23.
Adams, Alice. "Roses, Rhododendron." 1976: 1-14.
Adams, Bill. "The Foreigner." 1932: 3-15.
    "Way For a Sailor." 1923: 3-29.
Addington, Sarah. "'Hound Of Heaven.'" 1929: 1-19.
Agee, James. "A Mother's Tale." 1953: 1-18.
    "The Waiting." 1958: 1-20.
Aiken, Conrad. "The Dark City." 1922: 3-12.
Albee, George. "Fame Takes the J Car." 1933: 3-13.
    "Mighty, Mighty Pretty." 1949: 1-18.
Alexander, Sandra. "The Gift." 1925: 1-20.
Alexander, Sidney. "Part Of the Act." 1948: 1-19.
    "The White Boat." 1944: 1-16.
Algren, Nelson. "Beasts Of the Wild." 1957: 1-7.
    "Biceps." 1942: 1-18.
    "How the Devil Came Down Division Street." 1945: 1-7.
Alsop, G. F. "The Kitchen Gods." 1919: 3-23.
Amster, L. J. "Center Of Gravity." 1965: 1-44.
Andersen, U. S. "Turn Ever So Quickly." 1963: 1-14.
Anderson, Sherwood. "Another Wife." 1927: 50-58.
    "An Awakening." 1919: 24-33.
    "Brothers." 1921: 3-12.
    "I'm a Fool." 1922: 13-24.
    "The Lost Novel." 1929: 20-25.
    "The Man's Story." 1923: 30-49.
    "The Other Woman." 1920: 3-11.
    "The Return." 1925: 21-38.
Angell, Roger. "Flight Through the Dark." 1951: 1-9.
    "In an Early Winter." 1956: 1-17.
Angoff, Charles. "Jerry." 1946: 1-12.
    "Where Did Yesterday Go?" 1950: 1-4.
Appel, Benjamin. "Outside Yuma." 1935: 1-6.
    "Winter Meeting." 1934: 3-14.
Appel, Max. "Small Island Republics." 1981: 29-43.
Arkin, Frieda. "The Broomstick On the Porch." 1964: 1-14.
    "The Light Of the Sea." 1962: 1-15.
Asch, Nathan. "Gertrude Donovan." 1925: 39-52.

"Inland, Western Sea." 1951: 10-23.
Ashton, E. B. "Shadow Of a Girl." 1941: 1-13.
Aswell, James. "Shadow Of Evil." 1950: 5-32.
Atherton, Gertrude. "The Sacrificial Altar." 1916: 7-36.
Ayer, Ethan. "The Promise Of Heat." 1967: 1-12.
Ayre, Robert. "Mr. Sycamore." 1938: 1-53.

Babb, Sanora. "The Santa Ana." 1960: 1-10.
   "The Wild Flower." 1950: 33-41.
Babcock, Edwina Stanton. "Cruelties." 1918: 24-42.
   "The Excursion." 1917: 1-19.
   "Gargoyle." 1920: 12-35.
   "Mr. Cardeezer." 1923: 50-80.
   "Willum's Vanilla." 1919: 34-64.
Baker, Nicholson. "K. 590." 1982: 116-123.
Baldwin, James. "Sonny's Blues." 1958: 21-53.
   "Tell Me How Long the Train's Been Gone." 1968: 1-28.
   "This Morning, This Evening, So Soon." 1961: 1-40.
Ballard, James. "A Mountain Summer." 1953: 19-40.
Banks, Russell. "The Lie." 1975: 1-7.
   "Sarah Cole: A Type Of Love Story." 1985: 1-23.
   "With Ché In New Hampshire." 1971: 1-9.
Barber, Solon R. "The Sound That Frost Makes." 1931: 24-26.
Barich, Bill. "Hard To Be Good." 1983: 1-24.
Barnes, Djuna. "A Night Among the Horses." 1919: 65-73.
Barrett, William E. "Señor Payroll." 1944: 17-20.
Barthelme, Donald. "Basil From Her Garden." 1986: 1-9.
   "A City Of Churches." 1973: 1-5.
   "The Emerald." 1980: 1-26.
   "The New Music." 1979: 312-323.
   "The School." 1975: 8-11.
Bartlett, Frederick Orin. "Long, Long Ago." 1919: 74-81.
Battin, M. Pabst. "Terminal Procedure." 1976: 15-33.
Baum, Vicki. "This Healthy Life." 1943: 1-9.
Baumbach, Jonathan. "The Return Of Service." 1978: 354-362.
Baxter, Charles. "Gryphon." 1986: 10-27.
   "Harmony Of the World." 1982: 210-232.
Beal, M. F. "Gold." 1972: 1-15.
Beattie, Ann. "Janus." 1986: 28-33.
   "Winter: 1978." 1981: 44-76.
Beck, Warren. "The Blue Sash." 1939: 1-15.
   "Boundary Line." 1943: 10-22.
   "Edge Of Doom." 1950: 42-58.
   "The First Fish." 1945: 8-18.
   "Out Of Line." 1946: 13-25.
Becker, Stephen. "The Town Mouse." 1953: 41-52.
Beede, Ivan. "The Country Doctor." 1929: 26-37.
Beer, Thomas. "Onnie." 1917: 20-44.

Bell, Madison Smartt. "The Naked Lady." 1984: 13-18.
Bellow, Saul. "Notes Of a Dangling Man." 1944: 21-40.
   "A Sermon By Doctor Pep." 1950: 59-66.
   "A Silver Dish." 1979: 1-27.
Bemelmans, Ludwig. "The Valet Of the Splendide." 1942: 19-27.
Benedict, Dianne. "Unknown Feathers." 1984: 19-34.
Benedict, Libby. "Blind Man's Buff." 1938: 54-58.
Benefield, Barry. "Carrie Snyder." 1926: 1-18.
   "Guard Of Honor." 1925: 53-63.
   "Miss Willett." 1916: 37-51.
Benét, Stephen Vincent. "All Around the Town." 1941: 14-27.
   "A Tooth For Paul Revere." 1938: 59-73.
Bennett, Hal. "Dotson Gerber Resurrected." 1971: 10-23.
Bennett, Peggy. "Death Under the Hawthornes." 1950: 67-79.
   "A Fugitive From the Mind." 1951: 24-36.
Benson, Sally. "5135 Kensington: August, 1903." 1942: 28-40.
   "The Overcoat." 1935: 7-10.
Bercovici, Konrad. "The Beggar Of Alcazar." 1925: 64-80.
   "The Death Of Murdo." 1922: 25-41.
   "Fanutza." 1921: 13-27.
   "Ghitza." 1920: 36-48.
   "Seed." 1923: 81-97.
   "'There's Money In Poetry.'" 1929: 38-47.
Berge, Bill. "That Lovely Green Boat." 1952: 1-17.
Berriault, Gina. "Around the Dear Ruin." 1957: 8-18.
Berry, John. "Jawaharlal and the Three Cadavers." 1959: 1-14.
   "The Listener." 1961: 41-44.
Berryman, John. "The Lovers." 1946: 26-39.
Bessie, Alvah C. "Horizon." 1932: 16-24.
   "A Little Walk." 1933: 14-20.
   "No Final Word." 1934: 15-24.
   "Only We Are Barren." 1931: 27-46.
Betts, Doris. "The Proud and Virtuous." 1957: 19-31.
Biddle, Livingston, Jr. "The Vacation." 1949: 19-38.
Bingham, Sallie. "Winter Term." 1959: 15-25.
Bishop, Elizabeth. "The Farmer's Children." 1949: 39-47.
Bishop, Ellen. "Along a Sandy Road." 1930: 1-5.
Bishop, John Peale. "Toadstools Are Poison." 1933: 21-29.
Bishop, Michael. "Dogs' Lives." 1985: 24-43.
Blake, George. "A Place Not On the Map." 1967: 13-24.
Blake, James. "The Widow, Bereft." 1971: 24-66.
Blassington, Wyatt. "Man's Courage." 1957: 32-38.
Blattner, H. W. "Sound Of a Drunken Drummer." 1963: 15-56.
Bly, Carol. "The Dignity Of Life." 1983: 25-47.
Bolté, Mary. "The End Of the Depression." 1951: 37-44.
Bond, James. "A Change Of Season." 1983: 48-67.
Bond, Nelson S. "Mr. Mergenthwirker's Lobblies." 1938: 74-80.
Boogher, Susan M. "An Unknown Warrior." 1922: 42-48.

Booth, Frederick. "The Helpless Ones." 1922: 49-69.
    "Supers." 1916: 52-57.
Bowen, Robert O. "A Matter Of Price." 1955: 1-12.
    "The Other Side." 1952: 18-30.
Bowles, Jane. "Two Scenes." 1978: 310-315.
Bowles, Paul. "A Distant Episode." 1948: 20-31.
    "The Eye." 1979: 214-221.
    "The Frozen Fields." 1958: 54-72.
    "In the Red Room." 1984: 35-44.
    "Pastor Dowe At Tacaté." 1950: 80-101.
    "Under the Sky." 1949: 48-54.
Boyd, Albert Truman. "Elmer." 1933: 30-41.
Boyer, Agnes. "The Deserter." 1974: 1-5.
Boyle, Kay. "Anschluss." 1940: 1-19.
    "Frenchman's Ship." 1943: 23-40.
    "The Lost." 1952: 31-48.
    "Nothing Ever Breaks Except the Heart." 1942: 41-49.
    "Rest Cure." 1931: 47-54.
    "The Wild Horses." 1967: 25-36.
Brace, Ernest. "The Party Next Door." 1935: 11-27.
Bradbury, Ray. "The Big Black and White Game." 1946: 40-55.
    "The Day That It Rained Forever." 1958: 73-83.
    "I See You Never." 1948: 32-35.
    "The Other Foot." 1952: 49-60.
Bradford, Roark. "Child Of God." 1927: 72-85.
Bradshaw, George. "'The Picture Wouldn't Fit In the Stove.'" 1958: 84-95.
Bragdon, Clifford. "Love's So Many Things." 1932: 25-33.
    "Suffer Little Children." 1930: 6-20.
Brautigan, Richard. "The World War I Los Angeles Airplane." 1972: 16-19.
Brecht, Harold W. "Vienna Roast." 1927: 59-71.
Brennan, Frederick Hazlitt. "The Guardeen Angel." 1928: 1-12.
Brennan, Louis. "Poisoner In Motley." 1932: 34-43.
Brennan, Maeve. "The Eldest Child." 1969: 1-8.
Breuer, Bessie. "Bury Your Own Dead." 1946: 56-73.
Briskin, Mae Seidman. "The Boy Who Was Astrid's Mother." 1976: 34-53.
Broderick, Francis L. "Return By Faith." 1947: 1-16.
Brodkey, Harold. "Verona: A Young Woman Speaks." 1978: 65-71.
Bromell, Henry. "The Slightest Distance." 1973: 6-22.
Bromfield, Louis. "The Cat That Lived At the Ritz." 1928: 13-30.
    "Crime Passionnel." 1945: 19-29.
    "Tabloid News." 1931: 55-69.
Brookhouser, Frank. "My Father and the Circus." 1949: 55-59.
Brown, Carlton. "Suns That Our Hearts Harden." 1935: 28-40.
Brown, Katharine Holland. "Buster." 1918: 43-60.
Brown, Mary Ward. "The Cure." 1984: 45-55.

Brown, Morris. "The Snow Owl." 1956: 18-29.
Brown, Richard G. "Mr. Iscariot." 1964: 15-25.
Brown, Rosellen. "How To Win." 1975: 12-25.
  "The Wedding Week." 1979: 79-83.
Brown, T. K., III. "The Valley Of the Shadow." 1946: 74-86.
Brownell, Agnes Mary. "Dishes." 1919: 82-95.
Brush, Katharine. "Seven Blocks Apart." 1928: 31-50.
Bryan, Jack Y. "For Each Of Us." 1942: 50-66.
Bryner, Edna Clarke. "Forest Cover." 1922: 70-82.
  "The Life Of Five Points." 1920: 49-65.
Buckner, Robert. "The Man Who Won the War." 1937: 1-14.
Bulosan, Carlos. "My Brother Osong's Career In Politics." 1945:
  30-37.
Bumpus, Jerry. "Beginnings." 1974: 6-15.
  "Desert Matinee." 1975: 26-36.
Burke, James Lee. "The Convict." 1986: 34-47.
Burke, Morgan. "Champlin." 1924: 3-18.
Burlingame, Roger. "In the Cage." 1936: 1-15.
  "The Last Equation." 1937: 15-22.
Burman, Ben Lucien. "Minstrels Of the Mist." 1927: 86-102.
Burnet, Dana. "Beyond the Cross." 1923: 98-124. "Fog." 1916: 58-74.
Burnett, W. R. "The Ivory Tower." 1946: 87-109.
Burnett, Wanda. "Sand." 1932: 44-53.
Burnett, Whit. "The Cats Which Cried." 1934: 25-39.
  "A Day In the Country." 1931: 70-80.
  "Division." 1935: 41-97.
  "Serenade." 1933: 42-53.
  "Sherrel." 1932: 54-61.
  "Two Men Free." 1930: 21-33.
Burt, Maxwell Struthers. "The Blood-Red One." 1919: 96-107.
  "A Cup Of Tea." 1917: 45-69.
  "Experiment." 1921: 28-51.
  "The Water Hole." 1915: 15-34.
Busch, Frederick. "Bambi Meets the Furies." 1975: 37-46.
  "Long Calls." 1980: 27-43.
  "The Trouble With Being Good." 1977: 1-14.
Bush, Geoffrey. "A Great Reckoning In a Little Room." 1954: 1-13.
Butler, Frank. "Amid a Place Of Stone." 1959: 26-38.
  "To the Wilderness I Wander." 1957: 39-69.
Buzzell, Francis. "Lonely Places." 1917: 70-85.
  "Ma's Pretties." 1916: 75-84.
Byrne, Donn. "The Wake." 1915: 35-45.

Cabell, James Branch. "The Wedding Jest." 1919: 108-122.
Cady, Jack. "The Burning." 1966: 1-11.
  "I Take Care Of Things." 1971: 67-73.
  "Play Like I'm Sheriff." 1969: 9-20.
  "With No Breeze." 1970: 1-19.

Caldwell, Erskine. "The Cold Winter." 1935: 98-102.
    "Dorothy." 1931: 81-87.
    "The First Autumn." 1933: 54-59.
    "Handy." 1941: 28-34.
    "Horse Thief." 1934: 40-45.
    "The People Vs. Abe Lathan, Colored." 1940: 20-29.
    "Warm River." 1932: 62-69.
Caldwell, Price. "Tarzan Meets the Department Head." 1977: 15-23.
Caldwell, Ronald. "Vision In the Sea." 1939: 16-24.
Calisher, Hortense. "In Greenwich There Are Many Gravelled
    Walks." 1951: 45-59.
    "A Wreath For Miss Totten." 1952: 61-70.
Callaghan, Morley. "Big Jules." 1941: 35-42.
    "The Blue Kimono." 1936: 16-22.
    "The Cheat's Remorse." 1938: 81-85.
    "A Country Passion." 1928: 51-59.
    "The Faithful Wife." 1930: 34-38.
    "Father and Son." 1935: 103-114.
    "Getting On In the World." 1940: 30-36.
    "It Had To Be Done." 1939: 25-31.
    "Mr. and Mrs. Fairbanks." 1934: 46-51.
    "The Red Hat." 1932: 70-75.
    "A Sick Call." 1933: 60-67.
    "Soldier Harmon." 1929: 48-59.
    "The Voyage Out." 1937: 23-28.
    "The Young Priest." 1931: 88-94.
Camp, Wadsworth. "The Signal Tower." 1920: 66-82.
Canfield, Dorothy. "The Apprentice." 1948: 36-45.
    "At the Sign Of the Three Daughters." 1928: 60-76.
    "The Knot Hole." 1944: 41-61.
    "The Murder On Jefferson Street." 1936: 23-56.
    "Sex Education." 1947: 17-30.
Canin, Ethan. "Emperor Of the Air." 1985: 44-57.
    "Star Food." 1986: 48-65.
Cantwell, Robert. "The Land Of Plenty." 1933: 68-76.
Canzoneri, Robert. "Barbed Wire." 1971: 74-85.
Caperton, Helena Lefroy. "The Honest Wine Merchant." 1932: 76-79.
Capote, Truman. "The Headless Hawk." 1947: 31-55.
Cardozo, Nancy. "The Excursionists." 1955: 13-24.
    "The Unborn Ghosts." 1952: 71-85.
Carr, A. H. Z. "The Hunch." 1936: 57-69.
Carroll, Joseph. "At Mrs. Farrelly's." 1953: 53-61.
Carter, John Stewart. "The Keyhole Eye." 1963: 57-82.
    "To a Tenor Dying Old." 1964: 27-84.
Carver, Ada Jack. "Maudie." 1926: 19-35.
Carver, Raymond. "Cathedral." 1982: 3-17.
    "Where I'm Calling From." 1983: 68-83.
    "Will You Please Be Quiet, Please?" 1967: 37-66.

Casper, Leonard. "Sense Of Direction." 1951: 60-72.
Cassill, R. V. "Larchmoor Is Not the World." 1951: 73-88.
"The Life Of the Sleeping Beauty." 1953: 62-80.
Cather, Willa. "Double Birthday." 1929: 60-85.
Chaikin, Nancy G. "Bachelor Of Arts." 1955: 25-38.
"Beautiful, Helpless Animals." 1976: 54-67.
"The Climate Of the Family." 1952: 86-96.
"Waiting For Astronauts." 1975: 47-58.
Chambers, María Cristina. "John Of God, the Water Carrier." 1928: 77-93.
Cheever, John. "The Bella Lingua." 1959: 39-58.
"The Brothers." 1938: 86-99.
"The Country Husband." 1955: 39-63.
"The Enormous Radio." 1948: 46-56.
"Falconer." 1977: 24-42.
"Frère Jacques." 1939: 32-38.
"The Jewels Of the Cabots." 1973: 23-37.
"The Pleasures Of Solitude." 1943: 41-46.
"The Season Of Divorce." 1951: 89-99.
"A Vision Of the World." 1963: 83-91.
Cherkasski, Vladimir. "What Hurts Is That I Was In a Hurry." 1938: 100-109.
Cherry, Kelly. "Covenant." 1972: 20-47.
Chester, Alfred. "As I Was Going Up the Stair." 1958: 96-118.
"Berceuse." 1961: 45-57.
Chidester, Ann. "Wood Smoke." 1952: 97-107.
Childs, Marquis W. "The Woman On the Shore." 1934: 52-66.
Choy, Wayson S. "The Sound Of Waves." 1962: 16-31.
Christopher, Robert. "Jishin." 1950: 102-108.
Chute, Carolyn. "'Ollie, Oh. . . .'" 1983: 84-98.
Clark, Eleanor. "A Summer In Puerto Rico." 1974: 16-44.
Clark, Gean. "Indian On the Road." 1939: 39-51.
Clark, Valma. "Ignition." 1923: 125-143.
Clark, Walter Van Tilburg. "The Portable Phonograph." 1942: 67-74.
"The Wind and the Snow Of Winter." 1946: 110-127.
Clay, George R. "That's My Johnny-Boy." 1948: 57-72.
"We're All Guests." 1956: 30-63.
Clay, Richard. "A Beautiful Night For Orion." 1954: 14-47.
Clayton, John Bell. "Visitor From Philadelphia." 1948: 73-77.
Clayton, John J. "Cambridge Is Sinking!" 1973: 38-56.
Clearman, Mary. "Paths Unto the Dead." 1975: 59-68.
Cleaver, Eldridge. "The Flashlight." 1970: 20-52.
Clemons, Walter. "The Dark Roots Of the Rose." 1957: 70-92.
Coates, Grace Stone. "The Way Of the Transgressor." 1930: 39-45.
"Wild Plums." 1929: 86-91.
Coates, Robert M. "Getaway." 1959: 59-75.
"In a Foreign City." 1956: 64-75.
"The Need." 1953: 81-89.

"The Net." 1941: 43-53.
"Passing Through." 1939: 52-59.
Cobb, Irvin S. "Boys Will Be Boys." 1917: 86-127.
"The Chocolate Hyena." 1923: 144-169.
"Darkness." 1921: 52-81.
"The Great Auk." 1916: 85-114.
"No Dam' Yankee." 1928: 94-112.
Coffin, Lyn. "Falling Off the Scaffold." 1979: 131-149.
Coggeshall, Rosanne. "Lamb Says." 1982: 299-310.
Cohen, Bella. "The Laugh." 1925: 81-84.
Cohen, Rose Gollup. "Natalka's Portion." 1922: 83-99.
Cohn, David L. "Black Troubadour." 1939: 60-67.
Colcord, Lincoln. "An Instrument Of the Gods." 1921: 82-108.
Cole, Madelene. "Bus To Biarritz." 1935: 115-124.
Colwin, Laurie. "My Mistress." 1983: 99-116.
Comfort, Will Levington. "Chautonville." 1915: 46-54.
Connell, Evan S., Jr. "Arcturus." 1957: 93-127.
"The Fisherman From Chihuahua." 1955: 64-73.
Connolly, Myles. "The First Of Mr. Blue." 1928: 113-124.
Conroy, Frank. "Gossip." 1986: 66-82.
Coogan, Joe. "The Decline and Fall Of Augie Sheean." 1955: 74-83.
Cook, Whitfield. "Dear Mr. Flessheimer." 1938: 110-117.
Cooke, Charles. "Catalfalque." 1936: 70-79.
"Enter Daisy; To Her, Alexandra." 1937: 29-37.
"Triple Jumps." 1935: 125-134.
Coombes, Evan. "The North Wind Doth Blow." 1936: 80-86.
Coover, Robert. "The Magic Poker." 1970: 53-73.
"A Working Day." 1981: 77-109.
Copeland, Ann. "At Peace." 1977: 43-65.
Corle, Edwin. "Amethyst." 1934: 67-80.
Corley, Donald. "The Glass Eye Of Throgmorton." 1926: 36-55.
Corning, Howard McKinley. "Crossroads Woman." 1934: 81-90.
Corrington, John William. "The Actes and Monuments." 1976: 68-97.
"Old Men Dream Dreams, Young Men See Visions." 1973: 57-66.
"Pleadings." 1977: 66-101.
Costello, Mark. "Murphy's Xmas." 1969: 21-36.
Cournos, John. "The Samovar." 1923: 170-182.
"The Story Of the Stranger." 1932: 80-89.
Cousins, Margaret. "A Letter To Mr. Priest." 1948: 78-92.
Cram, Mildred. "Billy." 1924: 19-38.
Crew, Helen Coale. "The Parting Genius." 1920: 83-89.
Creyke, Richard Paulett. "Niggers Are Such Liars." 1938: 118-126.
Critchell, Laurence. "Flesh and Blood." 1946: 128-146.
Crowell, Chester T. "Take the Stand, Please." 1926: 56-70.
Cullinan, Elizabeth. "A Good Loser." 1978: 46-64.
Curley, Daniel. "The Day Of the Equinox." 1955: 84-95.
"A Story Of Love, Etc." 1964: 85-93.

D'Agostino, Guido. "The Dream Of Angelo Zara." 1943: 47-55.
Dahlberg, Edward. "Because I Was Flesh." 1962: 32-40.
Damon, Philip. "Growing Up In No Time." 1977: 102-110.
Danielson, Richard Ely. "Corporal Hardy." 1939: 68-81.
Davenport, Guy. "Robot." 1973: 67-98.
Davis, Olivia. "The Other Child." 1970: 74-83.
Davis, Wesley Ford. "The Undertow." 1956: 76-89.
Dawkins, Cecil. "A Simple Case." 1963: 92-108.
Deal, Borden. "Antæus." 1962: 41-50.
    "Exodus." 1949: 60-71.
Deasy, Mary. "Harvest." 1945: 38-48.
    "Morning Sun." 1953: 90-100.
    "A Sense Of Danger." 1946: 147-164.
Deck, John. "Greased Samba." 1968: 29-42.
DeJenkins, Lyll Becerra. "Tyranny." 1975: 69-79.
DeJong, David Cornel. "Home-Coming." 1935: 135-149.
    "Mama Is a Lady." 1941: 54-58.
    "So Tall the Corn." 1932: 90-100.
    "That Frozen Hour." 1942: 75-92.
Dell, Floyd. "Phantom Adventure." 1924: 39-52.
DeMarinis, Rick. "Gent." 1984: 56-71.
DeMott, Benjamin. "The Sense That In the Scene Delights." 1954:
    48-57.
DePaola, Daniel. "The Returning." 1965: 45-56.
Dethier, Vincent G. "The Moth and the Primrose." 1981: 110-128.
Dickerson, George. "Chico." 1963: 109-124.
    "A Mussel Named Ecclesiastes." 1966: 13-33.
DiDonato, Pietro. "Christ In Concrete." 1938: 127-140.
Diefenthaler, Andra. "Hansel." 1932: 101-107.
Dikeman, May. "The Sound Of Young Laughter." 1963: 125-139.
    "The Woman Across the Street." 1964: 95-107.
Dingle, A. E. "Bound For Rio Grande." 1926: 71-89.
Dobie, Charles Caldwell. "The Cracked Teapot." 1924: 53-69.
    "The Hands Of the Enemy." 1925: 85-104.
    "The Honey Pot." 1933: 77-90.
    "Laughter." 1917: 128-146.
    "The Open Window." 1918: 61-84.
Doctorow, E. L. "The Leather Man." 1985: 58-66.
Dolokhov, Adele. "Small Miracle." 1949: 72-80.
Dorrance, Ward. "The Devil On a Hot Afternoon." 1956: 90-104.
    "A Stop On the Way To Texas." 1954: 58-71.
    "The White Hound." 1949: 81-93.
Doughty, LeGarde S. "The Firebird." 1954: 72-78.
Downey, Harris. "Crispin's Way." 1953: 101-111.
    "The Hobo." 1956: 105-122.
    "The Hunters." 1951: 100-114.
    "The Song." 1957: 128-137.
    "The Vicar-General and the Wide Night." 1966: 35-57.

Drake, Albert. "The Chicken Which Became a Rat." 1971: 86-106.
Drake, Carlos. "The Last Dive." 1924: 70-73.
Draper, Edythe Squier. "The Voice Of the Turtle." 1930: 46-53.
Dreiser, Theodore. "The Lost Phoebe." 1916: 115-132.
   "Reina." 1923: 183-215.
Dubus, Andre. "Cadence." 1975: 80-99.
   "A Father's Story." 1984: 72-94.
   "If They Knew Yvonne." 1970: 84-107.
   "The Winter Father." 1981: 129-149.
Dudley, Henry Walbridge. "Query." 1926: 90-97.
Duke, Osborn. "Struttin' With Some Barbecue." 1953:   112-126.
Dwiggins, W. A. "La Dernière Mobilisation." 1915: 55-56.
Dwight, H. G. "The Emperor Of Elam." 1917: 147-207.
Dwyer, James Francis. "The Citizen." 1915: 57-76.
Dyer, Murray. "Samuel Blane." 1943: 56-69.

Eakin, Boyce. "Prairies." 1942: 93-104.
Eastlake, William. "The Dancing Boy." 1971: 107-117.
   "The Death Of Sun." 1973: 99-118.
   "Little Joe." 1955: 96-106.
   "A Long Day's Dying." 1964: 109-123.
   "The Quiet Chimneys." 1956: 123-133.
   "The Unhappy Hunting Grounds." 1957: 138-154.
Eastman, Elizabeth. "Like a Field Mouse Over the Heart." 1944: 62-80.
Eaton, Charles Edward. "The Motion Of Forgetfulness Is Slow." 1952:
   108-117.
Edmonds, Walter D. "Black Wolf." 1933: 91-107.
   "Death Of Red Peril." 1929: 92-103.
   "The Swamper." 1928: 125-149.
   "Water Never Hurt a Man." 1931: 95-103.
Edwards, Margaret. "Roses." 1985: 67-83.
Eisenberg, Frances. "Roof Sitter." 1940: 37-52.
Elkin, Samuel. "In a Military Manner." 1946: 165-183.
Elkin, Stanley. "The Conventional Wisdom." 1978: 223-247.
   "Criers and Kibbitzers, Kibbitzers and Criers." 1962: 51-80.
   "I Look Out For Ed Wolfe." 1963: 140-165.
   "The Transient." 1965: 57-91.
Ellin, Stanley. "The Day Of the Bullet." 1960: 11-28.
Elliott, George P. "Brother Quintillian and Dick the Chemist." 1955:
   107-122.
   "Children Of Ruth." 1952: 118-147.
   "Faq'." 1953: 127-136.
   "Is He Dead?" 1956: 134-166.
   "The NRACP." 1950: 109-142.
   "Words Words Words." 1960: 29-43.
Ellson, Hal. "The Rat Is a Mouse." 1939: 82-93.
Ely, David. "The Academy." 1966: 59-68.
Enright, Elizabeth. "Apple Seed and Apple Thorn." 1954: 79-85.

"The First Face." 1952: 148-150.
"The Temperate Zone." 1951: 115-120.
Epstein, Joseph. "The Count and the Princess." 1983: 117-140.
Epstein, Leslie. "Skaters On Wood." 1978: 1-25.
"The Steinway Quintet." 1977: 111-160.
Epstein, Seymour. "Wheat Closed Higher, Cotton Was Mixed." 1962: 81-95.
Erdrich, Louise. "Scales." 1983: 141-154.
Esslinger-Carr, Pat M. "The Party." 1974: 45-51.
Eustis, Helen. "The Good Days and the Bad." 1944: 81-100.
Evanier, David. "The One-Star Jew." 1980: 44-79.
Exall, Henry. "To the Least. . . ." 1941: 59-73.

Fante, John. "A Nun No More." 1941: 74-82.
Farrell, James T. "An American Student In Paris." 1968: 43-74.
"The Fall Of Machine Gun McGurk." 1940: 53-64.
"Helen, I Love You!" 1933: 108-114.
Fast, Howard. "The Man Who Looked Like Jesus." 1960: 44-63.
Faulkner, William. "The Bear." 1943: 70-86.
"Beyond." 1934: 91-104.
"Fool About a Horse." 1937: 38-54.
"Gold Is Not Always." 1941: 83-96.
"Hand Upon the Waters." 1940: 65-81.
"Lo!" 1935: 150-167.
"Mr. Acarius." 1966: 69-82.
"Smoke." 1932: 108-133.
"That Evening Sun Go Down." 1931: 104-121.
"That Will Be Fine." 1936: 87-105.
Fauset, Arthur Huff. "Symphonesque." 1926: 98-113.
Felsen, Henry Gregor. "Li Chang's Million." 1949: 94-99.
Fenton, Edward. "Burial In the Desert." 1945: 49-63.
Ferber, Edna. "The Gay Old Dog." 1917: 208-233.
"Home Girl." 1923: 216-239.
Ferry, James. "Dancing Ducks and Talking Anus." 1982: 18-36.
Fessier, Michael. "Black Wind and Lightning." 1938: 141-145.
"That's What Happened To Me." 1936: 106-112.
Fiedler, Leslie A. "The Fear Of Innocence." 1950: 143-190.
Field, Rachel. "Beginning Of Wisdom." 1943: 87-104.
Field, S. S. "Goodbye To Cap'm John." 1937: 55-66.
"Torrent Of Darkness." 1936: 113-133.
Fifield, William. "The Fishermen Of Patzcuaro." 1944: 101-116.
Fineman, Morton. "The Light Of Morning." 1945: 64-70.
"Tell Him I Waited." 1942: 105-115.
Finger, Charles J. "Adventures Of Andrew Lang." 1924: 74-94.
"The Lizard God." 1921: 109-129.
"The Shame Of Gold." 1922: 100-114.
Finley-Thomas, Elisabeth. "Mademoiselle." 1927: 103-117.
Finney, Charles G. "The Iowan's Curse." 1959: 76-90.

Fish, Horace. "The Wrists On the Door." 1919: 123-146.
Fisher, M. F. K. "The Hollow Heart." 1948: 93-98.
Fisher, Rudolph. "The City Of Refuge." 1925: 105-121.
    "Miss Cynthie." 1934: 105-117.
Fisher, Vardis. "A Partnership With Death." 1943: 105-114.
Fitzgerald, F. Scott. "Babylon Revisited." 1931: 122-142.
    "Crazy Sunday." 1933: 115-132.
    "Design In Plaster." 1940: 82-88.
    "Two For a Cent." 1922: 115-131.
Flandreau, Grace. "What Do You See, Dear Enid?" 1943: 115-121.
    "What Was Truly Mine." 1933: 133-139.
Flannagan, Roy. "The Doorstop." 1936: 134-141.
Fleming, Berry. "Strike Up a Stirring Music." 1944: 117-124.
Flythe, Starkey. "Walking, Walking." 1985: 84-95.
Foley, Martha. "Glory, Glory, Hallelujah!" 1937: 67-77.
    "Her Own Sweet Simplicity." 1936: 142-151.
    "Martyr." 1933: 140-144.
    "One With Shakespeare." 1931: 143-150.
    "She Walks In Beauty." 1934: 118-125.
Fontaine, Robert. "Day Of Gold and Darkness." 1947: 56-61.
Ford, Jesse Hill. "Big Boy." 1975: 100-110.
Ford, Richard. "Communist." 1986: 83-99.
Francis, H. E. "A Chronicle Of Love." 1976: 98-115.
    "One Of the Boys." 1967: 67-84.
    "The Sudden Trees." 1985: 96-115.
Frank, Waldo. "John the Baptist." 1922: 132-150.
    "Under the Dome." 1921: 130-141.
Frazee, Steve. "My Brother Down There." 1954: 86-122.
Freedley, Mary Mitchell. "Blind Vision." 1918: 85-91.
Freedman, David. "Mendel Marantz—Housewife." 1922: 151-170.
Freeman, Anne Hobson. "The Girl Who Was No Kin To the
    Marshalls." 1982: 251-259.
Freitag, George H. "An Old Man and His Hat." 1968: 75-78.
Frosher, Wingate. "A Death In the Family." 1953: 137-147.
Furniss, Ruth Pine. "Answer." 1930: 54-58.

Gale, Zona. "The Biography Of Blade." 1924: 95-99.
    "Evening." 1926: 114-119.
Gallagher, Tess. "Bad Company." 1986: 100-112.
Gallant, Mavis. "The Assembly." 1981: 150-157.
    "August." 1960: 64-101.
    "Lena." 1984: 95-105.
    "The Remission." 1980: 80-118.
    "Speck's Idea." 1980: 119-158.
Garber, Eugene K. "The Lover." 1977: 161-180.
Gardner, Herb. "Who Is Harry Kellerman and Why Is He Saying
    Those Terrible Things About Me?" 1968: 79-100.
Gardner, John. "Redemption." 1978: 248-261.

Garfinkle, Harold. "'Color Trouble.'" 1941: 97-119.
Garner, Hugh. "The Conversion Of Willie Heaps." 1952: 151-159.
Garrett, George. "An Evening Performance." 1960: 102-111.
    "The Old Army Game." 1962: 96-107.
Garrigan, Philip. "'Fly, Fly, Little Dove.'" 1948: 99-105.
Gass, William H. "In the Heart Of the Heart Of the Country." 1968: 101-124.
    "The Love and Sorrow Of Henry Pimber." 1961: 58-88.
    "Mrs. Mean." 1959: 91-120.
    "The Old Folks." 1980: 159-175.
    "The Pedersen Kid." 1962: 108-166.
Gavell, Mary Ladd. "The Rotifer." 1968: 125-136.
Geeslin, Hugh, Jr. "A Day In the Life Of the Boss." 1959: 121-136.
Gellhorn, Martha. "Miami—New York." 1948: 106-123.
    "Weekend At Grimsby." 1952: 160-180.
Gerald, John Bart. "Blood Letting." 1970: 108-114.
    "Walking Wounded." 1969: 37-48.
Gerould, Gordon Hall. "Imagination." 1918: 92-108.
Gerould, Katharine Fullerton. "An Army With Banners." 1925: 122-147.
    "Belshazzar's Letter." 1922: 171-194.
    "French Eva." 1921: 142-167.
    "Habakkuk." 1920: 90-115.
    "The Knight's Move." 1917: 234-255.
Gerry, Bill. "Understand What I Mean?" 1945: 71-81.
Gerstley, Adelaide. "The Man In the Mirror." 1947: 62-75.
Gertler, T. "In Case Of Survival." 1980: 176-195.
Gibbons, Robert. "Departure Of Husband." 1949: 100-105.
    "A Loaf Of Bread." 1942: 116-128.
    "Time's End." 1943: 122-134.
Gilbert, George. "In Maulmain Fever-Ward." 1918: 109-124.
Gilbert, Sister Mary. "The Model Chapel." 1962: 167-180.
Gilchrist, Jack. "Opening Day." 1965: 93-98.
Gilkyson, Walter. "Blue Sky." 1930: 59-73.
    "Coward's Castle." 1925: 148-166.
    "Enemy Country." 1936: 152-168.
Gill, Brendan. "The Test." 1945: 82-89.
Gillespie, Alfred. "Tonight At Nine Thirty-Six." 1970: 115-137.
Gilpatric, Guy. "The Flaming Chariot." 1931: 151-163.
Gizycka, Felicia. "The Magic Wire." 1941: 120-153.
Glasgow, Ellen. "The Past." 1921: 168-193.
Glaspell, Susan. "'Government Goat.'" 1919: 147-166.
    "His Smile." 1921: 194-206.
    "A Jury Of Her Peers." 1917: 256-282.
Glen, Emilie. "Always Good For a Belly Laugh." 1952: 181-189.
Glover, James Webber. "First Oboe." 1929: 104-111.
Godfrey, Dave. "Newfoundland Night." 1963: 166-174.
Godin, Alexander. "My Dead Brother Comes To America." 1934:

126-132.
Godschaux, Elma. "Chains." 1937: 78-94.
"Wild Nigger." 1935: 168-181.
Gold, Herbert. "A Death On the East Side." 1972: 48-74.
"Love and Like." 1959: 137-171.
Gold, Ivan. "A Change Of Air." 1954: 123-144.
"The Nickel Misery Of George Washington Carver Brown." 1961: 89-130.
Goodman, Henry. "The Button." 1923: 240-262.
"The Stone." 1919: 167-177.
Goodman, J. Carol. "The Kingdom Of Gordon." 1951: 121-127.
Goodwin, John B. L. "The Cocoon." 1947: 76-94.
Gordon, Armistead C. "The Silent Infare." 1916: 133-148.
Gordon, Caroline. "Frankie and Thomas and Bud Asbury." 1940: 89-108.
"Summer Dust." 1930: 74-86.
"Tom Rivers." 1934: 133-151.
Gordon, Ethel Edison. "The Value Of the Dollar." 1951: 128-138.
Gordon, William J. J. "The Pures." 1963: 175-184.
Goryan, Sirak. "The Broken Wheel." 1934: 152-163.
Goss, John Mayo. "Bird Song." 1947: 95-113.
Gottlieb, Elaine. "The Norm." 1946: 184-202.
Gowen, Emmett. "Fiddlers Of Moon Mountain." 1931: 164-178.
"Fisherman's Luck." 1933: 145-156.
Goyen, William. "Figure Over the Town." 1964: 125-135.
"Her Breath Upon the Windowpane." 1951: 139-143.
"A Tale Of Inheritance." 1961: 131-151.
Granit, Arthur. "Free the Canaries From Their Cages!" 1956: 167-183.
Grau, Shirley Ann. "The Beach Party." 1966: 83-94.
"Hunter's Home." 1958: 119-133.
Graves, John. "The Last Running." 1960: 112-125.
Gray, Peter. "Threnody For Stelios." 1943: 135-143.
Greenberg, Alvin. "The Power Of Language Is Such That Even a Single Word Taken Truly To Heart Can Change Everything." 1982: 182-192.
"The Real Meaning Of the Faust Legend." 1973: 119-131.
Greenberg, Joanne. "The Supremacy Of the Hunza." 1972: 75-92.
Greene, Frederick Stuart. "The Bunker Mouse." 1917: 283-306.
"The Cat Of the Cane-Brake." 1916: 149-161.
Greenwald, Tupper. "Corputt." 1924: 100-109.
"Wheels." 1926: 120-126.
Gregg, Frances. "Whose Dog——?" 1915: 77-79.
Gregory, Vahan Krikorian. "Athens, Greece, 1942." 1953: 148-153.
Grennard, Elliott. "Sparrow's Last Jump." 1948: 124-138.
Griffith, Beatrice. "In the Flow Of Time." 1949: 106-116.
Griffith, Paul. "The Horse Like September." 1947: 114-124.
Gropman, Donald. "The Heart Of This Or That Man." 1968: 137-148.

Groshong, James W. "The Gesture." 1965: 99-112.
Guérard, Albert J. "Turista." 1947: 125-140.
Gupta, Roberta. "The Café De Paris." 1982: 151-181.
Gustafson, Ralph. "The Human Fly." 1948: 139-147.
"The Pigeon." 1950: 191-200.

Haardt, Sara. "Little White Girl." 1935: 182-190.
Hagge, John. "Pontius Pilate." 1976: 116-132.
Hagopian, Richard. "Be Heavy." 1945: 90-98.
Hahn, Emily. "Adventure." 1930: 87-90.
"It Never Happened." 1945: 99-108.
Haines, William Wister. "Remarks: None." 1935: 191-209.
Hale, Nancy. "Brahmin Beachhead." 1952: 190-203.
"The Double House." 1935: 210-216.
"Simple Aveu." 1933: 157-160.
"A Summer's Long Dream." 1957: 155-170.
"Those Are As Brothers." 1942: 129-140.
"Who Lived and Died Believing." 1943: 144-165.
Hall, Donald. "A Day On Ragged." 1962: 181-199.
Hall, Elizabeth. "Two Words Are a Story." 1936: 169-183.
Hall, James B. "A Spot In History." 1953: 154-164.
Hall, James Norman. "Fame For Mr. Beatty." 1929: 112-122.
"Lord Of Marutea." 1934: 164-187.
Hall, Lawrence Sargent. "The Ledge." 1960: 126-142.
Hallet, Richard Matthews. "The Harbor Master." 1921: 207-239.
"Making Port." 1916: 162-180.
"Rainbow Pete." 1917: 307-325.
"To the Bitter End." 1919: 178-199.
Halper, Albert. "Going To Market." 1933: 161-169.
"The Poet." 1937: 95-104.
"Prelude." 1939: 94-108.
Hamer, Martin J. "Sarah." 1965: 113-123.
Hampl, Patricia. "Look At a Teacup." 1977: 181-187.
Hannum, Alberta Pierson. "Turkey Hunt." 1938: 146-152.
Hardwick, Elizabeth. "The Bookseller." 1981: 158-170.
"The Faithful." 1980: 196-209.
"The Golden Stallion." 1947: 141-170.
"The Mysteries Of Eleusis." 1946: 203-213.
"The Purchase." 1960: 143-164.
Hardy, W. G. "The Czech Dog." 1945: 109-114.
Hare, Amory. "Three Lumps Of Sugar." 1927: 118-122.
Harris, Eleanor E. "Home To Mother's." 1928: 150-165.
Harris, MacDonald. "Trepleff." 1967: 85-100.
Harris, Mark. "The Self-Made Brain Surgeon." 1961: 152-167.
Harris, Ruth McCoy. "Up the Road a Piece." 1947: 171-188.
Harrison, William. "The Snooker Shark." 1968: 149-160.
Hart, Frances Noyes. "Green Gardens." 1921: 240-252.
Hartman, Lee Foster. "The Judgment Of Vulcan." 1920: 116-147.

Hartwick, Elizabeth. "Evenings At Home." 1949: 117-126.
Hartwick, Harry. "Happiness Up the River." 1930:91-103.
Hauptman, William. "Good Rockin' Tonight." 1982: 54-74.
Harvor, Beth. "Pain Was My Portion." 1971: 118-133.
Hawthorne, Hazel. "More Like a Coffin." 1944: 125-127.
Hayden, Julie. "In the Words Of." 1973: 132-141.
Hazel, Robert. "White Anglo-Saxon Protestant." 1967: 101-134.
Heath, Mary. "The Breadman." 1972: 93-112.
Heath, Priscilla. "Farewell, Sweet Love." 1954: 145-162.
Hébert, Anne. "The House On the Esplanade." 1954: 163-173.
Hecht, Ben. "Life." 1915: 80-83.
    "Winkelburg." 1922: 195-202.
Hedin, Mary. "The Middle Place." 1979: 172-183.
    "Places We Lost." 1966: 95-112.
Heggen, Thomas. "Night Watch." 1947: 189-207.
Heinemann, Larry. "The First Clean Fact." 1980: 210-220.
Heller, Joseph. "Castle Of Snow." 1949: 127-134.
Helprin, Mark. "The Schreuderspitze." 1978: 72-97.

Hemingway, Ernest. "The Killers." 1927: 40-49.
    "My Old Man." 1923: 263-276.
    "The Snows Of Kilimanjaro." 1937: 105-126.
    "The Undefeated." 1926: 127-155.
    "Under the Ridge." 1940: 109-122.
Hempel, Amy. "Today Will Be a Quiet Day." 1986: 113-119.
Henderson, Robert. "Into the Wind." 1980: 221-230.
Herald, Leon Srabian. "Power Of Horizon." 1929: 123-129.
Herbst, Josephine. "I Hear You, Mr. and Mrs. Brown." 1931: 179-188.
Hergesheimer, Joseph. "The Meeker Ritual." 1919: 200-224.
    "The Token." 1922: 203-231.
    "Triall By Armes." 1927: 123-141.
Herman, Justin. "Smile For the Man, Dear." 1941: 154-160.
Hermann, John. "Aunt Mary." 1963: 185-195.
Herschberger, Ruth. "A Sound In the Night." 1949: 135-148.
Hersey, John. "Why Were You Sent Out Here?" 1948: 148-156.
Hervey, Harry. "The Young Men Go Down." 1924: 110-118.
Hess, Leonard L. "The Lesser Gift." 1924: 119-136.
Heth, Edward Harris. "Homecoming." 1937: 127-141.
    "Under the Ginkgo Trees." 1947: 208-220.
Heyward, DuBose. "The Half Pint Flask." 1927: 142-157.
Higgins, George V. "The Habits Of the Animals: The Progress Of the Seasons." 1973: 142-149.
Higgins, Joanna. "The Courtship Of Widow Sobcek." 1982: 37-53.
Higgins, Judith. "The Only People." 1968: 161-186.
    "His Smile." 1921: 194-206.
Hill, Pati. "Ben." 1958: 134-149.
Hoffman, William. "The Spirit In Me." 1975: 111-123.
Holmes, Edward M. "Drums Again." 1972: 113-122.

Holwerda, Frank. "Char On Raven's Bench." 1954: 174-184.
 "In a Tropical Minor Key." 1959: 172-189.
Hood, Hugh. "Getting To Williamstown." 1966: 113-124.
Hood, Mary. "Inexorable Progress." 1984: 106-122.
Hopper, James. "When It Happens." 1927: 158-168.
Horgan, Paul. "Black Snowflakes." 1964: 137-151.
 "A Distant Harbour." 1935: 217-227.
 "The Other Side Of the Street." 1931: 189-201.
 "The Peach Stone." 1943: 166-186.
 "The Surgeon and the Nun." 1937: 142-159.
 "To the Mountains." 1939: 109-138.
Horne, Lewis B. "Mansion, Magic, and Miracle." 1974: 52-66.
Horton, Philip. "What's In a Corner." 1952: 204-211.
Housepian, Marjorie Anaïs. "How Levon Dai Was Surrendered To
 the Edemuses." 1956: 184-194.
Houston, Noel. "A Local Skirmish." 1944: 128-134.
Howard, Maureen. "Sherry." 1965: 125-165.
Hudson, Helen. "The Tenant." 1968: 187-200.
Hughes, Langston. "Cora Unashamed." 1934: 188-197.
Hughes, Llewellyn. "Lady Wipers—Of Ypres." 1928: 166-179.
Hughes, Mary Gray. "The Foreigner In the Blood." 1969: 49-68.
 "The Judge." 1972: 123-137.
Hughes, Rupert. "Grudges." 1924: 137-154.
 "The Stick-in-the-Muds." 1920: 148-168.
Humphrey, G. "The Father's Hand." 1918: 125-130.
Humphrey, William. "The Pump." 1964: 153-160.
Humphreys, John Richard. "Michael Finney and the Little Men."
 1947: 221-237.
Hunt, Hugh Allyn. "Acme Rooms and Sweet Marjorie Russell."
 1967: 135-150.
Hunter, Evan. "The Analyst." 1975: 124-136.
Hunter, Laura. "Jerry." 1949: 149-156.
Hurlbut, Kaatje. "A Short Walk Into Afternoon." 1979: 44-55.
 "The Vestibule." 1961: 168-182.
Hurst, Fannie. "Get Ready the Wreaths." 1917: 326-360.
 "Give This Little Girl a Hand." 1928: 180-210.
 "Ice Water, Pl——!" 1916: 181-211.
 "Seven Candles." 1923: 277-306.
 "She Walks In Beauty." 1921: 253-287.
 "T. B." 1915: 84-117.
Hutter, Donald. "A Family Man." 1965: 167-185.
Hyman, Mac. "The Hundredth Centennial." 1955: 123-146.

Ignatow, Rose Graubart. "Down the American River." 1974: 67-86.
Ingersoll, Will E. "The Centenarian." 1919: 225-236.

Jackson, Charles [pseud. "Jack Tennison"]. "The Buffalo Wallow."
 1953: 165-175.

Jackson, Roberts. "Fly Away Home." 1953: 176-188.
Jackson, Shirley. "Birthday Party." 1964: 161-171.
    "The Bus." 1966: 125-137.
    "Come Dance With Me In Ireland." 1944: 135-140.
    "One Ordinary Day, With Peanuts." 1956: 195-204.
    "The Summer People." 1951: 144-156.
Jacobs, Theodore. "A Girl For Walter." 1961: 183-190.
Jacobsen, Josephine. "On the Island." 1966: 139-153.
Jafek, Bev. "You've Come a Long Way, Mickey Mouse." 1985: 116-125.
Jarrell, Randall. "Gertrude and Sidney." 1954: 185-205.
Jeffers, Lance. "The Dawn Swings In." 1948: 157-171.
Jenison, Madge. "True Believer." 1939: 139-158.
Jenkins, MacGregor. "Alcantara." 1929: 130-145.
Jenks, Almet. "No Way Down." 1954: 206-218.
Jitro, William. "The Resurrection and the Life." 1922: 232-241.
Joffe, Eugene. "In the Park." 1933: 170-172.
    "Siege Of Love." 1934: 198-209.
Johnson, Arthur. "Mr. Eberdeen's House." 1915: 118-144.
    "The Visit Of the Master." 1918: 131-148.
Johnson, Calvin. "Messengers." 1919: 237-268.
Johnson, Charles. "Exchange Value." 1982: 108-115.
Johnson, Curt. "Lemon Tree." 1980: 231-249.
Johnson, Fanny Kemble. "The Strange-Looking Man." 1917: 361-364.
Johnson, Josephine W. "The Author." 1950: 215-233.
    "Fever Flower." 1945: 115-122.
    "The Mother's Story." 1951: 157-167.
    "The Rented Room." 1944: 141-163.
    "Story Without End." 1946: 214-223.
Jones, Ann. "In Black and White." 1972: 138-152.
Jones, Howard Mumford. "Mrs. Drainger's Veil." 1919: 269-296.
Jones, Madison P., Jr. "Dog Days." 1953: 189-206.
Jordan, Virgil. "Vengeance Is Mine." 1915: 145-152.
Just, Ward. "Burns." 1973: 150-165.
    "Dietz At War." 1976: 133-144.
    "Three Washington Stories." 1972: 153-179.
Justice, Donald. "The Artificial Moonlight." 1984: 123-139.

Kalechofsky, Roberta. "His Day Out." 1972: 180-192.
Kantor, MacKinlay. "That Greek Dog." 1942: 141-155.
Kaplan, David Michael. "Doe Season." 1986: 120-135.
Kaplan, H. J. "The Mohammedans." 1944: 164-189.
Kaplan, James. "In Miami, Last Winter." 1978: 329-353.
Kaplan, Ralph. "The Artist." 1950: 234-249.
Karchmer, Sylvan. "Hail Brother and Farewell.'" 1950: 250-258.
Karmel, Ilona. "Fru Holm." 1951: 168-186.
Karmel-Wolfe, Henia. "The Last Day." 1962: 200-204.
    "The Month Of His Birthday." 1965: 187-197.
Kaser, Paul. "How Jerem Came Home." 1975: 137-143.

Kavaler, Rebecca. "The Further Adventures Of Brunhild." 1972: 193-211.
Kees, Weldon. "The Life Of the Mind." 1941: 161-173.
Kelly, Frank K. "With Some Gaiety and Laughter." 1936: 184-190.
Kelm, Karlton. "Tinkle and Family Take a Ride." 1936: 191-196.
Kenary, James S. "Going Home." 1973: 166-179.
Kerouac, Jack. "The Mexican Girl." 1956: 205-225.
Kerr, Baine. "Rider." 1977: 188-204.
King, Mary. "The Honey House." 1940: 123-144.
    "The White Bull." 1941: 174-194.
Kirk, Stephen. "Morrison's Reaction." 1984: 140-149.
Kittredge, Eleanor Hayden. "September Sailing." 1930: 104-123.
Kjelgaard, Jim. "Of the River and Uncle Pidcock." 1949: 157-165.
Klein, Norma. "The Boy In the Green Hat." 1969: 69-80.
Kline, Burton. "The Caller in the Night." 1917: 365-382.
    "In the Open Code." 1918: 149-153.
Knight, Eric. "Sam Small's Better Half." 1942: 156-173.
Knight, Laurette MacDuffie. "The Enchanted." 1943: 187-217.
Knight, Wallace E. "The Way We Went." 1973: 180-194.
Kober, Arthur. "Some People Are Just Plumb Crazy." 1941: 195-199.
Komroff, Manuel. "The Christian Bite." 1926: 156-170.
    "Death Of an Outcast." 1940: 145-154.
    "The Girl With the Flaxen Hair." 1937: 160-169.
    "Hamlet's Dagger." 1934: 210-217.
    "How Does It Feel To Be Free?" 1925: 167-173.
    "The Little Master Of the Sky." 1921: 288-299.
    "Napoleon's Hat Under Glass." 1932: 134-137.
    "A Red Coat For Night." 1930: 124-134.
    "That Blowzy Goddess Fame." 1936: 197-202.
    "What Is a Miracle?" 1939: 159-168.
    "The Whole World Is Outside." 1938: 153-159.
Konecky, Edith. "The Power." 1964: 173-190.
Krantz, David E. "Awakening and the Destination." 1937: 170-178.
Kreisel, Henry. "The Broken Globe." 1966: 155-165.
Kroll, Harry Harrison. "Second Wife." 1937: 179-194.
Krunich, Milutin. "Then Christs Fought Hard." 1926: 171-184.
Kuehn, Susan. "The Searchers." 1952: 212-224.
Kumin, Maxine. "The Missing Person." 1979: 234-242.
    "Opening the Door On Sixty-Second Street." 1974: 87-94.

LaFarge, Christopher. "Scorn and Comfort." 1941: 200-220.
LaFarge, Oliver. "Old Century's River." 1951: 187-200.
    "The Resting Place." 1955: 147-158.
LaFarge, Oliver, II. "North Is Black." 1927: 169-180.
Laidlaw, Clara. "The Little Black Boys." 1943: 218-231.
LaMar, Nathaniel. "Creole Love Song." 1956: 226-241.
Lambertson, Louise. "Sleet Storm." 1933: 173-186.
Lamkin, Speed. "Comes a Day." 1950: 259-273.

LaMotte, Ellen N. "Under a Wine-Glass." 1919: 297-304.
Lampman, Ben Hur. "Old Bill Bent To Drink." 1946: 224-242.
Lane, Rose Wilder. "Yarbwoman." 1927: 181-201.
Langdon, John. "The Blue Serge Suit." 1957: 171-184.
Lanning, George. "Old Turkey Neck." 1951: 201-209.
Lanux, Eyre De. "The S. S. Libertad." 1944: 190-196.
Lardas, Konstantinos. "The Broken Wings." 1973: 195-205.
Lardner, Ring W. "The Golden Honeymoon." 1922: 242-259.
    "Haircut." 1925: 174-185.
    "Travelogue." 1926: 185-196.
Larsen, Erling. "A Kind Of a Sunset." 1936: 203-209.
LaSalle, Peter. "Some Manhattan In New England." 1979: 102-114.
Laurence, Bethel. "The Call." 1952: 225-236.
Lavin, Mary. "At Sallygap." 1942: 385-409.
    "Happiness." 1969: 81-98.
    "Heart Of Gold." 1965: 199-222.
    "In the Middle Of the Fields." 1962: 205-220.
    "Love Is For Lovers." 1943: 232-255.
    "One Summer." 1966: 167-202.
    "Tom." 1974: 95-111.
    "The Yellow Beret." 1961: 191-206.
Leahy, Jack Thomas. "Hanging Hair." 1962: 221-234.
Lee, Lawrence. "The Heroic Journey." 1967: 151-160.
Leech, Margaret. "Manicure." 1929: 146-158.
Leenhouts, Grant. "The Facts In the Case." 1933: 187-201.
Leffland, Ella. "The Forest." 1970: 138-160.
LeGuin, Ursula K. "The Professor's Houses." 1983: 155-160.
    "Sur." 1983: 161-177.
Lerner, Mary. "Little Selves." 1916: 212-225.
LeSueur, Meridel. "Annunciation." 1936: 210-220.
    "The Girl." 1938: 160-170.
    "Persephone." 1927: 202-212.
    "Salutation To Spring." 1939: 169-182.
    "Spring Story." 1932: 138-152.
Leviant, Curt. "Mourning Call." 1966: 203-218.
Levin, Meyer. "The System Was Doomed." 1941: 221-230.
Lewis, Ethel G. "Portrait." 1951: 210-217.
Lewis, Janet. "At the Swamp." 1930: 135-141.
Lewis, Sinclair. "The Willow Walk." 1918: 154-190.
L'Heureux, John. "Clothing." 1985: 126-138.
    "A Family Affair." 1974: 112-141.
    "Fox and Swan." 1972: 212-225.
Liben, Meyer. "The Caller." 1946: 243-254.
Licht, Fred. "Shelter the Pilgrim." 1982: 75-92.
Lieberman, Elias. "A Thing Of Beauty." 1919: 305-311.
Liebling, A. J. "Run, Run, Run, Run." 1946: 255-276..
Lincoln, Victoria. "Down In the Reeds By the River." 1947: 238-250.
    "The Glass Wall." 1950: 274-300.

"Morning, A Week Before the Crime." 1948: 172-188.
Lineaweaver, John. "Mother Tanner." 1934: 218-223.
Linn, R. H. "The Intrigue Of Mr. S. Yamamoto." 1937:   195-199.
Lipsky, David. "Three Thousand Dollars." 1986: 136-149.
Litwak, Leo E. "In Shock." 1968: 201-214.
Livesay, Dorothy. "The Glass House." 1951: 218-227.
Lockwood, Scammon. "An Arrival At Carthage." 1932: 153-164.
Loeser, Katinka. "Beggarman, Rich Man, or Thief." 1963: 196-199.
Lolos, Kimon. "Mule No. 095." 1964: 191-201.
Lopate, Phillip. "The Chamber Music Evening." 1974: 142-166.
Loveridge, George. "The Latter End." 1954: 219-231.
Lowry, Robert. "Little Baseball World." 1947: 251-168.
"The Terror In the Streets." 1948: 189-199.
Ludlow, Don. "She Always Wanted Shoes." 1938: 171-176.
Ludwig, Jack. "Confusions." 1961: 207-225.
Lull, Roderick. "Don't Get Me Wrong." 1941: 231-244.
"Footnote To American History." 1949: 166-178.
"That Fine Place We Had Last Year." 1940: 155-169.
Lussu, Emilio. "Your General Does Not Sleep." 1940: 170-193.
Lynch, John A. "The Burden." 1948: 200-212.
Lynds, Dennis. "A Blue Blonde In the Sky Over Pennsylvania." 1965: 223-239.
Lyon, Harris Merton. "The Weaver Who Clad the Summer." 1915: 153-171.
Lyons, Augusta Wallace. "The First Flower." 1956: 242-248.

Mabry, T. D. "The Vault." 1949: 179-192.
Mabry, Thomas. "Lula Borrow." 1957: 185-233.
McAlmon, Robert. "Potato Picking." 1929: 159-168.
McCarthy, Tim. "The Windmill Man." 1978: 282-291.
McCarthy, Wilson. "His Friend the Pig." 1929: 169-180.
Macauley, Robie. "Legend Of Two Swimmers." 1958: 150-167.
"The Wishbone." 1951: 228-252.
McClaughlin, Ruth. "Seasons." 1979: 157-166.
McCleary, Dorothy. "Little Bride." 1938: 177-185.
"The Shroud." 1936: 221-236.
"Something Jolly." 1940: 194-213.
"Sunday Morning." 1935: 228-240.
"Winter." 1934: 224-246.
McClintic, Winona. "A Heart Of Furious Fancies." 1957: 234-240.
McCluskey, John. "John Henry's Home." 1976: 145-155.
McCord, Jean. "Somewhere Out Of Nowhere." 1958: 168-178.
McCoy, Esther. "The Cape." 1950: 308-316.
McCullers, Carson. "The Ballad Of the Sad Café." 1944: 205-264.
"Sucker." 1964: 217-226.
Macdonald, Agnes. "Vacia." 1949: 193-204.
MacDonald, Alan. "An Arm Upraised." 1939: 183-188.
MacDonald, Lachlan. "The Hunter." 1960: 165-190.

Best American Short Stories

MacDougall, Ursula. "Titty's Dead and Tatty Weeps." 1937: 200-206.
McElroy, Joseph. "The Future." 1981: 185-202.
McEwan, Ian. "Psychopolis." 1978: 192-211.
McGinnis, Allen. "Let Nothing You Dismay." 1937: 207-218.
McGrath, Elizabeth. "Fogbound In Avalon." 1981: 203-219.
McGregor, Matthew W. "Porkchops With Whiskey and Ice Cream."
    1969: 147-164.
McGuane, Thomas. "Sportsmen." 1986: 150-154.
McHugh, Vincent. "Parish Of Cockroaches." 1935: 241-245.
    "The Search." 1948: 213-221.
McIlroy, Christopher. "All My Relations." 1986: 155-179.
McKelway, St. Clair. "The Fireflies." 1963: 200-210.
    "First Marriage." 1961: 238-244.
McKenna, Edward L. "Battered Armor." 1928: 211-221.
    "I Have Letters For Marjorie." 1929: 181-192.
McKenna, Richard. "The Sons Of Martha." 1968: 215-234.
McKenzie, Miriam. "Déjà Vu." 1962: 246-256.
McLaughlin, Lissa. "The Continental Heart." 1982: 144-150.
McLaughlin, Robert. "Poor Everybody." 1945: 123-132.
MacLeod, Alistair. "The Boat." 1969: 99-116.
    "The Lost Salt Gift Of Blood." 1975: 144-161.
MacMillan, Ian. "Proud Monster—Sketches." 1982: 287-298.
McNamara, Eugene. "The Howard Parker Montcrief Hoax." 1975:
    178-196.
McNulty, John. "Don't Scrub Off These Names." 1945: 133-142.
McPherson, James Alan. "Gold Coast." 1969: 165-182.
    "The Silver Bullet." 1973: 206-220.
Madden, David. "The Day the Flowers Came." 1969: 117-128.
    "No Trace." 1971: 134-155.
Maddow, Ben. "'To Hell the Rabbis.'" 1962: 235-245.
Maier, Howard. "The World Outside." 1950: 301-307.
Malamud, Bernard. "The German Refugee." 1964: 203-215.
    "God's Wrath." 1973: 221-227.
    "Home Is the Hero." 1979: 284-311.
    "The Last Mohican." 1959: 190-211.
    "The Magic Barrel." 1955: 159-175.
    "The Maid's Shoes." 1960: 191-203.
    "Pictures Of Fidelman." 1969: 129-146.
    "The Prison." 1951: 253-258.
Maloney, Ralph. "Intimacy." 1972: 226-234.
Maltz, Albert. "The Happiest Man On Earth." 1939: 189-201.
    "Man On a Road." 1936: 237-244.
    "Sunday Morning On Twentieth Street." 1941: 245-254.
Mamet, Louis. "Episode From Life." 1935: 246-250.
    "The Pension." 1934: 247-256.
Mandell, Marvin. "The Æsculapians." 1972: 235-255.
March, William. "The Female Of the Fruit Fly." 1944: 197-204.
    "Fifteen From Company K." 1931: 202-213.

44

"The Last Meeting." 1938: 186-197.
"The Little Wife." 1930: 142-153.
"Maybe the Sun Will Shine." 1937: 219-255.
"Mist On the Meadow." 1932: 165-176.
"This Heavy Load." 1934: 257-266.
Marks, Jeannette. "The Sun Chaser." 1916: 226-261.
Marquand, J. P. "Good Morning, Major." 1927: 213-239.
Marquis, Don. "The Other Room." 1931: 214-233.
Marsh, Peter. "By the Yellow Lake." 1978: 212-222.
Marsh, Willard. "Beachhead In Bohemia." 1953: 207-213.
"Mexican Hayride." 1961: 226-237.
Marshall, Alan. "Death and Transfiguration." 1934: 267-281.
Marshall, Elizabeth. "The Hill People." 1953: 214-226.
Martenet, May Davies. "Father Delacroix." 1947: 269-281.
Mason, Bobbie Ann. "Graveyard Day." 1983: 178-190.
"Shiloh." 1981: 171-184.
Mason, Grace Sartwell. "The First Stone." 1926: 197-209.
"His Job." 1920: 169-186.
Matthews, Jack. "Another Story." 1970: 161-173.
"The Burial." 1975: 162-177.
"A Questionnaire For Rudolph Gordon." 1977: 205-209.
Maxwell, William. "Further Tales About Men and Women." 1966: 219-233.
"The Gardens Of Mont-Saint Michel." 1970: 174-193.
Mayhall, Jane. "The Darkness." 1947: 282-292.
"The Men." 1949: 205-211.
Medearis, Mary. "Death Of a Country Doctor." 1942: 174-200.
Meighan, Astrid. "Shoe the Horse and Shoe the Mare." 1944: 265-272.
Meinke, Peter. "The Piano Tuner." 1985: 139-149.
Meriwether, Susan. "Grimaldi." 1926: 210-219.
Merril, Judith. "Dead Center." 1955: 176-201.
Mian, Mary. "Exiles From the Creuse." 1944: 273-279.
Middleton, Elizabeth H. "Portrait Of My Son As a Young Man." 1955: 202-208.
Milburn, George. "The Apostate." 1933: 202-207.
"Heel, Toe, and a 1, 2, 3, 4." 1932: 177-186.
"A Pretty Cute Little Stunt." 1931: 234-242.
Miller, Arthur. "I Don't Need You Any More." 1960: 204-244.
"The Prophecy." 1962: 257-296.
"Search For a Future." 1967: 161-174.
Miller, Warren. "The Animals' Fair." 1945: 143-153.
Milton, Edith. "Coming Over." 1982: 233-250.
Milton, John R. "The Inheritance Of Emmy One Horse." 1969: 183-194.
Minot, Stephen. "Grubbing For Roots." 1976: 156-169.
"A Passion For History." 1977: 210-221.
"The Tide and Isaac Bates." 1974: 167-178.
Minot, Susan. "Throrofare." 1984: 150-160.

Mitchell, Beverly. "Letter From Sakaye." 1974: 179-193.
Mitchell, Don. "Diesel." 1971: 156-175.
Mitchell, W. D. "The Owl and The Bens." 1946: 277-291.
Molinaro, Ursule. "The Insufficient Rope." 1963: 211-219.
Moll, Elick. "To Those Who Wait." 1938: 198-207.
Molloy, Ruth Branning. "Twenty Below, At the End Of a Lane." 1956: 249-263.
Montague, Margaret Prescott. "The Today Tomorrow." 1923: 307-321.
Montgomery, Marion. "The Decline and Fall Of Officer   Fergerson." 1971: 176-201.
Moore, Brian. "The Apartment Hunter." 1967: 175-186.
Morang, Alfred. "Frozen Stillness." 1935: 251-253.
Morgan, Berry. "Andrew." 1967: 187-192.
Morgan, Patrick. "The Heifer." 1949: 212-218.
Moriconi, Virginia. "Simple Arithmetic." 1964: 227-240.
Morris, Edita. "A Blade Of Grass." 1937: 226-244.
    "Caput Mortuum." 1942: 201-209.
    "Heart Of Marzipan." 1944: 280-284.
    "Kullan." 1940: 214-228.
    "Mrs. Lancaster-Jones." 1935: 254-264.
    "Young Man In an Astrakhan Cap." 1943: 256-270.
Morris, Gouverneur. "A Postscript To Divorce." 1924: 155-166.
Morris, Ira V., Jr. "The Beautiful Fire." 1940: 229-243.
    "The Kimono." 1932: 187-197.
    "Marching Orders." 1937: 245-269.
    "The Sampler." 1933: 208-209.
    "A Tale From the Grave." 1926: 220-236.
Morris, Lloyd. "Footnote To a Life." 1933: 210-222.
    "Glimpse Into Another Country." 1984: 161-176.
    "Green Grass, Blue Sky, White House." 1970: 194-206.
    "Magic." 1971: 202-216.
    "Victrola." 1983: 191-200.
Morris, Wright. "Fellow-Creatures." 1985: 150-156.
Morse, Robert. "The Professor and the Puli." 1948: 222-235.
Morton, Frederic. "The Guest." 1965: 241-249.
Moseley, Amelia. "The Mountains Where Cithæron Is." 1981: 220-240.
Moseley, Katharine Prescott. "The Story Vinton Heard At Mallorie." 1918: 191-199.
Moseley, William. "The Preacher and Margery Scott."   1968: 235-246.
Mott, Frank Luther. "The Man With the Good Face." 1921: 300-320.
Mudrick, Marvin. "The Professor and the Poet." 1955: 209-218.
Muilenburg, Walter J. "At the End Of the Road." 1916: 262-271.
    "Heart Of Youth." 1915: 172-183.
Mukherjee, Bharati. "Angela." 1985: 157-167.
Mullen, Robert. "Light Without Heat." 1929: 193-205.
Munro, Alice. "Monsieur Les Deux Chapeaux." 1986: 180-206.
    "Spelling." 1979: 150-156.

"Wood." 1981: 241-254.
Myers, E. Lucas. "The Vindication Of Dr. Nestor." 1962: 297-323.

Nabokov, Vladimir. "'That In Aleppo Once. . . .'" 1944:   285-294.
    "Time and Ebb." 1946: 292-301.
Neagoe, Peter. "Ill-Winds From the Wide World." 1941: 255-268.
    "Shepherd Of the Lord." 1932: 198-215.
Neely, Jessica. "Skin Angels." 1986: 207-218.
Nelson, Kent. "Invisible Life." 1986: 219-240.
    "Looking Into Nothing." 1976: 170-180.
Nemerov, Howard. "A Delayed Hearing." 1958: 179-191.
    "A Secret Society." 1959: 212-227.
    "Unbelievable Characters." 1960: 245-261.
    "Yore." 1955: 219-229.
Neugeboren, Jay. "The Application." 1965: 251-258.
Newhouse, Edward. "My Brother's Second Funeral." 1950: 317-327.
Newman, Charles. "The Woman Who Thought Like a   Man." 1977:
    222-234.
Noland, Felix. "The Whipping." 1953: 227-238.
Norris, Hoke. "Take Her Up Tenderly." 1950: 328-336.
Noyes, Newbold. "The End Of the Path." 1915: 184-188.
Nugent, Beth. "City Of Boys." 1985: 168-182.

Oates, Joyce Carol. "By the River." 1969: 195-212.
    "The Fine White Mist Of Winter." 1963: 220-234.
    "First Views Of the Enemy." 1965: 259-270.
    "Gay." 1977: 235-255.
    "How I Contemplated the World From the Detroit House Of
        Correction and Began My Life Over Again." 1970: 207-222.
    "Nairobi." 1984: 177-183.
    "Presque Isle." 1981: 255-270.
    "Raven's Wing." 1985: 183-191.
    "Silkie." 1973: 228-237.
    "Theft." 1982: 311-358.
    "The Translation." 1978: 26-45.
    "Upon the Sweeping Flood." 1964: 241-256.
    "Where Are You Going, Where Have You Been?" 1967: 193-210.
O'Brien, Seumas. "The Whale and the Grasshopper." 1915: 189-195.
O'Brien, Tim. "Going After Cacciato." 1977: 256-274.
O'Connor, Flannery. "The Artificial Nigger." 1956: 264-284.
    "A Circle In the Fire." 1955: 230-248.
    "Everything That Rises Must Converge." 1962: 324-339.
    "An Exile In the East." 1979: 28-38.
    "Greenleaf." 1957: 241-263.
    "Parker's Back." 1966: 235-254.
    "A View Of the Woods." 1958: 192-212.
O'Connor, Philip F. "The Gift Bearer." 1971: 217-236.
O'Hara, Mary. "My Friend Flicka." 1942: 210-230.

Olive, Jeannie. "Society." 1961: 245-254.
Olsen, Paul "The Flag Is Down." 1970: 223-235.
Olsen, Tillie. "I Stand Here Ironing." 1957: 264-271.
"Requa I." 1971: 237-265.
"Tell Me a Riddle." 1961: 255-290.
Oppenheim, James. "He Laughed At the Gods." 1922: 260-269.
"The Rending." 1920: 187-197.
O'Reilly, Mary Boyle. "In Berlin." 1915: 196.
Ostroff, Anthony. "La Bataille Des Fleurs." 1958: 213-224.
Ostrow, Joanna. "Celtic Twilight." 1968: 247-268.
O'Sullivan, Vincent. "The Interval." 1917: 383-390.
"Master Of Fallen Years." 1921: 321-336.
Ozick, Cynthia. "The Dock-Witch." 1972: 256-289.
"A Mercenary." 1976: 181-208.
"Rosa." 1984: 184-222.
"The Shawl." 1981: 271-275.
"Yiddish In America." 1970: 236-287.

Paley, Grace. "Friends." 1980: 250-261.
"Telling." 1986: 241-257.
Panetta, George. "Papa, Mama and Economics." 1945: 154-163.
Pansing, Nancy Pelletier. "The Visitation." 1969: 213-232.
Parker, Dorothy. "The Banquet Of Crow." 1958: 225-235.
"The Cradle Of Civilization." 1930: 154-157.
"Here We Are." 1931: 243-252.
"A Telephone Call." 1928: 222-227.
Parker, Glidden. "Bright and Morning." 1950: 337-348.
Parker, Nancy Huddleston. "Early Morning, Lonely Ride." 1968: 269-282.
Pasinetti, P. M. "Family History." 1940: 244-284.
Patt, Esther. "The Butcherbirds." 1951: 259-267.
Patterson, Pernet. "'Conjur.'" 1929: 206-238.
Patton, Frances Gray. "The Game." 1954: 232-251.
"Paul, L." [pseud.]. "Fences." 1928: 228-245.
Paulding, Gouverneur. "The White Pigeon." 1930: 158-161.
Payne, Robert. "The Red Mountain." 1954: 252-267.
Peattie, Margaret Rhodes. "The Green Village." 1942: 231-244.
Peden, William. "Night In Funland." 1961: 291-299.
Pei, Lowry. "The Cold Room." 1984: 223-237.
Pelley, William Dudley. "The Toast To Forty-Five." 1918: 200-222.
Pendergast, Constance. "The Picnic." 1953: 239-256.
Pennell, Joseph Stanley. "On the Way To Somewhere Else." 1945: 164-169.
Penner, Jonathan. "Things To Be Thrown Away." 1984: 238-242.
Pentz, Albert Duverney. "The Big Stranger On Dorchester Heights." 1916: 272-274.
Pereda, Prudentio De. "The Spaniard." 1938: 208-217.
"The Way Death Comes." 1940: 285-295.

Perry, Lawrence. "'A Certain Rich Man——.'" 1917: 391-411.
Petesch, Natalie L. M. "Main Street Morning." 1978: 163-176.
Petry, Ann. "Like a Winding Sheet." 1946: 302-315.
Pfeffer, Irving. "All Prisoners Here." 1949: 219-237.
Phelan, R. C. "Birds, Clouds, Frogs." 1963: 235-245.
Phillips, Jayne Anne. "Something That Happened." 1979: 324-329.
Phillips, John. "Bleat Blodgette." 1968: 283-314.
Plath, Sylvia. "Johnny Panic and the Bible Of Dreams." 1969: 233-248.
    "Mothers." 1973: 238-247.
Polk, William. "The Patriot." 1930: 162-170.
Pooler, James. "Herself." 1940: 296-310.
Porter, Joe Ashby. "The Vacation." 1972: 290-308.
Porter, Katherine Anne. "The Cracked Looking-Glass." 1933: 223-253.
    "The Downward Path To Wisdom." 1940: 311-332.
    "The Grave." 1936: 245-250.
    "The Old Order." 1937: 270-284.
    "Theft." 1930: 171-176.
Portugal, Ruth. "Call a Solemn Assembly." 1945: 170-179.
    "Neither Here Nor There." 1944: 295-308.
    "The Stupendous Fortune." 1948: 236-248.
Post, Mary Brinker. "That's the Man!" 1948: 249-265.
Powers, J. F. "Death Of a Favorite." 1951: 268-285.
    "Lions, Harts, Leaping Does." 1944: 309-331.
    "Prince Of Darkness." 1947: 293-335.
Prashker, Ivan. "Shirt Talk." 1971: 266-274.
Pratt, Theodore. "The Owl That Kept Winking." 1945: 180-187.
Price, Reynolds. "Broad Day." 1976: 209-219.
    "The Names and Faces Of Heroes." 1964: 257-283.
    "Night and Day At Panacea." 1975: 197-211.
Prokosch, Frederic. "A Russian Idyll." 1938: 218-227.
Pulver, Mary Brecht. "The Path Of Glory." 1917: 412-440.
Purdy, Ken. "Change Of Plan." 1953: 257-262.
Putman, Clay. "The Old Acrobat and the Ruined City." 1950: 349-363.
    "Our Vegetable Life." 1953: 263-278.
Pynchon, Thomas. "Entropy." 1961: 300-313.

Radcliffe, Donald. "Song Of the Simidor." 1967: 211-238.
Rader, Paul. "The Tabby Cat." 1951: 286-294.
Randal, Vera. "Waiting For Jim." 1964: 285-297.
Raphaelson, Samson. "The Greatest Idea In the World." 1947: 336-349.
Rayner, George Thorp. "A Real American Fellow." 1938: 228-236.
Read, Allen. "Rhodes Scholar." 1931: 253-257
Reed, Louis. "Episode At the Pawpaws." 1933: 254-265.
Reese, Lizette Woodworth. "Forgiveness." 1924: 167-174.
Renwick, Joyce. "The Dolphin Story." 1982: 124-143.
Rhodes, Harrison. "Extra Men." 1918: 223-231.
Richler, Mordecai. "Some Grist For Mervyn's Mill." 1963: 246-268.

Richmond, Roaldus. "Thanks For Nothing." 1936: 251-263.
Rishel, Mary Ann Malinchak. "Staus." 1978: 363-380.
Robbins, Tom. "The Chink and the Clock People." 1977: 275-290.
Roberts, Elizabeth Madox. "The Haunted Palace." 1938: 237-253.
    "On the Mountain-Side." 1928: 246-257.
Roberts, Phyllis. "Hero." 1960: 262-277.
Robin, Ralph. "Mr. Pruitt." 1958: 236-258.
Robinson, Anthony. "The Farlow Express." 1957: 272-291.
Robinson, Leonard Wallace. "The Practice Of an Art." 1965: 271-282.
Robinson, Robert. "The Ill Wind." 1925: 186-194.
Robinson, Rosanne Smith. "The Impossible He." 1957:   292-304.
    "The Mango Tree." 1954: 268-277.
Robison, James. "Home." 1980: 262-271.
Robison, Mary. "Coach." 1982: 93-107.
Roche, Arthur Somers. "The Dummy-Chucker." 1920: 198-213.
Rogers, John. "Episode Of a House Remembered." 1949: 238-247.
Roof, Katharine Metcalf. "The Waiting Years." 1915: 197-218.
Rooke, Leon. "Mama Tuddi Done Over." 1980: 272-301.
Rooney, Frank. "Cyclists' Raid." 1952: 237-253.
Root, Waverley. "Carmencita." 1948: 266-273.
Rosenblatt, Benjamin. "In the Metropolis." 1922: 270-272.
    "The Menorah." 1916: 275-281.
    "Zelig." 1915: 219-225.
Rosenfeld, Isaac. "The Hand That Fed Me." 1945: 188-204.
Rosner, Anne F. "Prize Tomatoes." 1982: 260-286.
Rosten, Leo. "The Guy In Ward 4." 1959: 228-243.
Roth, Henry. "The Surveyor." 1967: 239-256.
Roth, Philip. "The Contest For Aaron Gold." 1956: 285-299. "The
    Conversion Of the Jews." 1959: 244-258.
    "Defender Of the Faith." 1960: 278-306.
Rothberg, Abraham. "Not With Our Fathers." 1950: 364-377.
    "Pluto Is the Furthest Place." 1966: 255-268.
    "Polonaise." 1975: 212-253.
Rothschild, Michael. "Dog In the Manger." 1974: 194-218.
    "Wondermonger." 1976: 220-273.
Rowell, Donna. "A War Marriage." 1945: 205-221.
Rubin, David. "Longing For America." 1967: 257-278.
Rubin, Louis D., Jr. "Finisterre." 1979: 243-269.
    "The St. Anthony Chorale." 1981: 276-292.
Rugel, Miriam. "Paper Poppy." 1969: 249-264.
Ruml, Wentzle, III. "For a Beautiful Relationship." 1946: 316-336.
Rush, Norman. "Bruns." 1984: 243-254.
    "In Late Youth." 1971: 275-290.
    "Instruments Of Seduction." 1985: 192-205.
Ryan, Paul. "The Sacred Thing." 1934: 282-284.

Sabsay, Nahum. "In a Park." 1934: 285-291.
St. Joseph, Ellis. "Leviathan." 1939: 202-220.
   "A Passenger To Bali." 1937: 285-315.
Salinger, J. D. "A Girl I Knew." 1949: 248-260.
Salter, James. "Foreign Shores." 1984: 255-270.
Sandberg, Peter L. "Calloway's Climb." 1974: 219-243.
Sandberg-Diment, Erik. "Come Away, Oh Human Child." 1973: 248-261.
Sandmel, Samuel. "The Colleagues Of Mr. Chips." 1961: 314-339.
Sandor, Marjorie. "The Gittel." 1985: 220-234.
Sanford, Annette. "Trip In a Summer Dress." 1979: 206-213.
Santiago, Danny. "The Somebody." 1971: 291-297.
Saroyan, William. "The Crusader." 1937: 316-324.
   "A Fresno Fable." 1977: 291-292.
   "The Hummingbird That Lived Through Winter." 1942: 245-249.
   "Isn't Today the Day?" 1974: 244-251.
   "Knife-Like, Flower-Like, Like Nothing At All In the World." 1943: 271-278.
   "Palo." 1952: 254-263.
   "Piano." 1939: 221-224.
   "The Presbyterian Choir Singers." 1940: 333-343.
   "Resurrection Of a Life." 1935: 265-274.
   "The Three Swimmers and the Educated Grocer." 1941: 269-279.
   "What a World, Said the Bicycle Rider." 1963: 269-279.
Sassoon, Babette. "The Betrayal." 1963: 280-314.
Saxon, Lyle. "Cane River." 1927: 240-254.
Sayles, John. "At the Anarchists' Convention." 1980: 302-311.
   "Breed." 1977: 293-316.
Sayre, Anne. "A Birthday Present." 1959: 259-273.
Schinto, Jeanne. "Caddies' Day." 1984: 271-278.
Schmitt, Gladys. "'All Souls.'" 1944: 332-344.
   "The King's Daughter." 1946: 337-354.
   "The Mourners." 1945: 222-237.
Schnabel, Dudley. "Load." 1932: 216-230.
Schneider, Philip H. "The Gray." 1974: 252-265.
Schoenstedt, Walter. "The Girl From the River Barge." 1939: 225-232.
Schorer, Mark. "Boy In the Summer Sun." 1938: 254-264.
   "What We Don't Know Hurts Us." 1947: 350-365.
Schott, Max. "Murphy Jones: Pearblossom, California." 1978: 177-191.
Schulberg, Budd Wilson. "The Real Viennese Roast." 1942: 259-268.
Schulberg, Stuart. "I'm Really Fine." 1952: 264-270.
Schumacher, Julie. "Reunion." 1983: 201-209.
Schwartz, Delmore. "An Argument In 1934." 1943: 279-291.
Schwartz, Lynne Sharon. "Plaisir D'Amour." 1979: 115-130.
   "Rough Strife." 1978: 262-281.
Scott, Evelyn. "The Old Lady." 1925: 195-206.
Seabrooke, Deborah. "Secrets." 1985: 206-219.
Seager, Allan. "Berkshire Comedy." 1939: 233-243.

"Fugue For Harmonica." 1936: 264-269.
"Game Chicken." 1947: 366-381.
"Pro Arte." 1938: 265-276.
"This Town and Salamanca." 1935: 275-284.
Seagre, Alfredo. "Justice Has No Number." 1949: 261-284.
Seaver, Edwin. "The Jew." 1928: 258-261.
Seide, Michael. "Bad Boy From Brooklyn." 1939: 244-258.
"Sacrifice Of Isaac." 1942: 250-258.
"Words Without Music." 1940: 344-356.
Selz, Thalia. "The Education Of a Queen." 1962: 340-377.
Sergel, Roger. "Nocturne: A Red Shawl." 1924: 175-190.
Sexton, John S. "The Pawnshop." 1927: 255-258.
Shapiro, Madelon. "An Island For My Friends." 1949: 285-294.
Sharp, Dolph. "The Tragedy In Jancie Brierman's Life." 1948: 274-293.
Shattuck, Roger. "Workout On the River." 1953: 279-294.
Shaw, Irwin. "Act Of Faith." 1947: 382-400.
"Gunners' Passage." 1945: 238-256.
"In the French Style." 1954: 278-292.
"Love On a Dark Street." 1962: 378-399.
"Main Currents Of American Thought." 1940: 357-367.
"Noises In the City." 1963: 315-326.
"Preach On the Dusty Roads." 1943: 292-300.
"Search Through the Streets Of the City." 1942: 269-278.
"Tip On a Dead Jockey." 1955: 249-281.
"Triumph Of Justice." 1941: 280-292.
"The Veterans Reflect." 1944: 345-357.
Shay, Frank. "Little Dombey." 1927: 259-278.
Shedd, Margaret. "My Public." 1943: 301-309.
Sheean, Vincent. "The Hemlock Tree." 1934: 292-305.
Sheltzline, David. "Country Of the Painted Freaks." 1973: 262-275.
Shepley, John. "The Machine." 1956: 300-323.
Sherman, Richard. "Now There Is Peace." 1934: 306-311.
Sherwood, Robert E. "'Extra! Extra!'" 1926: 237-243.
Shiffrin, A. B. "The Black Laugh." 1924: 191-197.
Shipley, Margaret. "The Tea Bowl Of Ninsei Nomura." 1969: 265-274.
Shirley, Sylvia. "The Red Dress." 1947: 401-415.
Shore, Wilma. "The Butcher." 1941: 293-301.
Shultz, Henry. "Oreste." 1953: 294-320.
Shumway, Naomi. "Ike and Us Moons." 1933: 266-279.
Sidney, Rose. "Butterflies." 1920: 214-235.
Siegel, Jules. "In the Land Of the Morning Calm, Déjà Vu." 1970: 288-307.
Silko, Leslie. "Lullaby." 1975: 254-263.
Simpson, Mona. "Lawns." 1986: 258-278.
Sinetos, L. Hluchan. "Telling the Bees." 1978: 292-302.
Singer, Isaac Bashevis. "The Colony." 1969: 275-286.
"The Key." 1970: 308-317.

"A Party In Miami Beach." 1979: 84-96.
"A Sacrifice." 1965: 283-289.
"The Safe Deposit." 1980: 312-324.
Singmaster, Elsie. "Penance." 1916: 282-293.
"The Survivors." 1915: 226-234.
Slesinger, Tess. "A Life In the Day Of a Writer." 1936: 270-281.
Slocombe, George. "The Seven Men Of Rouen." 1940: 368-380.
Smiley, Jane. "Lily." 1985: 235-255.
Smith, Gordon Arthur. "Feet Of Gold." 1916: 294-321.
Smith, John Campbell. "Run, Run Away, Brother." 1959: 305-319.
Smith, R. E. "The Gift Horse's Mouth." 1982: 193-209.
Somerlott, Robert. "Eskimo Pies." 1965: 291-298.
Sorrells, Robert T. "The Blacktop Champion Of Ickey Honey." 1978: 136-162.
Sorrentino, Gilbert. "Decades." 1978: 316-328.
Spencer, Elizabeth. "The Visit." 1965: 299-311.
Spingarn, Lawrence P. "The Ambassador." 1968: 315-322.
Springer, Fleta Campbell. "The Rotter." 1920: 236-265.
"Solitaire." 1918: 232-257.
Stafford, Jean. "Children Are Bored On Sunday." 1949: 295-304.
"The Healthiest Girl In Town." 1952: 271-288.
"The Interior Castle." 1947: 416-432.
"The Nemesis." 1951: 295-311.
"A Reasonable Facsimile." 1958: 259-280.
"The Shorn Lamb." 1954: 293-305.
"The Tea Time Of Stouthearted Ladies." 1965: 313-324.
"The Wedding: Beacon Hill." 1945: 257-271.
Stallings, Laurence. "Gentleman In Blue." 1932: 231-242.
Stanley, May. "Old Man Ledge." 1925: 207-227.
Stark, Irwin. "The Bridge." 1946: 355-399.
"Shock Treatment." 1947: 433-439.
Stark, Sharon Sheehe. "Best Quality Glass Company, New York." 1983: 210-221.
"The Johnstown Polka." 1985: 256-272.
Steele, Wilbur Daniel. "Ching, Ching, Chinaman." 1917: 441-467.
"The Dark Hour." 1918: 258-267.
"Down On Their Knees." 1916: 322-348.
"From the Other Side Of the South." 1922: 273-292.
"How Beautiful With Shoes." 1933: 280-300.
"Out Of Exile." 1920: 266-292.
"Out Of the Wind." 1926: 244-263.
"The Shame Dance." 1921: 337-361.
"Six Dollars." 1925: 228-252.
"The Yellow Cat." 1915: 235-256.
Stegner, Wallace. "Beyond the Glass Mountain." 1948: 294-304.
"Chips Off the Old Block." 1943: 310-326.
"Goin' To Town." 1941: 302-314.
"In the Twilight." 1942: 279-290.

"Maiden In a Tower." 1955: 282-294.
"The Traveler." 1952: 289-297.
"The Women On the Wall." 1947: 440-460.
Stein, Gerald. "For I Have Wept." 1965: 325-343.
Steinbeck, John. "The Chrysanthemums." 1938: 277-287.
"How Edith McGillcuddy Met R. L. Stevenson." 1942: 291-302.
Stern, James. "The Woman Who Was Loved." 1946: 400-418.
Stern, Morton. "Four Worms Turning." 1940: 381-386.
Stern, Richard. "Dr. Cahn's Visit." 1980: 325-329.
"Wissler Remembers." 1981: 293-302.
Stevens, James. "The Great Hunter Of the Woods." 1931: 258-266.
"The Romantic Sailor." 1928: 262-266.
Stewart, Ramona. "The Promise." 1950: 378-389.
Stewart, Solon K. "The Contract Of Corporal Twing." 1923: 322-338.
Stiles, George. "A Return." 1944: 358-377.
Still, James. "A Master Time." 1950: 390-398.
"Mrs. Razor." 1946: 419-424.
"A Ride On the Short Dog." 1952: 298-304.
Stimson, F. J. "By Due Process Of Law." 1923: 339-361.
Stone, Robert. "Porque No Tiene, Porque Le Falta." 1970: 318-343.
Storm, Ethel. "The Three Telegrams." 1920: 293-311.
Storm, Hans Otto. "The Two Deaths Of Kaspar Rausch." 1940: 387-421.
Strater, Edward L. "The Other Road." 1926: 264-281.
Street, Julian. "The Bird Of Serbia." 1918: 268-292.
Street, Penelope. "The Magic Apple." 1972: 309-323.
Strong, Joan. "The Hired Man." 1950: 399-406.
Strong, Jonathan. "Xavier Fereira's Unfinished Book: Chapter One." 1971: 298-315.
Stuart, Alison. "Death and My Uncle Felix." 1943: 327-336.
Stuart, David. "Bird Man." 1955: 295-303.
Stuart, Jesse. "The Accident." 1967: 279-290.
"Dawn Of Remembered Spring." 1943: 337-344.
"Eustacia." 1939: 259-273.
"Hair." 1937: 325-339.
"Huey, the Engineer." 1938: 288-305.
"Love." 1941: 315-318.
"Rich Men." 1940: 422-432.
"The Storm." 1942: 303-312.
Sturgeon, Theodore. "The Man Who Lost the Sea." 1960: 307-317.
Sturm, Carol. "The Kid Who Fractioned." 1967: 291-302.
Styron, William. "Shadrach." 1979: 56-78.
Suckow, Ruth. "Four Generations." 1924: 198-210.
"Midwestern Primitive." 1928: 267-284.
"Renters." 1923: 362-384.
Sulkin, Sidney. "The Plan." 1948: 305-320.
Sullivan, Alan. "In Portofino." 1927: 279-288.
Sullivan, Richard. "The Women." 1943: 345-359.

Sultan, Stanley. "The Fugue Of the Fig Tree." 1953: 321-331.
Surmelian, Leon Z. "My Russian Cap." 1944: 378-384.
Swados, Harvey B. "The Amateurs." 1938: 306-308.
  "A Glance In the Mirror." 1960: 318-333.
  "Herman's Day." 1955: 304-330.
  "Joe, the Vanishing American." 1958: 281-298.
  "The Letters." 1952: 305-330.
  "The Man In the Toolhouse." 1959: 274-310.
  "A Story For Teddy." 1964: 299-324.
Sylvester, Harry. "Beautifully and Bravely." 1940: 433-449.
  "A Boxer: Old." 1935: 285-297.
  "The Crazy Guy." 1939: 274-282.
Synon, Mary. "The Bounty-Jumper." 1915: 257-274.
  "None So Blind." 1917: 468-482.

Tallent, Elizabeth. "Ice." 1981: 303-311.
Targan, Barry. "The Man Who Lived." 1975: 264-277.
  "Old Vemish." 1974: 266-305.
  "The Rags Of Time." 1980: 330-355.
  "Surviving Adverse Seasons." 1976: 274-313.
Tartt, Ruby Pickens. "Alabama Sketches." 1945: 272-282.
Tate, Allen. "The Immortal Woman." 1934: 312-326.
Taylor, Kressmann. "The Pale Green Fishes." 1954: 306-327.
Taylor, Peter. "At the Drugstore." 1963: 327-353.
  "Daphne's Lover." 1970: 344-366.
  "The Fancy Woman." 1942: 313-342.
  "The Hand Of Emmagene." 1976: 314-332.
  "In the Miro District." 1978: 98-135.
  "Miss Leonora When Last Seen." 1961: 340-367.
  "The Old Forest." 1980: 356-408.
  "Rain In the Heart." 1945: 283-302.
  "The Scout Master." 1946: 425-463.
  "There." 1965: 345-370.
  "Venus, Cupid, Folly and Time." 1959: 311-339.
  "Who Was Jesse's Friend and Protector?" 1960: 334-353.
  "A Wife Of Nashville." 1950: 407-431.
Taylor, Robert, Jr. "Colorado." 1983: 222-235.
Tennenbaum, Silvia. "A Lingering Death." 1979: 270-283.
"Tennison, Jack." See Jackson, Charles.
Terrell, Upton. "Money At Home." 1934: 327-335.
Terry, Walter S. "The Bottomless Well." 1966: 269-282.
Thayer, Harriet Maxon. "Kindred." 1921: 362-385.
Thielen, Benedict. "Lieutenant Pearson." 1937: 340-353.
  "Night and the Lost Armies." 1940: 450-458.
  "The Psychologist." 1941: 319-331.
  "Souvenir Of Arizona." 1935: 298-305.
  "The Thunderstorm." 1939: 283-291.
Thomas, Dorothy. "The Joybell." 1933: 301-313.

Thomas, Elisabeth Wilkins. "Traveling Salesman." 1936: 282-292.
Thompson, Jean. "My Pigeon Pair." 1942: 343-354.
    "Paper Covers Rock." 1979: 222-233.
Thompson, Lovell. "The Iron City." 1937: 354-379.
Thurber, James. "The Catbird Seat." 1943: 360-369.
    "You Could Look It Up." 1942: 355-371.
Thurm, Marian. "Starlight." 1983: 236-248.
Thurman, Richard. "Not Another Word." 1958: 299-316.
Tildesley, Alice L. "Half-Past Ten." 1916: 349-356.
Toomer, Jean. "Blood-Burning Moon." 1923: 385-393.
Towne, Charles Hanson. "Shelby." 1921: 386-400.
Tracy, Virginia. "The Giant's Thunder." 1926: 282-310.
Traven, B. "The Third Guest." 1954: 328-362.
Travers, Robert. "The Big Brown Trout." 1967: 303-314.
Treichler, Jessie. "Homecoming." 1943: 370-390.
Trilling, Lionel. "Of This Time, Of That Place." 1944: 385-422.
    "The Other Margaret." 1946: 464-496.
Tucci, Noccolò. "The Desert In the Oasis." 1963: 354-379.
    "The Siege." 1947: 461-475.
Tushnet, Leonard. "The Klausners." 1971: 316-328.
Tüting, Bernhard Johann. "The Family Circle." 1932: 243-252.
Tyler, Anne. "Your Place Is Empty." 1977: 317-337.

Updike, John. "Deaths Of Distant Friends." 1983: 249-254.
    "Gesturing." 1980: 409-419.
    "A Gift From the City." 1959: 340-358.
    "The Man Who Loved Extinct Mammals." 1974: 333-339.
    "Pigeon Feathers." 1962: 400-419.
    "Son." 1974: 306-311.
    "Still Of Some Use." 1981: 312-316.
Upson, William Hazlett. "The Model House." 1931: 267-282.
    "The Vineyard At Schloss Ramsburg." 1930: 177-200.

Valgardson, W. D. "Bloodflowers." 1971: 329-346.
Van Den Bark, Melvin. "Two Women and Hog-Back Ridge." 1924: 211-227.
Van Dine, Warren L. "The Poet." 1924: 228-239.
Van Doren, Mark. "I Got a Friend." 1955: 331-337.
    "Nobody Say a Word." 1952: 331-335.
    "Still, Still So." 1953: 332-343.
Van Scoyk, Bob. "Home From Camp." 1958: 317-320.
Vanderhaeghe, Guy. "Reunion." 1983: 255-268.
Vatsek, Joan. "The Bees." 1942: 372-384.
Venable, Edward C. "At Isham's." 1918: 293-304.
Villa, José Garcia. "The Fence." 1933: 314-320.
    "Untitled Story." 1932: 253-263.
Vines, Howell. "The Mustydines Was Ripe." 1936: 293-304.
Virgo, Seán. "Home and Native Land." 1979: 39-43.

Vivante, Arturo. "Honeymoon." 1974: 312-317.
Vorse, Mary Heaton. "DeVilmarte's Luck." 1918: 305-324.
"The Other Room." 1919: 312-325.
"The Promise." 1923: 394-413.
"The Wallow Of the Sea." 1921: 401-417.
Vreuls, Diane. "Beebee." 1983: 269-284.
Vukelich, George. "The Scale Room." 1955: 338-348.

Wakefield, Dan. "Autumn Full Of Apples." 1966: 283-287.
Waksler, Norman. "Markowitz and the Gypsies." 1980: 420-438.
Waldman, Milton. "The Home Town." 1925: 253-269.
Waldron, Daniel. "Evensong." 1952: 336-346.
Walker, Alice. "The Revenge Of Hannah Kemhuff." 1974: 318-332.
Ward, Leo L. "The Quarrel." 1932: 264-272.
"The Threshing Ring." 1931: 283-297.
Ware, Edmund. "So-Long, Oldtimer." 1928: 285-296.
Warner, Elizabeth. "An Afternoon." 1944: 423-429.
Warren, Robert Penn. "Cass Mastern's Wedding Ring." 1945: 303-343.
"Chrismas Gift." 1938: 309-319.
"Have You Seen Sukie?" 1964: 325-336.
"How Willie Proudfit Came Home." 1939: 292-318.
"Meet Me In the Green Glen." 1972: 324-346.
Weathers, Winson. "The Games That We Played." 1968: 323-330.
Weaver, Gordon. "Hog's Heart." 1980: 439-454.
Weaver, John D. "Bread and Games." 1947: 476-489.
Weeks, Raymond. "The Hound-Tuner Of Callaway." 1927: 289-307.
Weesner, Theodore. "Stealing Cars." 1972: 347-372.
Weidman, Jerome. "Houdini." 1941: 332-340.
"Philadelphia Express." 1943: 391-399.
Weigel, Henrietta. "Love Affair." 1946: 497-524.
"Saturday Is a Poor Man's Port." 1957: 320-330.
Weisbrod, Rosine. "The Ninth Cold Day." 1970: 367-378.
Weller, George. "Strip-Tease." 1941: 341-355.
Welty, Eudora. "Asphodel." 1943: 400-411.
"A Curtain Of Green." 1939: 319-326.
"Going To Naples." 1955: 349-385.
"The Hitch-Hikers." 1940: 459-475.
"Lily Daw and the Three Ladies." 1938: 320-329.
"The Whole World Knows." 1948: 321-340.
Werner, Heinz. "Black Tobias and the Empire." 1939: 327-335.
Wescott, Glenway. "Fire and Water." 1925: 270-286.
"A Guilty Woman." 1929: 239-255.
"In a Thicket." 1924: 240-247.
Wesely, Donald. "A Week Of Roses." 1953: 344-352.
West, Jessamyn. "First Day Finish." 1945: 344-355.
"The Illumination." 1944: 430-442.
"The Picnickers." 1963: 380-399.

"Road To the Isles." 1949: 305-314.

"The Singing Lesson." 1946: 525-539.

West, Ray B., Jr. "The Last Of the Grizzly Bears." 1951: 312-337.

Weston, Christine. "The Forest Of the Night." 1953: 353-362.

"Four Annas." 1956: 324-335.

"Loud Sing Cuckoo." 1952: 347-360.

"The Man In Gray." 1954: 363-372.

Wheelwright, John T. "The Roman Bath." 1920: 312-319.

White, E. B. "The Second Tree From the Corner." 1948: 341-346.

White, Ellington. "The Perils Of Flight." 1961: 368-384.

White, Max. "A Pair Of Shoes." 1935: 306-312.

White, Robin. "House Of Many Rooms." 1958: 321-336.

Whitehand, Robert. "American Nocturne." 1936: 305-311.

Whitehill, Joseph. "One Night For Several Samurai." 1966: 289-325.

Whitman, Stephen French. "Amazement." 1920: 320-347.

Williams, Ben Ames. "Sheener." 1920: 348-358.

Williams, Calvin. "On the Sidewalk." 1936: 312-315.

Williams, Joy. "Bromeliads." 1978: 303-309.

"Health." 1986: 279-288.

"The Skater." 1985: 273-282.

Williams, Lawrence. "The Hidden Room." 1947: 490-504.

Williams, Tennessee. "Happy August the 10th." 1973: 276-288.

"The Resemblance Between a Violin Case and a Coffin." 1951: 338-350.

"Three Players Of a Summer Game." 1953: 363-383.

Williams, Thomas. "The Buck In Trotevale's." 1959: 359-380.

Williams, William Carlos. "The Venus." 1929: 256-264.

Willoughby, Barrett. "The Devil Drum." 1925: 287-310.

Wilner, Herbert. "Dovisch In the Wilderness." 1966: 327-357.

"The Quarterback Speaks To His God." 1979: 184-205.

Wilson, Anne Elizabeth. "The Miracle." 1931: 298-302.

Wilson, Ethel. "The Window." 1959: 381-394.

Wilson, Harry Leon. "Flora and Fauna." 1923: 414-439.

Wilson, Robley, Jr. "Living Alone." 1979: 167-171.

Wilson, William E. "The Lone Pioneer." 1936: 316-326.

Wilson, William S. "Anthropology: What Is Lost In Rotation." 1977: 338-348.

Wimberly, Lowry Charles. "White Man's Town." 1931: 303-314.

Wincelberg, Simon. "The Conqueror." 1953: 384-397.

Winn, Janet Bruce. "Dried Rose Petals In a Silver Bowl." 1968: 331-341.

Winslow, Joyce Madelon. "Benjamin Burning." 1969: 287-303.

Winters, Emmanuel. "God's Agents Have Beards." 1944: 443-451.

Wiser, William. "House Of the Blues." 1967: 315-331.

Wister, Owen. "The Right Honorable the Strawberries." 1927: 1-39.

Woiwode, Larry. "Change." 1981: 317-330.

"Firstborn." 1983: 285-316.

"The Suitor." 1971: 347-359.

Wolfe, Thomas. "Only the Dead Know Brooklyn." 1936: 327-331.
"The Sun and the Rain." 1935: 313-318.
Wolfe, Tobias. "The Rich Brother." 1986: 289-306.
Wolfert, Ira. "The Indomitable Blue." 1954: 373-395.
"Off the Highway." 1938: 330-340.
"The Way the Luck Runs." 1939: 336-352.
Wood, Clement. "The Coffin." 1922: 293-301.
Wood, Frances Gilchrist. "Shoes." 1924: 248-257.
"Turkey Red." 1920: 359-373.
"The White Battalion." 1918: 325-332.
Woods, Glennyth. "Death In a Cathedrale." 1946: 540-561.
Woodward, Gordon. "Escape To the City." 1957: 331-345.
Worthington, Marjorie. "Hunger." 1942: 410-422.
Wright, Eugene. "The White Camel." 1939: 353-373.
Wright, Richard. "Almos' a Man." 1941: 356-370.
"Big, Black, Good Man." 1958: 337-347.
"Bright and Morning Star." 1939: 374-414.
Wright, Wilson. "Arrival On a Holiday." 1937: 380-387.
Wylie, Elinor. "Gideon's Revenge." 1925: 311-321.

Yamamoto, Hisaye. "Yoneko's Earthquake." 1952: 361-371.
Yellen, Samuel. "Reginald Pomfret Skelton." 1956: 336-350.
Yentzen, Vurrell. "The Rock." 1954: 396-409.
Yezierska, Anzia. "'The Fat Of the Land.'" 1919: 326-349.
Yglesias, Jose. "The American Sickness." 1975: 278-290.
"The Guns In the Closet." 1972: 373-389.
Yngve, Rolf. "The Quail." 1979: 97-101.
Young, Elisabeth Larsh. "Counterclockwise." 1960: 354-377.
Yu-Hwa, Lee. "The Last Rite." 1965: 371-384.

Zara, Louis. "Resurgam." 1940: 476-480.
Zuckerman, William. "A Ship To Tarshish." 1945: 362-378.
Zugsmith, Leane. "Home Is Where You Hang Your Childhood."
1934: 336-346.
"Room In the World." 1937: 388-394.
"This Is a Love Story." 1945: 356-361.

Index to

Prize Stories: The O. Henry Awards

Introduction

"Lord, but English people are funny!"
This was the perplexed mental ejaculation that young Lieutenant
Skipworth Cary, of Virginia, found his thoughts constantly
reiterating during his stay in Devonshire. Had he been, he
wondered, a confiding fool, to accept so trustingly Chev
Sherwood's suggestion that he spend a part of his leave, at least,
in Bishopsthorpe, where Chev's people lived?

With these words there began in 1919 the publication of an annual volume of short stories that would come to exert enormous influence on the development and the achievement of American literature. For with these words—the first sentences of the story "England To America" by Margaret Prescott Montague—the Society of Arts and Sciences opened *O. Henry Memorial Award Prize Stories 1919*—the first volume of a series of annual collections that would prove to be a long-term benefit and a stimulus to the growth and the maturity of the American short story. And perhaps seldom would the work of a committee of advisors, coordinated by a chairperson/editor, so well serve the interests of a national literature.

The short stories chosen for inclusion in *O. Henry Memorial Award Prize Stories 1919* were not promising of literary greatness. Most of the authors of that day are not well remembered in American literary history—authors such as Ben Ames Williams, Edison Marshall, Francis Gilchrist Wood, Melville Davisson Post, G. F. Alsop, Thomas Grant Springer, and Louise Rice; but among the authors of 1919 O. Henry stories whose names are occasionally still encountered are Wilbur Daniel Steele, Albert Payson Terhune, Fannie Hurst, James Branch Cabell, and Edna Ferber. Nevertheless, the 1919 *Prize Stories* volume was financially successful, even when compared to the competing series, *Best Short Stories,* which had been established in 1915.

The organization that started the O. Henry *Prize Stories* was founded in New York City in 1883 by Herbert Spencer. The original group, called the Twilight Club, later became the Society of Arts and Sciences. At a dinner at the Hotel McAlpin in the spring of 1919 the Society agreed to establish a memorial—perhaps a statue or a plaque—to the prolific "O. Henry" (pseudonym of William Syndey Porter), who wrote numerous popular stories about the four million citizens of New York City between 1902 and his death in 1910.

Under the leadership of John F. Tucker, a committee of the Society decided, at a meeting in December 1918 at the Hotel Biltmore, to

establish annual prizes for the American authors who best carried on the art of short story writing—the literary genre associated with the name O. Henry. The memorial fund, raised by gifts from the membership of the Society of Arts and Sciences, would allow an annual first prize of $500 and a second prize of $250, the recipients to be chosen by a Committee of Award. (The annual prize monies varied, and in 1922 a third annual award—for the best brief story—was added.) The two (or three) best stories and several of the remaining stories considered for high honor were then to be published by Doubleday, Page, and Company, in an anthology edited by Blanche Colton Williams, who taught English at Hunter College and in extension/summer sessions at Columbia University and who published volumes such as *A Handbook On Story Writing* and *Our Short Story Writers*.

Given the social-club and academic-institution background of the O. Henry Memorial Committee of Award, it is not surprising that the annual readers, a group coordinated by Blanche Colton Williams, reflected the mainly conservative values of the New York City social and literary establishment. For instance, the first Committee of Award consisted of Professor Williams, Ph.D., and Edward J. Wheeler, Litt.D.; Ethel Watts Mumford; Robert Wilson Neal, M.A.; and Merle St. Croix Wright, D.D. Further, this Committee of Award was aided annually by an Honorary Committee, the membership of which consisted of over twenty such literary figures as Gertrude Atherton, Hamlin Garland, William Allen White, Max Eastman, Robert Morss Lovett, and Edward E. Hale. For the 1919 prizes, the Committee of Award narrowed its list of superior stories by American authors in American periodicals to thirty-two; after further voting by members of the committee, fifteen stories were chosen for inclusion in the memorial anthology, thirteen outstanding stories to follow the two best stories of 1919.

The organization and operation of the Society of Arts and Sciences to choose and publish the annual O. Henry short story volumes became necessarily much simplified over the next years of the annual's existence. By 1921, for instance, there were in operation only a small Committee on Award and an even smaller Committee of Administration. By 1924, there were only six preliminary readers of the year's published short stories, some of these readers having dual membership on a selection committee. A final committee of seven judges, composed of some members of the selection committee and some newly involved individuals, then chose the prize stories and the other stories for inclusion in the forthcoming anthology.

By 1924, royalties from sales of the annual volumes made it possible to remunerate the annual readers and judges, even after payment of the annual award monies. In 1927, when Doubleday, Doran became publisher for the annual volume, there were only first judges and final judges, groups with some overlapping membership. In 1928, the name of the Society of Arts and Sciences disappeared

from the title page of the anthology, leaving Doubleday as sponsor of the anthology. Blanche Colton Williams was listed only as author of the introduction to the volume, although, it was understood, credit was due her for the organization of the whole volume. Therefore, with the appearance of the 1929 volume, Williams was given title-page credit for selecting and editing the contents of the anthology, although she acknowledged annually the aid of a small group of advisors in selecting the prize awards.

In her introductions to the annual volumes from 1919 through 1932, Williams scrupulously documented the membership of the various Committees of Award and the Honorary Committees, she summarized the reasonings of the committee members as they ranked the years' stories, and she stated their (or at least her) criteria that short fiction must meet to become, in the view of the O. Henry organization, superior and award-winning. Although most of the annual introductions read like committee minutes, Williams occasionally provided useful comments. The most lengthy and detailed statement of criteria appeared in the 1922 volume, in a passage that Williams wrote and that she called the "credo":

> I believe certain laws govern the creation of the short story.
>
> I believe the short story should be short enough to be read at a single sitting. . . .
>
> I believe in a unified effect. If the unity is of time and place as well as action, so much the better. But I accept a story unified in other ways, as through character, or theme, or atmosphere, or the wise use of the angle of narration.
>
> I believe that every good story is based upon a struggle, not upon a tableau or picture. I admit that a complication enlarges and enriches the primary struggle.
>
> I believe in the aids of suspense, of clues, of dramatic forecast, of surprise and all the other arts at a story teller's command. For I know that to-day's sophistication is not so easily appeased as was the simplicity of yesterday. Nor do I forget that surprise was esteemed even in the folk ballads of Chaucer's day. . . .
>
> I believe that development through scenes contributes to the reader's entertainment, since every reader prefers the action of characters, as far as possible, without the interpolation of the author.
>
> I believe that an underlying truth, which is not propaganda or didacticism, exists at the basis of every good story.
>
> I believe that every story which lives, even momentarily, exists through a triangle of forces: the author's afflatus conveyed through the characters and firing the reader.
>
> I believe that if a story lives beyond threescore hours and ten it must be possessed of the intangible quality known as style.

Prize Stories: The O. Henry Awards

Williams elaborated these comments by noting that good stories are not condensed novels or biographies; good stories are not too long; good stories conceal their artistry; good stories are convincing and complete; good stories have coherent structure; and good stories are emotionally convincing. No longer acceptable to cultivated taste was "the professional, suave, utterly emasculated and conventional story of silk-sheathed heroines, charming villains, and even more charming heroes"—the kind of story that unfortunately flourished because it was sought after by too many readers unaware of the higher art of fiction exemplified in the annual selections of the Committees of Award.

Given the academic background and genteel taste of the annual Committees of Award, the record of the O. Henry volumes in discovering new talent was only moderately praiseworthy in the early years, although stories by some authors of lasting reputation were published: F. Scott Fitzgerald in 1920; Mary Heaton Vorse in 1922; Floyd Dell in 1923; Stephen Vincent Bénet in 1924; Mary Austin, Sherwood Anderson, and Julian Street in 1925; Ernest Hemingway, Louis Bromfield, and Ruth Suckow in 1927; Zona Gale in 1928; Dorothy Parker in 1929; William Faulkner in 1932; and James Gould Cozzens, Kay Boyle, and J. P. Marquand in 1932. Too often the O. Henry committee members appear to have rewarded the writings of comfortable, tame, established authors at the expense of the innovative, perhaps occasionally "distasteful" work of younger, rebellious writers.

Another factor that limited the judges in their annual voting on stories was their reading of only the prestigious and best-known magazines that published short fiction in America. In 1932, Williams stated proudly: "About fifty magazines, among them two or three flourishing weeklies, have been considered with no small conscientiousness for fourteen years, or 168 months; a total of some 8,000 or more from the beginning of 1919 through April, 1932." Coming in 1932, after the birth, life, and death of far more than fifty periodicals that existed to publish exciting, vigorous American short fiction in the years 1919-32, Williams' pride in the scope of the O. Henry prize stories today seems uninformed, misplaced, and overstated. By contrast, Edward O'Brien, in reading for his *Best Short Stories* volumes, was hugely ambitious and successful in finding and reading the exciting and numerous "little" or "literary" magazines of the day.

Study of a list of the first, second, and special O. Henry prizewinners in these years (see the complete list published elsewhere in this volume) reveals the limitations of the selection of prizewinners by committee, especially by a committee of self-perpetuating judges with circumscribed viewpoints. In summarizing her work with the annual O. Henry volumes, Williams in her final introduction—to the 1932 anthology—gave as valedictory a distinguished list of annual judges with whom she had worked since 1919; but her list of prize

recipients from 1919 forward, though lengthy, is embarrassingly short of writers who have earned lasting distinction.

Although she had published fourteen commercially successful volumes, consisting of 229 short stories, in her tenure as editor of *O. Henry Memorial Award Prize Stories*, Blanche Colton Williams had not met the high standard of innovation and improvement in American short fiction exemplified by Edward O'Brien, the more daring editor of the rival series, *Best Short Stories.*

The next series editor was Harry Hanson, literary editor of the New York *World-Telegram.* Given his background as a working journalist and columnist, Hansen brought to the selecting of new O. Henry award stories a more adventurous taste and a real-world knowledge largely absent from Williams and her circle. It is significant that the committee members chosen by Hansen to vote with him on the annual prize stories were mostly journalists with a similarly keen professional sense of the daring and contemporary. For example, even though Blanche Williams remained for 1933 on Hansen's board, her judgment was supplemented that year with that of William Soskin, literary editor of the *New York Evening Post,* and J. Donald Adams, editor of the *New York Times Book Review.* In the nine years of his tenure as editor of the *Prize Story* volumes, Hansen chose an occasional academic judge; but his typical judges were individuals such as Joseph Henry Jackson, literary editor for the *San Francisco Chronicle;* Lewis Gannett, daily book reviewer for the *New York Times;* Edmund Weeks, editor of *Atlantic;* Clifton Fadiman, critic for the *New Yorker;* and Herschel Brickell, literary editor for the *New York Post.*

Further, whereas Blanche Colton Williams had in her "credo" given allegiance to some of the fictional devices that O. Henry himself had used to great profit in his fiction—elements such as underlying moralism, surprise endings, and traditional structure—Hansen in each of his nine introductions to volumes in the series carefully distanced himself from the short story desiderata that obtained in O. Henry's day. In his very first volume, for 1933, Hansen wrote: "If I interpret the spirit of this award aright, it is to get as far away from professional precepts and crystallized attitudes as we can and allow full play for the author. O. Henry was not academic; he found his themes in everyday living and wrote of familiar objects and people; his narrative was succinct and vivid, filled with the life and color of his city, and he was going somewhere. The O. Henry Memorial Award carries forward his spirit without demanding that anyone write like him or his time." No clearer separation could have been made between the new editor and the old.

And Hansen and his fellow judges were successful in the 1930s in finding and publishing outstanding short story writers, including authors who wrote about contemporary social and economic conditions in the Great Depression as well as others who delighted in the never-ending fascination of human character skillfully revealed. In

1933, there were Conrad Aiken, Erskine Caldwell, and Marjorie Kinnan Rawlings; in 1934, Caroline Gordon, William Saroyan, John Steinbeck, and Thomas Wolfe; in 1935, Kay Boyle and Nelson Algren; in 1936, James Gould Cozzens, William March, and Alvah C. Bessie; in 1937, John O'Hara, Jesse Stuart, and Robert Penn Warren; in 1938, Richard Wright and Daniel Fuchs; in 1939, Irwin Shaw and Eudora Welty; in 1940, Katherine Anne Porter.

Not only in admiring and rewarding these outstanding, innovative writers of the American short story did Hansen reveal the vitality and contemporaneity of his literary standards, but he also provided succinct statements of his position as a short story judge. In 1934, he summarized the dichotomy between traditional plot and the innovative fictionalizing evident after the world war: "The argument is related to the old one of classicism versus impressionism, of the perfect whole against the suggestive part, of the Phidean statue against the half-formed figures rising from Rodin's marble block." Taking the side of organic, nontraditional fiction, Hansen declared: "Many of the stories by new writers reveal [a full] sense of life, and many authors dig deep into new material, telling tales about people whose lives have been veiled from us and whose ways of speech are far removed from the polished give and take of the well-groomed story. For dipping into the current of this writing the editor offers no apology."

As Hansen broadened the acceptable form (or formlessness) of current fiction, he bravely took all boundaries from around the subjectmatter allowable in short fiction: "The story teller has the world for his parish. No form of human experience, no phase of life, lived vicariously or in actuality, is foreign to the writer's inquiry; to-day, more than ever, he may say what he thinks and feels in the manner he thinks best." And these generous and wise literary criteria of Harry Hansen, so much needed to vitalize the O. Henry *Prize Stories* volumes of the 1930s, are potent reminders in any age of what should really matter in the reading and judging of fiction.

Quietly, with no farewell, Harry Hansen gave up the editorship of the *Prize Stories* anthologies with the 1940 volume, although he remained on the panel of judges to aid his successor in publishing the 1941 volume. One of the judges for the 1937 prizes, Herschel Brickell, literary editor for the *New York Post,* assumed the editorial duties for bringing out the annual volumes—work that he maintained and enjoyed from 1941 through 1951. A working journalist like Hansen, Brickell brought no new criteria or procedures to his *Prize Stories* volumes; his importance to the series lies in his continuance of Hansen's common-sense and realistic standards, firmly in place from 1933 through 1940.

In his introduction to the 1941 volume, Brickell briefly stated his position as editor: "I shall try to keep the flexibility and catholicity of taste that have been characteristic of the selections of stories for inclusion in preceding volumes. I believe the short story to be a living

organism which cannot, except to its detriment, be bound by hard-and-fast rules, and which should even be left free of definition. . . . I attach great value to originality in theme and treatment, and to style, which seems to me of supreme importance in the brief narrative. The very nature of the short story demands the best qualities of writing." Reminding himself of the danger of imposed rigid criteria, Brickell added, in tribute to Edward O'Brien, the recently deceased editor of *Best Short Stories:* "It is greatly to be desired that someone like Mr. O'Brien will always be on hand to help shatter whatever mold the short story falls into and to see that it maintains above everything else its vital freedom of form."

One modest innovation instituted by Brickell was the awarding annually of a special prize to the author of the best first-published story in the year's commercial periodicals—really, an award to encourage new talent to write and publish with the O. Henry prize standards always in view. Further, Brickell acknowledged the aid of an assistant, who screened the year's short fiction and from whose choices Brickell selected the best twenty stories, from which annual committees of three judges—a healthy mix of journalists, academic, and authors—chose reward recipients. Muriel Fuller, described as "a veteran at the job," worked with Brickell in 1941, assumed assistant-editor credit on the title pages from 1942 through 1946, and in 1947 returned to being only an aide to Brickell.

Brickell was especially proud of a further innovation in 1951, his last year as editor: cash payment to the nonprizewinning authors whose twenty or so stories constituted the O. Henry volumes. Income from the annual volumes thereafter allowed award of the prizes, with the editor and the contributing authors sharing the remaining royalty payments. And in each year of Brickell's editorship, *Prize Stories* certainly found and republished fiction by promising authors: in 1941, John Cheever and Walter Van Tilburg Clark; in 1942, Wallace Stegner and Carson McCullers; in 1943, Pearl Buck; in 1946, Truman Capote, Andrew Lytle, John Berryman, and Jessamyn West; in 1947, Paul Bowles, Ray Bradbury, and Jean Stafford; in 1948, Caroline Gordon; in 1949, Hortense Calisher, J. D. Salinger and Shirley Jackson; in 1950, Peter Taylor; and, in 1951, Evan S. Connell, Jr., John Hersey, and Arthur Miller.

Herschel Brickell confidently wrote at the end of his introduction to the 1951 volume of *Prize Stories:* "The future of the short story seems perfectly secure, and since at its best short fiction is a valid and vital commentary on life, there is reason to rejoice."

So much an expected event had the appearance of Herschel Brickell's *Prize Stories* become that, with the editor's unexpected death in May 1952, the publishers had no ready replacement to select the stories and to award the prizes. After thirty-three years of annual publication, the O. Henry *Prize Stories* might well have ended with those final, optimistic words of Herschel Brickell about the future of the American short story. Indeed, no volumes of *Prize Stories* were

published in 1952 and 1953. Yet the desired rescue of the series soon came, and from an unexpected place.

In their introduction to the 1954 O. Henry volume, Paul Engle and Hansford Martin wrote: "It is with a great deal of pleasure and a certain sense of fitness that the editors welcome the O. Henry Prize Stories to the State University of Iowa, and to the Writers' Workshop there. Henceforth the collection will be edited from the campus, with a staff of readers selected from graduate writing students representing all sections of the country." In "a community so genial to fiction" and with the available prize monies doubled for the awards, the revived series of anthologies could now be edited by members of the most vital and innovative creative-writing department in the nation, while the prize-winning stories would be selected by Paul Engle, the most distinguished teacher of fiction writing in the nation.

The introduction to the 1954 volume of *Prize Stories* stated the credo of the new editors as shortly and forthrightly as possible: "It is the editors' conviction that the only thing a short story *should be* is a brief fictional narrative that achieves an æsthetic effect of emotional depth which, at first glance, would seem to be out of proportion to the apparently simple scope of the work. The good short story does not merely fulfill the announcement of its superficial intent, it exceeds it; and it is this extended accomplishment which moves the short story from the realm of entertainment into that of literature."

Hoping to select, reward, and publish fiction that would succeed in "permanently entertaining us after all," the University of Iowa creative-writing teachers rejected stricter definitions of the short story; in their annual introductions they refused to impose their academic will on their readers; they welcomed, if not required, innovation and experiment; and they discovered no huge number of new writers who became lastingly important to American literature, but only a few writers and future creative-writing professors who subsequently influenced the course of the American short story: Richard Wilbur, R. V. Cassill, and Flannery O'Connor (1954); Shirley Ann Grau (1955); Saul Bellow and Howard Nemerov (1956); and Irwin Shaw and Mary McCarthy (1957). The main complaint made by the University of Iowa editors of the O. Henry series was that there was no lack of good story writers but instead too few serious periodicals publishing superior short fiction in the United States.

Just why *Prize Stories* left the University of Iowa after the 1959 anthology appeared is unknown; probably one of the periodic money shortages to which the academic world is subject required that the O. Henry memorial series take up residence elsewhere, away from the most exciting creative-writing department in the nation. The series now returned east, to the Doubleday publishing firm, whose editors again attempted permanent continuation of the yearly anthologies.

Probably as an acknowledged temporary measure, Doubleday chose Mary Stegner to edit the 1960 volume of *Prize Stories,* the volume to be introduced by her husband, the writer Wallace Stegner

Prize Stories: The O. Henry Awards

(although he received no credit on the title page of the volume). Mary Stegner did not state the editorial principles that she employed in selecting the prize-winning and other stories anthologized in her volume, and she included only two new authors whose names reoccurred prominently in American fiction: Philip Roth and James Purdy. Wallace Stegner's introduction to his wife's volume was written by a husband reacting to the mass of short stories that had for months cluttered his home: "I was surprised at the number of magazines, surprised at the total offering of stories, surprised how few of them were at all serious, surprised at how few even of the serious ones will stand up to a critical reading." But, most tellingly, he wrote, "I have thought the level of short-story writing in America is higher than in fact it is."

Yet, despite his disappointment at the material available to Mary Stegner for compiling her 1960 story volume, Wallace Stegner did in a few sentences of criticism describe and define the ideal short story better than had any editor of the O. Henry *Prize Stories* volumes since 1919:

> It must be made of recognizable human experience, but how cunningly articulated, how clearly seen, how passionately probed! It must, in the terms of an antiquated psychology, involve us both head and heart; it must not only stand the tests of logic, reality, probability, significance, but it must give us the very feel of things; must not only persuade us but move us as if these important, poignant, funny, or terrible happenings were the involvement of our own lives. Intelligence, rare as it is, is not enough. . . . At its best, the miracle that we call the short story can present us with a section of life—people, place, event—so arranged that it *acts* as its own meaning as it moves, and needs no caption or abstract formulation or extension. In four or five thousand words it can make us care so much about the lives of people we never heard of fifteen minutes before that it wrings bitter tears from us. At is very best, as in Chekhov, the light it casts on one man or woman can seem to illuminate the world.

Whatever the reason for hiring Mary Stegner to edit only the fortieth, 1961 volume of *Prize Stories,* Doubleday then turned to an academic person, this time a prestigious scholar of recent literature associated with the eastern literary avant-garde. Richard Poirier proved to be a sound choice to nurture and develop the O. Henry volumes toward their highest level.

Poirier edited the O. Henry volumes by himself for only three years, from 1961 through 1963; in 1964 he gained the editorial help of William Abrahams, who assumed complete editorship of the series with the 1966 volume. But in the three years of Poirier's intense work with the *Prize Stories* anthologies, the introductions written by Poirier

and the stories selected and rewarded by him brought to the long-running series—so it seems in retrospect—needed literary modernism and contemporary relevance.

Poirier made his introductions into lectures on the nature and importance of the short story. In the 1961 volume, he wrote of the difficulty of finding, from over five hundred stories worth some annual notice, only a dozen "worth recommending for more permanent attention than they would receive left in the attic with the periodicals that originally printed them." Not totally to blame were commercial magazines with their need to fill space with fiction of some kind. More to blame were the quality "literary journals": "Except in periods of considerable creative vitality and experimentation, of which this is not one, the exclusively literary journals tend to contribute not to the reinvigoration of fiction, but to a deadening refinement of already prevalent themes and techniques. They are becoming the house organs of Advanced Creative Writing classes." Thus, dissatisfied with almost all the current fiction that he read, Poirier set forth criteria for fiction that might evoke his admiration; and such desirable fiction was to be defined by one attribute—its style.

By "style," Poirier meant not surrender to commercial methods or even sophisticated methods of storytelling but instead the building of fiction on the writer's own voice, the rebelliously different and unteachable ordering of private reality that each day the artist goes through in knowing existence. In creating fiction raised to the level of art through the brilliance of the self-fashioned voice or style, the writer may well lose the ordinary devices of surface reality, logical ordering, tacit or subtle statement of theme, and definable boundaries. The reward for readers of such fiction is to be shocked freshly at the recognition of true art, art above social or psychological background, art often without any of the signs of traditional storytelling.

Of his best chosen stories of 1961, Poirier wrote: "They are significant because they can be read with pleasure by adults who do not associate significance with being bored or being uplifted, who tend rather to associate it with those forms of excitement and wonder that never die out of the language of the masters."

However the public or the literary establishment reacted to these demands—the most stringent standards applied to any collection of American short stories—Poirier continued in subsequent O. Henry volumes to lay forth his requirements for prize-winning fiction. In the 1962 volume, he took as his topic the attitudes of the finest short story writers to politics, by which term Poirier meant all of organized social life. Again, he disliked received opinions; he admired private, original stylistic organizing of fictive responses to the world's events.

Thinking of the relationship of the writer to his society, the editor stated about own responsibilities that the O. Henry volumes ideally "should announce the yearly emergence of new writers whose personal grasp of their material necessarily reveals itself in departures from routine, in their impatience with values that belong not

to their personal discoveries but to conventions, either social or literary, of earlier fiction." Poirier believed strongly in new fiction as exciting new organizations of words and images, and he arranged the contents of his anthologies to effect meaningful juxtapositions of style as he recognized and rewarded it.

In 1963, Richard Poirier wrote of the relationship of the writer to special coteries—special groups organized by society to define humans by race, by economic class, by religion, by profession, and by attitude. Instead of writing to or for a national consciousness, writers might better apply their voice, their style, to recognizable groups with common experience, although the criterion of new style even for common experience would not be relaxed. In the 1964 volume, the editor continued his argument for the purity of the art of writing fiction, for fiction should never be disguised as sociology, as psychology, or as any other discipline; "a story is a story, not a study," Poirier announced.

Had Richard Poirier continued writing such theoretical introductions to the *Prize Stories* volumes, his words might have come to be, if collected, a major document in the evolution of postmodern fiction. But, beginning in 1965, the annual introductions to the O. Henry volumes were written by William Abrahams, with Poirier remaining as coeditor through 1966. Not that Abrahams differed substantially from Poirier in his refined taste for original and important fiction, but he chose to confine his introductions to surveys of the current short story scene and to let the contents of the annual anthologies demonstrate by example the standards that he and Poirier shared. As Poirier had in his theorizing resembled Edward O'Brien in the formative years of *Best Short Stories,* so Abrahams resembled Harry Hansen and Herschel Brickell of the competing series in applying stringent criteria and demanding the excitement of originality in the writing of creative fiction.

In his introductions to the *Prize Stories* volumes starting in 1965, Abrahams occasionally defended himself against charges that, having in mind the criterion of high style over traditional storytelling values, he prescribed the writing processes that he then admired and collected; Abrahams correctly noted that he read magazines for good stories, not that he recommended stories for good magazines. He repeatedly lamented the decline of markets for the best short stories in mass-circulation or in limited-circulation magazines. He worried about the nation's literary future when, of a thousand annual short stories, two hundred were poor, two hundred were good, and six hundred were cause for regret. He saw periodicals disappear from the list of available markets for fine short stories, and he saw too many periodicals choose to publish "new journalism" articles instead of innovative new fiction. He defended his personal preference for nonnaturalistic fiction, while admitting that often one-half of the annual stories that he republished maintained the realistic background of literary tradition.

Prize Stories: The O. Henry Awards

Abrahams did institute one important change in the procedures of the O. Henry editorship: in 1970 he announced that occasionally he would award a special prize to a writer of short stories whose long-term and distinguished achievement in the genre had proved remarkable. The winners of this special award have been Joyce Carol Oates in 1970, John Updike in 1976; Alice Adams in 1982, and—again—Joyce Carol Oates in 1986.

And, after twenty years as editor of the O. Henry volumes, Abrahams could happily admit that he had not become bored with reading and judging fiction and that the American short story remained a creature of vitality and vivacity.

That such a confident assertion could be made and defended is greatly creditable to the labors of William Abrahams in editing the *Prize Stories* volumes. In the years of his editorship, which began in 1965, Abrahams could claim honor and wisdom in rewarding short stories by Donald Barthelme, Harry Mark Petrakis, Jay Neugeboren, John Barth, Anne Tyler, Grace Paley, Robert Hemenway, Alice Adams, Rosellen Brown, Renata Adler, Cynthia Ozick, E. L. Doctorow, Gail Godwin, Ann Beattie, John Irving, Donald Justice, Louise Erdrich, and dozens of other writers of short fiction who may yet earn their place in the canon of outstanding contemporary American fiction.

Under the editorship of William Abrahams, *Prize Stories: The O. Henry Awards* has gained and maintained first-rank importance in the development and achievement of excellence in American literature.

Volumes

O. Henry Memorial Award Prize Stories: 1919. Chosen By the Society Of Arts and Sciences. Introduction By Blanche Colton Williams. Garden City: Doubleday, Page & Company, 1920.

O. Henry Memorial Award Prize Stories: 1920. Chosen By` the Society Of Arts and Sciences. Introduction By Blanche Colton Williams. Garden City: Doubleday, Page & Company, 1921.

O. Henry Memorial Award Prize Stories Of 1921. Chosen By the Society Of Arts and Sciences. Introduction By Blanche Colton Williams. Garden City: Doubleday, Page & Company, 1922.

O. Henry Memorial Award Prize Stories Of 1922. Chosen By the Society Of Arts and Sciences. Introduction By Blanche Colton Williams. Garden City: Doubleday, Page & Company, 1923.

O. Henry Memorial Award Prize Stories Of 1923. Chosen By the Society Of Arts and Sciences. Introduction By Blanche Colton Williams. Garden City: Doubleday, Page & Company, 1924.

O. Henry Memorial Award Prize Stories Of 1924. Chosen By the Society Of Arts and Sciences. Introduction By Blanche Colton Williams. Garden City: Doubleday, Page & Company, 1925.

O. Henry Memorial Award Prize Stories Of 1925. Chosen By the Society Of Arts and Sciences. Introduction By Blanche Colton Williams. Garden City: Doubleday, Page & Company, 1926.

O. Henry Memorial Award Prize Stories Of 1926. Chosen By the Society Of Arts and Sciences. Introduction By Blanche Colton Williams. Garden City: Doubleday, Page & Company, 1927.

O. Henry Memorial Award Prize Stories Of 1927. Chosen By the Society Of Arts and Sciences. Introduction By Blanche Colton Williams. Garden City: Doubleday, Page & Company, 1928.

O. Henry Memorial Award Prize Stories Of 1928. Introduction By Blanche Colton Williams. Garden City: Doubleday, Doran & Company, 1928

O. Henry Memorial Award Prize Stories Of 1929. Selected and Edited By Blanche Colton Williams. Garden City: Doubleday, Doran & Company, 1930.

O. Henry Memorial Award Prize Stories Of 1930. Selected and Edited By Blanche Colton Williams. Garden City: Doubleday, Doran & Company, 1930.

O. Henry Memorial Award Prize Stories Of 1931. Selected and Edited By Blanche Colton Williams. Garden City: Doubleday, Doran & Company, 1931.

O. Henry Memorial Award Prize Stories Of 1932. Selected and Edited

By Blanche Colton Williams. Garden City: Doubleday, Doran & Company, 1932.

O. Henry Memorial Award Prize Stories Of 1933. Selected and Edited By Harry Hansen. Garden City: Doubleday, Doran & Company, 1933.

O. Henry Memorial Award Prize Stories Of 1934. Selected and Edited By Harry Hansen. Garden City: Doubleday, Doran & Company, 1934.

O. Henry Memorial Award Prize Stories Of 1935. Selected and Edited By Harry Hansen. Garden City: Doubleday, Doran & Company, 1935.

O. Henry Memorial Award Prize Stories Of 1936. Selected and Edited By Harry Hansen. Garden City: Doubleday, Doran & Company, 1936.

O. Henry Memorial Award Prize Stories Of 1937. Selected and Edited By Harry Hansen. Garden City: Doubleday, Doran & Company, 1937.

O. Henry Memorial Award Prize Stories Of 1938. Selected and Edited By Harry Hansen. New York: Doubleday, Doran & Company, 1938.

O. Henry Memorial Award Prize Stories Of 1939. Selected and Edited By Harry Hansen. New York: Doubleday, Doran & Company, 1939.

O. Henry Memorial Award Prize Stories Of 1940. Selected and Edited By Harry Hansen. New York: Doubleday, Doran & Company, 1941.

O. Henry Memorial Award Prize Stories Of 1941. Selected and Edited By Herschel Brickell. Garden City: Doubleday, Doran & Company, 1942.

O. Henry Memorial Award Prize Stories Of 1942. Selected and Edited By Herschel Brickell and Muriel Fuller. Garden City: Doubleday, Doran & Company, 1942.

O. Henry Memorial Award Prize Stories Of 1943. Selected and Edited By Herschel Brickell and Muriel Fuller. Garden City: Doubleday, Doran & Company, 1944.

O. Henry Memorial Award Prize Stories Of 1944. Selected and Edited By Herschel Brickell and Muriel Fuller. Garden City: Doubleday, Doran & Company, 1944.

O. Henry Memorial Award Prize Stories Of 1945. Selected and Edited By Herschel Brickell and Muriel Fuller. Garden City: Doubleday, Doran & Company, 1945.

O. Henry Memorial Award Prize Stories Of 1946. Selected and Edited By Herschel Brickell and Muriel Fuller. Garden City: Doubleday & Company, 1946.

Prize Stories Of 1947: The O. Henry Awards. Selected and Edited By Herschel Brickell. Garden City: Doubleday & Company, 1948.

Prize Stories Of 1948: The O. Henry Awards. Selected and Edited By Herschel Brickell. Garden City: Doubleday & Company, 1948.

Prize Stories: The O. Henry Awards

Prize Stories Of 1949: The O. Henry Awards. Selected and Edited By
Herschel Brickell. Garden City: Doubleday & Company, 1949.
Prize Stories Of 1950: The O. Henry Awards. Selected and Edited By
Herschel Brickell. Garden City: Doubleday & Company, 1950.
Prize Stories Of 1951: The O. Henry Awards. Selected and Edited By
Herschel Brickell. Garden City: Doubleday & Company, 1951.
[1952 No Volume Published]
[1953 No Volume Published]
Prize Stories 1954: The O. Henry Awards. Selected and Edited By Paul
Engle and Hansford Martin. Garden City: Doubleday & Company,
1954.
Prize Stories 1955: The O. Henry Awards. Selected and Edited By Paul
Engle and Hansford Martin. Garden City: Doubleday & Company,
1955.
Prize Stories 1956: The O. Henry Awards. Selected and Edited By Paul
Engle and Hansford Martin. Garden City: Doubleday & Company,
1956.
Prize Stories 1957: The O. Henry Awards. Selected and Edited By Paul
Engle and Constance Urdang. Garden City: Doubleday &
Company, 1957.
Prize Stories 1958: The O. Henry Awards. Selected and Edited By Paul
Engle and Curt Harnack. Garden City: Doubleday & Company,
1958.
Prize Stories 1959: The O. Henry Awards. Selected and Edited By Paul
Engle, Curt Harnack, and Constance Urdang. Garden City:
Doubleday & Company, 1959
Prize Stories 1960: The O. Henry Awards. Edited By Mary Stegner.
Garden City: Doubleday & Company, 1960.
Prize Stories 1961: The O. Henry Awards. Edited By Richard Poirier.
Garden City: Doubleday & Company, 1961.
Prize Stories 1962: The O. Henry Awards. Edited and With an
Introduction By Richard Poirier. Garden City: Doubleday &
Company, 1962.
Prize Stories 1963: The O. Henry Awards. Edited and With an
Introduction By Richard Poirier. Garden City: Doubleday &
Company, 1963.
Prize Stories 1964: The O. Henry Awards. Edited and With an
Introduction By Richard Poirier. Garden City: Doubleday &
Company, 1964.
Prize Stories 1965: The O. Henry Awards. Edited By Richard Poirier
and William Abrahams and With an Introduction By William
Abrahams. Garden City: Doubleday & Company, 1965.
Prize Stories 1966: The O. Henry Awards. Edited By Richard Poirier
and William Abrahams and With an Introduction By William
Abrahams. Garden City: Doubleday & Company, 1966.
Prize Stories 1967: The O. Henry Awards. Edited and With an
Introduction By William Abrahams. Garden City: Doubleday &
Company, 1967.

Prize Stories: The O. Henry Awards

Prize Stories 1968: The O. Henry Awards. Edited and With an
Introduction By William Abrahams. Garden City: Doubleday &
Company, 1968.
Prize Stories 1969: The O. Henry Awards. Edited and With an
Introduction By William Abrahams. Garden City: Doubleday &
Company, 1969.
Prize Stories 1970: The O. Henry Awards. Edited By and With an
Introduction By William Abrahams. Garden City: Doubleday &
Company, 1970.
Prize Stories 1971: The O. Henry Awards. Edited By and With an
Introduction By William Abrahams. Garden City: Doubleday &
Company, 1971.
Prize Stories 1972: The O. Henry Awards. Edited By and With an
Introduction By William Abrahams. Garden City: Doubleday &
Company, 1972.
Prize Stories 1973: The O. Henry Awards. Edited By and With an
Introduction By William Abrahams. Garden City: Doubleday &
Company, 1973.
Prize Stories 1974: The O. Henry Awards. Edited and With an
Introduction By William Abrahams. Garden City: Doubleday &
Company, 1974.
Prize Stories 1975: The O. Henry Awards. Edited and With an
Introduction By William Abrahams. Garden City: Doubleday &
Company, 1975.
Prize Stories 1976 The O. Henry Awards. Edited and With an
Introduction By William Abrahams. Garden City: Doubleday &
Company, 1976.
Prize Stories 1977: The O. Henry Awards. Edited and With an
Introduction By William Abrahams. Garden City: Doubleday &
Company, 1977.
Prize Stories 1978: The O. Henry Awards. Edited and With an
Introduction By William Abrahams. Garden City: Doubleday &
Company, 1978.
Prize Stories 1979: The O. Henry Awards. Edited and With an
Introduction By William Abrahams. Garden City: Doubleday &
Company, 1979.
Prize Stories 1980: The O. Henry Awards. Edited and With an
Introduction By William Abrahams. Garden City: Doubleday &
Company, 1980.
Prize Stories 1981: The O. Henry Awards. Edited and With an
Introduction By William Abrahams. Garden City: Doubleday &
Company, 1981.
Prize Stories 1982: The O. Henry Awards. Edited and With an
Introduction By William Abrahams. Garden City: Doubleday &
Company, 1982.
Prize Stories 1983: The O. Henry Awards. Edited and With an
Introduction By William Abrahams. Garden City: Doubleday &
Company, 1983.

Prize Stories: The O. Henry Awards

Prize Stories 1984: The O. Henry Awards. Edited and With an
  Introduction By William Abrahams. Garden City: Doubleday &
  Company, 1984.
Prize Stories 1985: The O. Henry Awards. Edited and With an
  Introduction By William Abrahams. Garden City: Doubleday &
  Company, 1985.
Prize Stories 1986: The O. Henry Awards. Edited and With an
  Introduction By William Abrahams. Garden City: Doubleday &
  Company, 1986.
Prize Stories 1987: The O. Henry Awards. Edited and With an
  Introduction By William Abrahams. Garden City: Doubleday &
  Company, 1987.

Prize-Winning Stories by Year

[FP = First Published Story]
[SP = Special Prize]
[SS = Short-Short Story]

1919
1. Montague, Margaret Prescott. "England to America."
2. Steele, Wilbur Daniel. "For They Know Not What They Do."

1920
1. Burt, Maxwell Struthers. "Each In His Generation."
2. Hart, Frances Noyes. "Contact."

1921
1. Marshall, Edison. "The Heart of Little Shikara."
2. Jackson, Charles Tenney. "The Man Who Cursed the Lilies."
SP: Steele, Wilbur Daniel. "The Marriage In Kairwan."

1922
1. Cobb, Irvin S. "Snake Doctor."
2. Lane, Rose Wilder. "Innocence."
SS: Buckley, F. R. "Gold-Mounted Guns."

1923
1. Smith, Edgar Valentine. "Prelude."
2. Connell, Richard. "A Friend of Napoleon."
SS: Folson, Elizabeth Irons. "Towers of Fame."

1924
1. Irwin, Inez Haynes. "The Spring Flight."
2. Crowell, Chester T. "Margaret Blake."
SS: Newman, Frances. "Rachel and Her Children."

1925
1. Street, Julian. "Mr. Bisbee's Princess."
2. Williams, Wythe. "Splendid With Swords."
SS: Austin, Mary. "Papago Wedding."

1926
1. Steele, Wilbur Daniel. "Bubbles."
2. Anderson, Sherwood. "Death In the Woods."

SS: Wetjen, Albert Richard. "Command."

1927
1. Bradford, Roark. "Child of God."
2. Hemingway, Ernest. "The Killers."
SS: Bromfield, Louis. "The Scarlet Woman."

1928
1. Duranty, Walter. "The Parrot."
2. Douglas, Marjorie Stoneman. "The Peculiar Treasure of Kings."
SS: Gale, Zona. "Bridal Pond."

1929
1. Parker, Dorothy. "Big Blonde."
2. Howard, Sidney. "The Homesick Ladies."
SS: Brush, Katharine. "Him and Her."

1930
1. Burnett, W. R. "Dressing-Up."
1. John, William M. "Neither Jew Nor Greek."
2. Roberts, Elizabeth Madox. "The Sacrifice of Maidens."
SS: Connelly, Marc. "Coroner's Inquest."

1931
1. Steele, Wilbur Daniel. "Can't Cross Jordan By Myself."
2. Swain, John D. "One Head Well Done."
3. Bradley, Mary Hastings. "The Five Minute Girl."
SS: LaFarge, Oliver. "Haunted Ground."

1932
1. Benét, Stephen Vincent. "An End To Dreams."
2. Cozzens, James Gould. "Farewell To Cuba."
SS: Granberry, Edwin. "A Trip To Czardis."

1933
1. Rawlings, Marjorie Kinnan. "Gal Young Un."
2. Buck, Pearl S. "The Frill."
SS: Hale, Nancy. "To the Invader."

1934
1. Paul, Louis. "No More Trouble For Jedwick."
2. Gordon, Caroline. "Old Red."
SS: Saroyan, William. "The Daring Young Man On the Flying Trapeze."

1935
1. Boyle, Kay. "The White Horses of Vienna."

2. Thomas, Dorothy. "The Home Place."
SS: Johnson, Josephine W. "John the Six."

1936
1. Cozzens, James Gould. "Total Stranger."
2. Benson, Sally. "Suite 2049."
SS: March, William. "A Sum In Addition."

1937
1. Benét, Stephen Vincent. "The Devil and Daniel Webster."
2. Moll, Elick. "To Those Who Wait."
3. Coates, Robert M. "The Fury."

1938
1. Maltz, Albert. "The Happiest Man On Earth."
2. Wright, Richard. "Fire and Cloud."
3. Steinbeck, John. "The Promise."

1939
1. Faulkner, William. "Barn Burning."
2. Still, James. "Bat Flight."
3. DeJong, David Cornel. "Calves."

1940
1. Benét, Stephen Vincent. "Freedom's a Hard-Bought Thing."
2. Lull, Roderick. "Don't Get Me Wrong."
3. Havill, Edward. "The Kill."

1941
1. Boyle, Kay. "Defeat."
2. Welty, Eudora. "A Worn Path."
3. Abbett, Hallie Southgate. "Eighteenth Summer."

1942
1. Welty, Eudora. "The Wide Net."
2. Stegner, Wallace. "Two Rivers."
3. Schramm, Wilbur L. "Windwagon Smith."
FP: Wylie, Jeanne E. "A Long Way To Go."

1943
1. Welty, Eudora. "Livvie Is Back."
2. Canfield, Dorothy. "The Knot Hole."
3. Fifield, William. "The Fishermen of Patzcuaro."
FP: Laidlaw, Clara. "The Little Black Boys."

1944
1. Shaw, Irwin. "Walking Wounded."
2. Breuer, Bessie. "Home Is a Place."

3. Beems, Griffith. "The Stagecoach."
FP: Critchell, Laurence. "Flesh and Blood."

1945
1. Clark, Walter Van Tilburg. "The Wind and the Snow of Winter."
2. Shaw, Irwin. "Gunners' Passage."
3. Lampman, Ben Hur. "Old Bill Bent To Drink."
FP: Critchell, Captain Laurence. "Flesh and Blood."

1946
1. Goss, John Mayo. "Bird Song."
2. Shedd, Margaret. "The Innocent Bystander."
3. Ullman, Victor. "Sometimes You Break Even."
FP: Meyer, Cord, Jr. "Waves Of Darkness."

1947
1. Clayton, John Bell. "The White Circle."
2. Burdick, Eugene L. "Rest Camp On Maui."
3. Parsons, Elizabeth. "The Nightingales Sing."
FP: Lewis, Robert. "Little Victor."

1948
1. Capote, Truman. "Shut a Final Door."
2. Stegner, Wallace. "Beyond the Glass Mountain."
3. Bradbury, Ray. "Powerhouse."
FP: Grennard, Elliott. "Sparrow's Last Jump."

1949
1. Faulkner, William. "A Courtship."
2. Van Doren, Mark. "The Watchman."
3. Dorrance, Ward. "The White Hound."

1950
1. Stegner, Wallace. "The Blue-Winged Teal."
2. Leiper, Gudger Bart. "The Magnolias."
3. Lowry, Robert. "Be Nice to Mr. Campbell."

1951
1. Downey, Harris. "The Hunters."
2. Welty, Eudora. "The Burning."
3. Capote, Truman. "The House Of Flowers."

1952
[No Volume Published]

1953
[No Volume Published]

1954
1. Mabry, Thomas. "The Indian Feather."
2. Putman, Clay. "The News From Troy."
3. Wilbur, Richard. "A Game Of Catch."

1955
1. Stafford, Jean. "In the Zoo."
2. O'Connor, Flannery. "A Circle In the Fire."
3. Buechner, Frederick. "The Tiger."

1956
1. Cheever, John. "The Country Husband."
2. Buechner, James. "Pepicelli."
3. Cassill, R. V. "The Prize."

1957
1. O'Connor, Flannery. "Greenleaf."
2. Gold, Herbert. "Encounter In Haiti."
3. Elliott, George P. "Miracle Play."

1958
1. Gellhorn, Martha. "In Sickness As In Health."
2. Calisher, Hortense. "What a Thing, To Keep a Wolf In a Cage!"
3. Steiner, George. "The Deeps Of the Sea."

1959
1. Taylor, Peter. "Venus, Cupid, Folly and Time."
2. Elliott, George P. "Among the Dangs."
3. Turner, Thomas C. "Something To Explain."

1960
1. Hall, Lawrence Sargent. "The Ledge."
2. Roth, Philip. "Defender Of the Faith."
3. White, Robin. "Shower Of Ashes."

1961
1. Olsen, Tillie. "Tell Me a Riddle."
2. Gold, Ivan. "The Nickel Misery Of George Washington Carver Brown."
3. Price, Reynolds. "One Sunday In Late July."

1962
1. Porter, Katharine Anne. "Holiday."
2. Pynchon, Thomas. "Under the Rose."
3. Cole, Tom. "Familiar Usage In Leningrad."

1963
1. O'Connor, Flannery. "Everything That Rises Must Converge."

2. Krause, Ervin D. "The Snake."
3. Selz, Thalia. "The Education Of a Queen."

1964
1. Cheever, John. "The Embarkment For Cythera."
2. Oates, Joyce Carol. "Stigmata."
3. Shedd, Margaret. "The Everlasting Witness."

1965
1. O'Connor, Flannery. "Revelation."
2. Friedman, Sanford. "Ocean."
3. Humphrey, William. "The Ballad Of Jesse Neighbours."

1966
1. Updike, John. "The Bulgarian Poetess."
2. Howard, Maureen. "Sherry."
3. Cole, Tom. "On the Edge Of Arcadia."

1967
1. Oates, Joyce Carol. "In the Region Of Ice."
2. Barthelme, Donald. "See the Moon?"
3. Strong, Jonathan. "Supperburger."

1968
1. Welty, Eudora. "The Demonstrators."
2. Broner, E. M. "The New Nobility."
3. Katz, Shlomo. "My Redeemer Cometh. . . ."

1969
1. Malamud, Bernard. "Man In the Drawer."
2. Oates, Joyce Carol. "Accomplished Desires."
3. Barth, John. "Lost In the Funhouse."

1970
1. Hemenway, Robert. "The Girl Who Sang With the Beatles."
2. Eastlake, William. "The Biggest Thing Since Custer."
3. Rindfleisch, Norval. "A Cliff Of Fall."
SP: Oates, Joyce Carol. "Unmailed, Unwritten Letters."
   "How I Contemplated the World From the Detroit House Of
   Correction and Began My Life Over Again."

1971
1. Hecht, Florence M. "Twin Bed Bridge."
2. Cardwell, Guy A. "Did You Once See Shelly?"
3. Adam, Alice. "Gift Of Grass."

1972
1. Bakti, John. "Strange-Dreaming, Cow-Eyed Charlie."

    2. Oates, Joyce Carol. "Sol Bird Says: Relate! Communicate! Liberate!"
    3. Rascoe, Judith. "Small Sounds and Tilting Shadows."

1973
    1. Oates, Joyce Carol. "The Dead."
    2. Malamud, Bernard. "Talking Horse."
    3. Brown, Rosellen. "Mainlanders."

1974
    1. Adler, Renata. "Brownstone."
    2. Henson, Robert. "Lizzie Borden In the P.M."
    3. Adams, Alice. "Alternatives."

1975
    1. Brodkey, Harold. "A Story In an Almost Classical Mode."
    1. Ozick, Cynthia. "Usurpation (Other People's Stories)."
    [No Second Or Third Prizes]

1976
    1. Brodkey, Harold. "His Son, In His Arms, In Light, Aloft."
    2. Sayles, John. "I-80 Nebraska, M. 409-M.205."
    3. Adams, Alice. "Roses, Rhododendron."
    SP: Updike, John. "Separating."

1977
    1. Leffland, Ella. "Last Courtesies"
    1. Hazzard, Shirley. "A Long Short Story."
    [No Second Or Third Prizes]

1978
    1. Allen, Woody. "The Kugelmass Episode."
    2. Schorer, Mark. "A Lamp."
    3. Henson, Robert. "The Upper and the Lower Millstones."

1979
    1. Weaver, Gordon. "Getting Serious."
    2. Bromell, Henry. "Travel Stories."
    3. Hecht, Julie. "I Want You, I Need You, I Love You."

1980
    1. Bellow, Saul. "A Silver Dish."
    2. Hallinan, Nancy. "Women In a Roman Courtyard."
    3. Michaels, Leonard. "The Men's Club."

1981
    1. Ozick, Cynthia. "The Shawl."
    [No Second Or Third Prizes]

1982
1. Kenney, Susan. "Facing Front."
2. McElroy, Joseph. "The Future."
3. Brooks, Ben. "A Postal Creed."
SP: Adams, Alice. "Greyhound People."
   "To See You Again."

1983
1. Carver, Raymond. "A Small, Good Thing."
2. Oates, Joyce Carol. "My Warszawa."
3. Morris, Wright. "Victrola."

1984
1. Ozick, Cynthia. "Rosa."
[No Second Or Third Prizes]

1985
1. Smiley, Jane. "Lily."
1. Dybek, Stuart. "Hot Ice."
[No Second or Third Prizes]

1986
1.Walker, Alice. "Kindred Spirits."
[No Second Or Third Prizes]
SP: Oates, Joyce Carol. "Master Race."

1987
1. Erdrich, Louise. "Fleur."
1. Johnson, Joyce. "The Children's Wing."
[No Second Or Third Prizes]

Author Index

Abbett, Hallie Southgate. "Eighteenth Summer." 1941: 31-46.
Abbott, Lee K., Jr. "Living Alone In Iota." 1984: 118-126.
Adams, Alice. "Alaska." 1984: 96-105.
    "Alternatives." 1974: 54-67.
    "Beautiful Girl." 1978: 67-75.
    "Flights." 1977: 186-198.
    "Gift Of Grass." 1971: 58-66.
    "The Girl Across the Room." 1979: 319-327.
    "Greyhound People." 1982: 289-300.
    "Molly's Dog." 1986: 118-129.
    "Ripped Off." 1972: 177-185.
    "Roses, Rhododendron." 1976: 52-65.
    "Snow." 1981: 94-104.
    "The Swastika On Our Door." 1973: 107-124.
    "Tide Pools." 1987: 65-80.
    "To See You Again." 1982: 301-311.
    "Truth Or Consequences." 1980: 345-357.
    "Verlie I Say Unto You." 1975: 99-110.
Adams, Bill. "Home Is the Sailor." 1928: 55-72.
    "Jukes." 1927: 34-52.
    "The Lubber." 1933: 75-92.
Adams, Thomas E. "Sled." 1962: 217-225.
Adler, Renata. "Brownstone." 1974: 13-25.
Aiken, Conrad. "Hello, Tib." 1941: 61-67.
    "Impulses." 1933: 95-109.
Aldrich, Bess Streeter. "The Man Who Caught the Weather." 1928: 89-97.
Alexander, Charles. "As a Dog Should." 1922: 44-55.
Algren, Nelson. "A Bottle Of Milk For Mother." 1941: 71-89.
    "The Brothers' House." 1935: 63-67.
    "The Captain Is Impaled." 1950: 52-67.
Allen, Maryland. "The Urge." 1921: 45-65.
Allen, Woody. "The Kugelmass Episode." 1978: 15-25.
Alsop, G. F. "The Kitchen Gods." 1919: 253-273.
Anderson, Sherwood. "Alice." 1929: 65-71.
    "Death In the Woods." 1926: 23-35.
    "The Return." 1925: 77-93.
Ansell, Helen Essary. "The Threesome." 1963: 182-194.
Appel, Benjamin. "Awroopdedoop!" 1937: 45-52.
    "Pigeon Flight." 1934: 55-62.
Appel, Max. "Paddycake, Paddycake . . . A Memoir." 1978: 76-86.
Arensberg, Ann. "Art History." 1975: 151-168.

"Group Sex." 1980: 271-294.
Arking, Linda. "Certain Hard Places." 1975: 251-282.
Arnold, Len. "Portrait Of a Woman." 1933: 113-116.
Ashworth, John. "High Diver." 1949: 43-57.
Austin, Mary. "Papago Wedding." 1925: 73-76.
Avery, Stephen Morehouse. "Never In This World." 1928: 73-88.

Babcock, Edwina Stanton. "Dunelight." 1925: 94-111.
Baker, Dorothy. "Keeley Street Blues." 1939: 65-76.
Baldwin, James. "Come Out the Wilderness." 1959: 208-233.
Ballantyne, Sheila. "Perpetual Care." 1977: 87-104.
Banks, Russell. "With Ché At Kitty Hawk." 1975: 297-315.
Barrett, Richmond Brooks. "Art For Art's Sake." 1922: 56-70.
Barth, John. "Lost In the Funhouse." 1969: 63-85.
Barthelme, Donald. "Basil From Her Garden." 1987: 115-123.
    "Margins." 1965: 103-107.
    "See the Moon?" 1967: 19-29.
    "Subpoena." 1972: 265-268.
Batki, John. "Strange-Dreaming Charlie, Cow-Eyed Charlie." 1972:
    1-15.
Baumbach, Jonathan. "The Life and Times Of Major Fiction." 1984:
    186-198.
    "Passion?" 1979: 173-186.
Bausch, Richard. "What Feels Like the World." 1987: 144-159.
Bayer, Ann. "Department Store." 1975: 343-349.
Beagle, Peter S. "Come Lady Death." 1965: 149-164.
Beattie, Ann. "The Cinderella Waltz." 1980: 389-407.
    "In the White Night." 1985: 46-50.
Beems, Griffith. "Leaf Unfolding." 1931: 79-98.
    "The Stagecoach." 1944: 29-41.
Beer, Thomas. "Mummery." 1921: 66-83.
    "Tact." 1922: 71-90.
Bellah, James Warner. "Fear." 1927: 53-83.
Bellow, Saul. "The Gonzaga Manuscripts." 1956: 76-102.
    "A Silver Dish." 1980: 11-39.
Benedict, Elizabeth. "Feasting." 1983: 246-255.
Benét, Stephen Vincent. "The Devil and Daniel Webster." 1937: 3-17.
    "An End To Dreams." 1932: 3-15.
    "Freedom's a Hard-Bought Thing." 1940: 3-21.
    "Johnny Pye and the Fool-Killer." 1938: 109-134.
    "The King Of the Cats." 1929: 73-89.
    "The Professor's Punch." 1935: 71-84.
    "Uriah's Son." 1924: 53-70.
Bennett, James W. "The Kiss Of the Accolade." 1922:   91-112.
Bennett, Peggy. "Death Under the Hawthorns." 1950:   68-80.
Benson, Sally. "Retreat." 1941: 93-102.
    "Suite 2049" 1936: 25-31.
Berkman, Sylvia. "Ellen Craig." 1960: 86-107.
    "Pontifex." 1963: 95-107.

Berriault, Gina. "The Birthday Party." 1966: 197-204.
    "The Island Of Ven." 1987: 124-131.
    "The Stone Boy." 1958: 99-110.
    "Sublime Child." 1960: 108-118.
Berry, John. "New Shoes." 1950: 81-88.
Berryman, John. "The Imaginary Jew." 1946: 65-73.
    "Wash Far Away." 1976: 230-251.
Bessie, Alvah C. "A Personal Issue." 1936: 41-52.
Bienen, Leigh Buchanan. "My Life As a West African Gray Parrot."
    1983: 175-188.
Bingham, Robert. "The Unpopular Passenger." 1955: 62-67.
Bingham, Sallie. "The Banks Of the Ohio." 1964: 70-80.
    "Bare Bones." 1966: 235-243.
Bird, Virginia. "For Nancy's Sake." 1937: 55-61.
    "Havoc Is a Circle." 1936: 55-63.
Blackman, M. C. "Hot Copy." 1928: 98-114.
Blake, George. "A Modern Development." 1970: 71-82.
Blanton, Lowell D. "The Long Night." 1958: 155-165.
Blassingame, Wyatt. "Man's Courage." 1957: 152-158.
Boone, Jack H., and Merle Constiner. "Big Singing." 1932: 49-68.
Boswell, Robert. "The Darkness Of Love." 1987: 25-64.
Bowles, Paul. "The Echo." 1947: 61-75.
    "Pastor Dowe At Tacaté." 1949: 58-78.
Boyle, Kay. "Anschluss." 1939: 79-102.
    "The Canals Of Mars." 1943: 79-88.
    "Defeat." 1941: 3-14.
    "The First Lover." 1932: 71-76.
    "Poor Monsieur Panalitus." 1940: 59-69.
    "St. Stephen's Green." 1981: 59-66.
    "Summer Evening." 1950: 89-101.
    "Their Name Is Macaroni." 1942: 91-102.
    "The White Horses Of Vienna." 1935: 3-20.
    "Winter Night." 1946: 74-84.
Brace, Ernest. "Silent Whistle." 1936: 67-87.
Bradbury, Ray. "Homecoming." 1947: 76-88.
    "Powerhouse." 1948: 26-34.
Bradford, Roark. "Careless Love." 1930: 55-68.
    "Child Of God." 1927: 1-14.
    "River Witch." 1928: 115-133.
Bradley, Mary Hastings. "The Five-Minute Girl." 1931: 53-67.
    "The Life Of the Party." 1938: 137-150.
Brady, Mariel. "Peter Projects." 1925: 112-129.
Brand, Millen. "The Pump." 1939: 105-118.
Branda, Eldon. "The Dark Days Of Christmas." 1968: 246-258.
Brecht, Harold W. "Two Heroes." 1925: 130-148.
Breuer, Bessie. "Bury Your Own Dead." 1945: 61-74.
    "Home Is a Place." 1944: 19-28.
    "Pigeons En Casserole." 1943: 91-103.
    "The Skeleton and the Easter Lily." 1947: 89-97.

Brodkey, Harold. "His Son, In His Arms, In Light, Aloft." 1976: 15-32.
    "A Story In an Almost Classical Mode." 1975: 13-60.
    "Verona: A Young Woman Speaks." 1978: 238-244.
Bromell, Henry. "Photographs." 1973: 243-251.
    "Travel Stories." 1979: 35-56.
Bromfield, Louis. "The Apothecary." 1929: 93-119.
    "The Scarlet Woman." 1927: 25-33.
Broner, E. M. "The New Nobility." 1968: 18-49.
Brookhouser, Frank. "Request For Sherwood Anderson." 1946: 85-90.
    "She Did Not Cry At All." 1948: 49-61.
Brooks, Ben. "A Postal Creed." 1982: 52-61.
Brooks, Roy Patchen. "Without Hal." 1940: 73-83.
Brower, Brock. "Storm Still." 1968: 168-194.
Brown, Cambray. "Episode In a Machine Age." 1928: 134-147.
Brown, Margery Finn. "In the Forests Of Riga the Beasts Are Very Wild Indeed." 1972: 209-218.
Brown, Rosellen. "A Letter To Ismael In the Grave." 1972: 186-191.
    "Mainlanders." 1973: 55-63.
    "Why I Quit the Gowanus Liberation Front." 1976: 261-276.
Brown, T. K., III. "A Drink Of Water." 1958: 179-201.
Brush, Katharine. "Football Girl." 1932: 79-83.
    "Good Wednesday." 1931: 101-117.
    "Him and Her." 1929: 55-62.
    "Night Club." 1927: 84-96.
    "Speakeasy." 1929: 123-142.
Buchan, Perdita. "It's Cold Out There." 1970: 51-70.
Buchwald, Emilie Bix. "The Present." 1959: 129-135.
Buck, Pearl S. "The Enemy." 1943: 107-126.
    "The Frill." 1933: 47-59.
    "Shanghai Scene." 1934: 65-70.
Buckley, F. R. "Gold-Mounted Guns." 1922: 36-43.
Buechler, James. "Pepicelli." 1956: 41-59.
    "The Second Best Girl." 1967: 93-104.
Buechner, Frederick. "The Tiger." 1955: 53-61.
Bumpus, Jerry. "The Idols Of Afternoon." 1976: 201-210.
Burdick, Eugene L. "Rest Camp On Maui." 1947: 9-21.
Burgess, Jackson. "The Magician." 1961: 145-153.
Burnett, W. R. "Dressing-Up." 1930: 3-13.
Burt, Katherine Newlin. "Herself." 1930: 71-88.
Burt, Maxwell Struthers. "Each In His Generation." 1920: 3-22.
    "The Fawn." 1939: 121-130.
Busch, Frederick. "Is Anyone Left This Time Of Year?" 1974: 77-86.

Cabell, James Branch. "Porcelain Cups." 1919: 210-227.
Cain, James M. "Dead Man." 1936: 91-104.
Caldwell, Erskine. "Country Full Of Swedes." 1933: 119-136.
    "Man and Woman." 1938: 153-159.
    "Maud Island." 1934: 73-85.

"The People Vs. Abe Lathan, Colored." 1939: 133-144.
Calisher, Hortense. "A Christmas Carillon." 1955: 68-84.
　"The Middle Drawer." 1949: 79-88.
　"The Night Club In the Woods." 1956: 103-120.
　"The Scream On 57th Street." 1964: 141-166.
　"What a Thing, To Keep a Wolf In a Cage!" 1958: 47-62.
Cameron, Peter. "Excerpts From Swan Lake." 1986: 110-117.
　"Homework." 1985: 222-228.
Canfield, Dorothy. "Ancestral Home." 1932: 87-106.
　"The Knot Hole." 1943: 19-39.
　"Sex Education." 1946: 91-102.
Capote, Truman. "The House Of Flowers." 1951: 32-45.
　"Miriam." 1946: 103-114.
　"Shut a Final Door." 1948: 1-14.
Caputi, Anthony. "The Derby Hopeful." 1979: 242-254.
Cardwell, Guy A. "Did You Once See Shelley?" 1971: 28-57.
Carkeet, David. "The Greatest Slump Of All Time." 1982: 271-288.
Carr, Archie. "The Black Beach." 1956: 121-132.
Carver, Ada Jack. "Redbone." 1925: 149-169.
　"Singing Woman." 1927: 97-108.
　"Treeshy." 1926: 47-68.
Carver, Raymond. "Are You a Doctor?" 1975: 111-118.
　"Put Yourself In My Shoes." 1974: 215-228.
　"A Small, Good Thing." 1983: 1-25.
　"What Is It?" 1973: 147-155.
Casper, Leonard. "Sense Of Direction." 1951: 46-60.
Cassill, R. V. "The Inland Years." 1955: 85-102.
　"The Prize." 1956: 60-75.
　"The War In the Air." 1954: 51-66.
　"When Old Age Shall This Generation Waste." 1957: 245-261.
Cavanaugh, Arthur. "What I Wish (Oh, I Wish) I Had　Said." 1965: 233-247.
Chapman, Elisabeth Cobb. "With Glory and Honour." 1927: 109-125.
Chapman, Mariston. "Treat You Clever." 1929: 145-161.
Chase, Mary Ellen. "Salesmanship." 1931: 121-127.
Chasin, Helen. "Fatal." 1980: 239-247.
Cheever, John. "The Country Husband." 1956: 15-40.
　"The Embarkment For Cythera." 1964: 1-29.
　"The Five-Forty-Eight." 1955: 103-116.
　"I'm Going To Asia." 1941: 105-110.
　"The Jewels Of the Cabots." 1973: 184-200.
　"The Journal Of an Old Gent." 1957: 159-181.
　"The Pot Of Gold." 1951: 61-77.
　"The President Of the Argentine." 1977: 297-303.
　"The Trouble Of Marcie Flint." 1959: 289-305.
　"Vega." 1950: 102-118.
Chester, Alfred. "The Head Of a Sad Angel." 1956: 133-164.
Chidester, Ann. "Mrs. Ketting and Clark Gable." 1950: 119-129.

Chittendon, Gerald. "The Victim Of His Vision." 1921:   84-112.
Clark, Walter Van Tilburg. "The Ascent Of Ariel Goodbody." 1943:
    129-139.
    "The Buck In the Hills." 1944: 52-62.
    "Hook." 1941: 113-136.
    "The Portable Phonograph." 1942: 105-113.
    "The Wind and the Snow Of Winter." 1945: 1-14.
Clay, Richard. "Very Sharp For Jagging." 1954: 67-91.
Clayton, John Bell. "The White Circle." 1947: 1-8.
Clayton, John J. "Bodies Like Mouths." 1978: 186-204.
    "Cambridge Is Sinking!" 1974: 87-104.
Clearman, Mary. "Lambing Out." 1972: 65-82.
Cleaver, Eldridge. "The Flashlight." 1971: 226-260.
Clemons, Walter. "A Summer Shower." 1958: 145-154.
Coates, Robert M. "The Fury." 1937: 35-42.
    "In a Foreign City." 1956: 165-177.
    "Let's Not Talk About It Now." 1940: 87-94.
Coatsworth, Elizabeth. "Bremen's." 1949: 89-99.
    "The Visit." 1936: 107-109.
Cobb, Irvin S. "A Colonel Of Kentucky." 1932: 109-133.
    "An Episode At Pintail Lake." 1928: 148-168.
    "Faith, Hope and Charity." 1930: 91-109.
    "Snake Doctor." 1922: 1-22.
Cobb, Jane. "The Hot Day." 1947: 98-110.
Colby, Nathalie. "Glass Houses." 1936: 113-125.
Cole, Madelene. "Bus To Biarritz." 1934: 89-100.
Cole, Tom. "Familiar Usage In Leningrad." 1962: 79-98.
    "On the Edge Of Arcadia." 1966: 57-73.
    "Saint John Of the Hershey Kisses." 1970: 149-183.
Colwin, Laurie. "The Lone Pilgrim." 1977: 231-242.
Combes, Evan. "Kittens Have Fathers." 1932: 137-146.
Connell, Evan S., Jr. "I Came From Yonder Mountain." 1951: 78-86.
    "I'll Take You To Tennessee." 1949: 100-109.
Connell, Richard. "A Friend Of Napoleon." 1923: 19-37.
    "The Law Beaters." 1928: 169-179.
    "The Most Dangerous Game." 1924: 71-92.
Connelly, Marc. "Coroner's Inquest." 1930: 47-52.
Conrad, Barnaby. "Cayetano the Perfect." 1949: 110-122.
Cook, Charles. "Nothing Can Change It." 1939: 147-160.
Cook, Whitfield. "The Unfaithful." 1943: 143-152.
Cooper, Courtney Ryley. "The Elephant Forgets." 1930:   113-128.
Corfman, Eunice Luccock. "To Be an Athlete." 1969: 147-167.
Corrington, John William. "The Actes and Monuments." 1976:
    107-140.
Cox, James Trammell. "That Golden Crane." 1963: 195-215.
Cozzens, James Gould. "Farewell To Cuba." 1932: 19-36.
    "Total Stranger." 1936: 3-21.
Cram, Mildred. "Stranger Things." 1921: 127-155.
Cramer, Alice Carver. "The Boy Next Door." 1949: 123-134.

Critchell, Laurence. "Flesh and Blood." 1945: 47-60.
Crowell, Chester T. "Margaret Blake." 1924: 25-44.
Culver, Monty. "Black Water Blues." 1951: 87-97.
Curley, Daniel. "Love In the Winter." 1965: 199-212.
Currie, Ellen. "O Lovely Appearance Of Death." 1961: 154-180.
    "Tib's Eve." 1959: 136-149.

Daly, Maureen. "Sixteen." 1938: 163-168.
Daniels, Roger. "Bulldog." 1927: 126-148.
Davenport, Guy. "The Richard Nixon Freischütz Rag." 1976: 66-74.
    "Robot." 1974: 186-214.
Davis, Christopher. "A Man Of Affairs." 1966: 181-195.
Davis, Robert Gorham. "An Interval Like This." 1942: 117-124.
Deasy, Mary. "The Holiday." 1947: 111-123.
    "Long Shadow On the Lawn." 1945: 75-89.
    "The People With the Charm." 1962: 137-152.
DeFord, Miriam Allen. "Pride." 1934: 103-109. .
    "The Silver Knight." 1930: 131-142.
DeJong, David Cornel. "Calves." 1939: 51-62.
    "The Chicory Neighbors." 1937: 65-73.
    "The Record." 1947: 162-168.
    "Seven Boys Take a Hill." 1941: 139-152.
    "Snow-On-the-Mountain." 1942: 127-136.
Dell, Floyd. "Phantom Adventure." 1923: 46-58.
Derieux, Samuel A. "Comet." 1921: 156-168.
    "The Sixth Shot." 1922: 113-123.
    "The Trial in Tom Belcher's Store." 1919: 192-209.
Detzer, Karl W. "The Wreck Job." 1926: 69-90.
Dickinson, Charles. "Risk." 1984: 50-65.
DiFranco, Anthony. "The Garden Of Redemption." 1986: 152-161.
Dillon, Millicent G. "All the Pelageyas." 1980: 409-422.
    "Monitor." 1987: 160-169.
Disch, Thomas M. "Getting Into Death." 1975: 223-238.
    "Xmas." 1979: 309-318.
Dixon, Stephen. "Layaways." 1982: 152-165.
    "Mac In Love." 1977: 268-278.
Dobie, Charles Caldwell. "The False Talisman." 1931: 131-149.
    "Horse and Horse." 1924: 93-112.
    "The Thrice Bereft Widow Of Hung Gow." 1926: 91-108.
Doctorow, E. L. "Ragtime." 1975: 169-184.
Donohue, H. E. F. "Joe College." 1970: 93-112.
Dorrance, Ward. "The White Hound." 1949: 30-42.
Douglas, Ellen. "On the Lake." 1963: 230-260.
Douglas, Marjory Stoneman. "He Man." 1927: 149-174.
    "The Peculiar Treasure Of Kings." 1928: 22-48.
Downey, Harris. "The Hunters." 1951: 1-16.
    "The Mulhausen Girls." 1949: 135-149.
Driftmier, Lucile. "For My Sister." 1936: 129-139.
Dubus, Andre. "The Pitcher." 1980: 373-388.

Dunn, Robert. "Hopeless Acts Performed Properly, With Grace."
    1980: 225-237.
Duranty, Walter. "The Parrot." 1928: 1-21.
Dybek, Stuart. "Blight." 1987: 81-102.
    "Hot Ice." 1985: 20-45.
    "Pet Milk." 1986: 12-16.

Eastlake, William. "The Biggest Thing Since Custer." 1970: 17-28.
    "The Death Of Sun." 1974: 242-260.
    "Flight Of the Circle Heart." 1959: 194-207.
Eastman, Elizabeth. "Like a Field Mouse Over the Heart." 1944: 63-82.
Eaton, Charles Edward. " The Case Of the Missing Photographs."
    1972: 192-208.
Edmonds, Walter D. "The Cruise Of the Cashalot." 1932: 149-161.
    "Escape From the Mine." 1936: 143-168.
    "Honor Of the County." 1934: 113-140.
Eisenberg, Deborah. "Translations In a Foreign Currency." 1986:
    130-151.
Elder, Walter. "You Can Wreck It." 1947: 124-142.
Eliot, Ethel Cook. "Maternal." 1925: 170-182.
Ellerbe, Alma, and Paul Ellerbe. "'Done Got Over.'" 1927: 175-191.
Elliott, George P. "Among the Dangs." 1959: 46-72.
    "A Family Matter." 1954: 92-132.
    "Miracle Play." 1957: 48-54.
    "Miss Cudahy Of Stowes Landing." 1955: 117-139.
Engberg, Susan. "Lambs Of God." 1969: 261-290.
    "Pastorale." 1978: 87-105.
    "A Stay By the River." 1977: 279-296.
Enright, Elizabeth. "The Eclipse." 1958: 111-118.
    "A Gift Of Light." 1960: 119-132.
    "I Forgot Where I Was." 1946: 115-122.
    "The Operator." 1955: 141-154.
    "The Sardillion." 1950: 130-137.
    "The Trumpeter Swan." 1949: 150-161.
Erdrich, Louise. "Fleur." 1987: 1-14.
    "Saint Marie." 1985: 103-115.
Eustis, Helen. "An American Home." 1947: 143-155.

Faragoh, Francis Edwards. "The Distant Street." 1923: 59-74.
Faulkner, William. "Barn Burning." 1939: 3-29.
    "By the People." 1957: 121-140.
    "A Courtship." 1949: 1-16.
    "Hand Upon the Waters." 1940: 97-116.
    "Lion." 1936: 171-191.
    "A Name For the City." 1951: 98-115.
    "The Old People." 1941: 155-169.
    "Race At Morning." 1956: 178-193.
    "Thrift." 1931: 153-169.
    "Turn About." 1932: 165-192.

"Two Soldiers." 1942: 139-158.
"Wash." 1934: 143-157.
Fauset, Arthur Huff. "Symphonesque." 1926: 109-124.
Faust, Irvin. "Melanie and the Purple People Eaters." 1983: 90-107.
"The Year Of the Hot Jock." 1986: 208-225.
Fenton, Edward. "Burial In the Desert." 1945: 90-104.
Ferber, Edna. "April 25th, As Usual." 1919: 274-298.
Fetler, Andrew. "Shadows On the Water." 1977: 66-86.
"The Third Count." 1984: 139-160.
Fifeld, William. "The Fishermen Of Patzcuaro." 1943: 43-59.
Filer, Tom. "The Last Voyage." 1959: 257-276.
Fineman, Morton. "Soldier Of the Republic." 1944: 83-90.
Finney, Ernest J. "The Investigator." 1967: 115-129.
Fisher, Vardis. "The Scarecrow." 1934: 161-168.
Fitzgerald, F. Scott. "The Camel's Back." 1920: 43-70.
"Family In the Wind." 1933: 139-161.
Fleming, Berry. "Strike Up a Stirring Music." 1944: 91-99.
Flowers, Sandra Hollin. "Hope Of Zion." 1981: 117-126.
Flythe, Starkey, Jr. "Point Of Conversion." 1972: 83-93.
Folsom, Elizabeth Irons. "Towers Of Fame." 1923: 38-45.
Forbes, Esther. "Break-Neck Hill." 1920: 71-80.
Ford, Jesse Hill. "The Bitter Bread." 1967: 51-58.
"How the Mountains Are." 1961: 181-190.
"To the Open Water." 1966: 225-233.
Foster, Joseph O'Kane. "Gideon." 1939: 163-177.
Fowler, Janet. "A Day For Fishing." 1960: 133-145.
Fowler, Mary Dewees. "Man Of Distinction." 1955: 155-172.
Francis, H. E. "A Chronicle Of Love." 1976: 277-295.
Franklin, F. K. "Nigger Horse." 1968: 129-144.
Friedman, Sanford. "Ocean." 1965: 21-51.
Frost, Frances M. "The Heart Being Perished." 1933: 165-171.
Fuchs, Daniel. "The Amazing Mystery At Storick, Dorschi,
Pflaumer, Inc." 1938: 171-189.
"Twilight In Southern California." 1955: 173-189.
Fuller, Blair. "All Right." 1978: 106-128.
"Bakti's Hand." 1974: 126-137.

Gale, Zona. "Bridal Pond." 1928: 49-54.
"Crisis." 1936: 195-200.
Gallico, Paul. "The Snow Goose." 1941: 173-194.
Gardner, John. "The Things." 1974: 105-116.
Gellhorn, Martha. "In Sickness As In Health." 1958: 15-45.
Gerber, Merrill Joan. "'I Don't Believe This.'" 1986: 95-104.
Gerould, Christopher. "The End Of the Party." 1932: 195-199.
Gerry, Bill. "Understand What I Mean?" 1945: 105-115.
Gertler, T. "In Case Of Survival." 1980: 249-270.
Gewertz, Kenneth. "I Thought Of Chatterton, the Marvelous Boy."
1982: 114-135.
Gidney, James B. "The Muse and Mr. Parkinson." 1948: 62-71.

Gill, Brendan. "Fat Girl." 1972: 94-115.
Gilpatric, Guy. "Black Art and Ambrose." 1920: 81-93.
Glenn, Isa Urquhart. "The Wager." 1923: 75-91.
Godchaux, Elma. "Chains." 1936: 203-223.
Godwin, Gail. "Amanuensis: A Tale Of the Creative Life." 1980:
    321-344.
Gold, Herbert. "A Celebration For Joe." 1956: 194-202.
    "A Death On the East Side." 1972: 235-264.
    "Encounter In Haiti." 1957: 37-47.
    "Love and Like." 1960: 146-182.
    "The Smallest Part." 1979: 203-212.
    "The Witch." 1954: 133-141.
Gold, Ivan. "The Nickel Misery Of George Washington   Carver
    Brown." 1961: 58-100.
Goldberg, Lester. "Shy Bearers." 1979: 74-85.
Goldman, Miriam. "Fireflies." 1967: 71-76.
Goodloe, Abbie Carter. "Claustrophobia." 1926: 125-138.
Goodman, Ivy. "Baby." 1981: 212-216.
    "White Boy." 1982: 186-195.
Gordon, Caroline. "The Enemy." 1938: 193-199.
    "Frankie and Thomas and Bud Asbury." 1939: 181-204.
    "Old Red." 1934: 19-41.
    "The Petrified Woman." 1948: 72-84.
Gordon, Ethel Edison. "War Front: Louisiana." 1945:   116-124.
Gordon, Mary. "The Only Son Of the Doctor." 1983: 203-215.
Goss, John Mayo. "Bird Song." 1946: 1-17.
    "Evening and Morning Prayer." 1949: 162-171.
Gottlieb, Elaine. "The Lizard." 1972: 154-165.
Govan, Christine Noble. "Miss Winters and the Wind." 1947: 156-161.
Goyen, William. "Bridge Of Music, River Of Sand." 1976: 153-157.
Graeve, Oscar. "A Death On Eight' Avenue." 1926: 139-152.
Granat, Robert. "My Apples." 1958: 273-292.
    "To Endure." 1960: 183-190.
Granberry, Edwin. "A Trip to Czardis." 1932: 39-46.
Granit, Arthur. "Free the Canaries From Their Cages!" 1957:
    182-198.
Gration, Gwen. "Teacher." 1968: 116-128.
Grau, Shirley Ann. "Eight O'Clock One Morning." 1962: 153-159.
    "Joshua." 1955: 190-214.
Graves, John. "The Aztec Dog." 1962: 201-216.
    "The Green Fly." 1955: 215-225.
Green, Eleanor. "The Dear Little Doves." 1942: 161-168.
Greene, Mary Francis. "The Silent Day." 1948: 85-96.
Greene, Philip L. "The Dichotomy." 1971: 267-283.
    "One Of You Must Be Wendell Corey." 1966: 149-159.
Grennard, Elliott. "Sparrow's Last Jump." 1948: 35-48.
Griffith, Patricia Browning. "Dust." 1976: 89-106.
    "Nights At O'Rear's." 1970: 135-148.
Grinnell, Sarah. "Standby." 1943: 155-163.

Grinstead, David. "A Day In Operations." 1970: 205-217.
Grossberg, Elmer. "Black Boy's Good Time." 1943: 167-177.

Haardt, Sara. "Absolutely Perfect." 1933: 175-187.
Hackett, Francis. "Unshapely Things." 1925: 183-191.
Hale, Nancy. "Always Afternoon." 1938: 203-212.
  "The Most Elegant Drawing Room In Europe." 1968: 97-115.
  "A Slow Boat To China." 1958: 167-177.
  "Sunday Lunch." 1966: 161-170.
  "Sunday—1913." 1942: 171-191.
  "That Woman." 1940: 119-143.
  "Those Are As Brothers." 1941: 197-209.
  "To the Invader." 1933: 63-71.
  "To the North." 1937: 77-98.
  "Who Lived and Died Believing." 1943: 181-200.
Hall, James B. "Estate and Trespass: A Gothic Story." 1954: 142-150.
  "In the Time Of Demonstrations." 1951: 116-129.
  "A Kind Of Savage." 1968: 211-229.
Hall, Lawrence Sargent. "The Ledge." 1960: 21-38.
Hallet, Richard Matthews. "Misfortune's Isle." 1930: 145-169.
Halley, Anne. "The Sisterhood." 1976: 252-260.
Hallinan, Nancy. "Women In a Roman Courtyard." 1980: 41-55.
Hamill, Katharine. "Leora's Father." 1935: 87-100.
Hamilton, R. C. "Da Vinci Is Dead." 1985: 116-131.
Hardwick, Elizabeth. "The People On the Roller Coaster." 1945:
  125-136.
  "What We Have Missed." 1946: 123-132.
Harnden, Ruth. "Rebellion." 1954: 151-159.
Harris, MacDonald. "Second Circle." 1959: 165-177.
Harris, Marilyn. "Icarus Again." 1968: 284-295.
Hart, Frances Noyes. "'Contact!'" 1920: 23-42.
Harter, Evelyn. "The Stone Lovers." 1971: 137-147.
Hartley, Lodwick. "Mr. Henig's Wall." 1948: 97-107.
Hartman, Lee Foster. "The Judgment Of Vulcan." 1920: 94-122.
  "Mr. Smith." 1928: 180-195.
Hauser, Marianne. "The Other Side Of the River." 1948: 108-124.
Havill, Edward. "The Kill." 1940: 45-56.
Hazzard, Shirley. "A Long Story Short." 1977: 42-65.
Hecht, Florence M. "Twin Bed Bridge." 1971: 1-27.
Hecht, Julie. "I Want You, I Need You, I Love You." 1979: 57-73.
Heden, Mary. "Ladybug, Fly Away Home." 1977: 179-185.
Heerman, Elizabeth Alexander. "Fifty-Two Weeks For   Florette."
  1921: 169-192.
Held, John, Jr. "A Man Of the World." 1930: 173-181.
Heller, Steve. "The Crow Woman." 1985: 148-173.
  "The Summer Game." 1979: 86-100.
Helprin, Mark. "Leaving the Church." 1976: 171-185.
  "The Schreuderspitze." 1978: 265-291.

Hemenway, Robert. [pseud. "Stephen Patch"]. "The Girl Who Sang With the Beatles." 1970: 1-16.
"Troy Street." 1974: 138-154.
Hemingway, Ernest. "The Killers." 1927: 15-24.
Henderson, Robert. "Immortality." 1960: 191-202.
Henson, Robert. "Lizzie Borden In the P.M. " 1974: 26-53.
"The Upper and the Lower Millstone." 1978: 41-66.
Hersey, John. "Peggety's Parcel Of Shortcomings." 1951: 130-139.
Heth, Edward Harris. "Big Days Beginning." 1936: 227-242.
Heyert, Murray. "The New Kid." 1945: 137-150.
Heyward, Du Bose. "Crown's Bess." 1925: 192-202.
Highsmith, Patricia. "The Heroine." 1946: 113-148.
Hill, Richard. "Out In the Garage." 1974: 68-76.
Hilton, Charles. "Gods Of Darkness." 1937: 101-108.
Hoagland, Edward. "The Final Fate Of the Alligators." 1971: 330-340.
Hochstein, Rolaine. "She Should Have Died Hereafter." 1985: 271-281.
"What Kind Of a Man Cuts His Finger Off?" 1974: 155-166.
Holt, T. E. "Charybdis." 1982: 80-98.
Hope, Marjorie. "That's My Brother." 1944: 100-108.
Hopper, James. "Célestine." 1923: 92-103.
Horgan, Paul. "The Trunk." 1936: 245-250.
Horn, R. DeS. "The Jinx Of the 'Shandon Belle.'" 1922: 124-138.
Horne, Lewis. "Taking Care." 1987: 235-250.
Howard, Maureen. "Bridgeport Bus." 1962: 239-250.
"Sherry." 1966: 17-56.
Howard, Sidney. "The Homesick Ladies." 1929: 29-51.
Hubbell, Catherine. "Monday At Six." 1945: 151-159.
Hudson, Helen. "The Theft." 1976: 141-152.
Hull, Alexander. "The Argosies." 1920: 123-140.
Hull, Helen R. "His Sacred Family." 1922: 139-158.
Hume, Cyril. "Forrester." 1931: 173-191.
Humphrey, William. "The Ballad Of Jesse Neighbours." 1965: 53-70.
"The Hardys." 1950: 138-151.
Hunt, Hamlen. "Only By Chance Are Pioneers Made."   1938: 215-230.
"The Saluting Doll." 1937: 111-119.
Hurst, Fanny. "'Humoresque.'" 1919: 148-179.
Hutchins, M. P. "Innocents." 1946: 149-176.

Ingles, James Wesley. "The Wind Is Blind." 1948: 125-135.
Inman, Robert. "I'll Call You." 1971: 168-196.
Irving, John. "Interior Space." 1981: 20-51.
Irwin, Inez Haynes. "The Spring Flight." 1924: 1-24.

Jackson, Charles Tenney. "The Horse Of Hurricane Reef." 1922: 159-176.
"The Man Who Cursed the Lilies." 1921: 29-44.
Jackson, David. "The English Gardens." 1962: 161-199.
Jackson, Josephine. "On the Island." 1966: 71-91.
Jackson, Shirley. "The Lottery." 1949: 172-180.

Jacobs, Marguerite. "Singing Eagles." 1926: 153-172.
Jacobsen, Josephine. "Jack Frost." 1978: 148-158.
   "The Jungle Of Lord Lion." 1971: 197-207.
   "The Mango Community." 1985: 282-298.
   "Nel Bagno." 1976: 75-88.
   "A Walk With Raschid." 1973: 201-215.
Janeway, Elizabeth. "Child Of God." 1948: 136-147.
Jauss, David. "Shards." 1983: 189-202.
Jaynes, Clare. "The Coming Of Age." 1942: 195-203.
John, William M. "Neither Jew Nor Greek." 1930: 17-31.
Johnson, Curt. "Trespasser." 1973: 231-242.
Johnson, Diane. "An Apple, An Orange." 1973: 168-183.
Johnson, Greg. "Crazy Ladies." 1986: 17-30.
Johnson, Josephine W. "Alexander To the Park." 1942: 207-215.
   "Dark." 1934: 171-175.
   "The Glass Pigeon." 1943: 203-212.
   "John the Six." 1935: 57-59.
   "Night Flight." 1944: 109-115.
Johnson, Joyce. "The Children's Wing." 1987: 15-24.
Johnson, Nora. "The Jungle Of Injustice." 1982: 99-113.
Johnson, Nunnally. "The Actor." 1928: 196-210.
   "Mlle. Irene the Great." 1930: 185-202.
Johnson, Willis. "Prayer For the Dying." 1984: 170-185.
Johnston, Mary. "Elephants Through the Country." 1929: 165-186.
Just, Ward. "About Boston." 1985: 174-198.
   "The Costa Brava, 1959." 1986: 55-69.
Justice, Donald. "The Artificial Moonlight." 1984: 199-213.
   "The Lady." 1950: 152-166.
   "Vineland's Burning." 1954: 160-166.

Kantor, MacKinlay. "Silent Grow the Guns." 1935: 103-121.
Katterjohn, Elsie. "Teachers." 1936: 253-264.
Katz, Shlomo. "My Redeemer Cometh. . . ." 1968: 50-77.
Kelly, Eleanor Mercein. "Basquerie." 1926: 173-212.
   "Monkey Motions." 1927: 192-207.
Kenney, Susan. "Facing Front." 1982: 1-31.
Kensinger, Faye Riter. "A Sense Of Destination." 1951: 140-153.
Kentfield, Calvin. "In the Caldron." 1960: 203-220.
   "Near the Line." 1968: 78-96.
Kerr, Sophie. "Wild Earth." 1921: 193-228.
King, Mary. "Chicken On the Wind." 1940: 147-166.
Klass, Perri. "Not a Good Girl." 1984: 226-232.
   "The Secret Lives Of Dieters." 1983: 301-309.
Klein, Norma. "The Burglar." 1963: 108-119.
   "Magic." 1968: 145-167.
   "The Wrong Man." 1974: 175-185.
Knickerbocker, Conrad. "Diseases Of the Heart." 1967: 159-168.
Kniffin, Harry Anable. "The Tribute." 1921: 229-233.
Knight, Eric. "The Marne." 1936: 267-269.

Knight, Ruth Adams. "What a Darling Little Boy!" 1944: 116-123.
Koch, Claude. "Bread and Butter Questions." 1985: 71-88.
Kornblatt, Joyce R. "Offerings." 1986: 44-54.
Kotzwinkle, William. "Swimmer In the Secret Sea." 1975: 350-380.
Krause, Ervin D. "The Quick and the Dead." 1961: 191-208.
    "The Snake." 1963: 17-22.
Krysl, Marilyn. "Looking For Mother." 1980: 153-162.
Kuehn, Susan. "The Hunt." 1950: 167-180.
    "The Rosebush." 1947: 169-180.
Kunasz, Paul. "I'd Give It All Up For Tahiti." 1941: 213-219.
Kurtz, M. R. "Waxing Wroth." 1967: 147-158.

LaFarge, Christopher. "The Three Aspects." 1948: 148-156.
LaFarge, Oliver. "Haunted Ground." 1931: 71-75.
    "Old Century's River." 1951: 154-169.
Laidlaw, Clara. "The Little Black Boys." 1943: 63-75.
Laing, Alexander. "The Workmanship Has To Be Wasted." 1942:
    219-227.
Lampkin, Speed. "Comes a Day." 1950: 181-195.
Lampman, Ben Hur. "Blinker Was a Good Dog." 1943: 215-219.
    "Old Bill Bent To Drink." 1945: 33-46.
Lane, Rose Wilder. "Innocence." 1922: 23-35.
    "Old Maid." 1933: 191-213.
Langdon, John. "The Blue Serge Suit." 1957: 107-120.
Lanning, George. "Something Just For Me." 1964: 167-189.
Larson, Charles R. "Up From Slavery." 1971: 300-320.
Larsson, Genevieve. "Witch Mary." 1923: 104-119.
Lavers, Norman. "Big Dog." 1987: 170-187.
Lavin, Mary. "Single Lady." 1949: 181-197.
Leach, Peter. "The Fish Trap." 1974: 167-174.
Leaton, Anne. "The Passion Of Marco Z——." 1979: 117-124.
Leavitt, David. "Counting Months." 1984: 66-85.
Leech, Margaret. "Manicure." 1929: 189-201.
Leffland, Ella. "Last Courtesies." 1977: 17-41.
Leiper, Gudger Bart. "The Magnolias." 1950: 18-36.
Lemmon, Robert S. "The Bamboo Trap." 1923: 120-133.
LeSueur, Meridel. "Breathe Upon These Slain." 1946: 177-194.
Leviant, Curt. "Ladies and Gentlemen, the Original Music Of the
    Hebrew Alphabet." 1978: 205-237.
Levin, Mary. "The Sand Castle." 1945: 160-171.
Lewis, O. F. "Alma Mater." 1920: 141-147.
    "The Get-Away." 1921: 234-242.
    "Old Peter Takes an Afternoon Off." 1922: 177-195.
Lewis, Robert. "Little Victor." 1947: 37-60."
L'Heureux, John. "Brief Lives In California." 1981: 247-257.
    "The Comedian." 1986: 31-43.
    "The Priest's Wife." 1980: 359-372.
Liberman, M. M. "Big Buick To the Pyramids." 1957: 272-280.
Lish, Gordon. "For Jeromé—With Love and Kisses." 1984: 255-292.

"Resurrection." 1986: 105-109.
Litwak, Leo. "In Shock." 1969: 101-113.
  "The Making Of a Clerk." 1958: 119-143.
Lloyd, Lynda. "Poor Boy." 1983: 285-300.
Logan, Andy. "The Visit." 1941: 49-60.
Loomis, Alfred E. "Professional Aid." 1931: 195-210.
Lott, James. "The Janeites." 1987: 103-114.
Love, Peggy Harding. "The Jersey Heifer." 1951: 170-181.
Loveridge, George. "The Fur Coat." 1944: 124-134.
Lowry, P. H. "Too Young To Have a Gun." 1954: 167-179.
Lowry, Robert. "Be Nice To Mr. Campbell." 1950: 37-51.
Ludwig, Jack. "Thoreau In California." 1961: 209-245.
  "A Woman Of Her Age." 1965: 213-231.
Luhrs, Marie. "Mrs. Schwellenbach's Receptions." 1931: 213-221.
Lull, Roderick. "Don't Get Me Wrong." 1940: 25-41.
Lumpkin, Grace. "The Treasure." 1940: 169-177.
Lynch, John A. "The Burden." 1947: 181-193.
Lytle, Andrew. "The Guide." 1946: 195-217.

Mabry, Thomas. "The Indian Feather." 1954: 21-39.
McCarthy, Mary. "The Hounds Of Summer." 1965: 249-285.
  "Yellowstone Park." 1957: 292-309.
Macauley, Robie. "The Chevigny Man." 1956: 203-220.
  "Dressed In Shade." 1967: 169-188.
  "The Invaders." 1951: 182-191.
McClatchy, J. D. "Allonym." 1972: 219-234.
McCleary, Dorothy. "Little Elise." 1935: 125-138.
  "Mother's Helper." 1940: 181-205.
  "Not Very Close." 1946: 218-225.
McClure, J. G. "The Rise Of the Proletariat." 1963: 159-181.
McCorkle, Susannah. "Ramona By the Shore." 1975: 119-141.
McCullers, Carson. "The Jockey." 1942: 231-237.
  "The Sojourner." 1951: 192-201.
  "Sucker." 1965: 189-197.
  "A Tree. A Rock. A Cloud." 1943: 223-231.
McCully, Emily Arnold. "How's Your Vacuum Cleaner Working?"
  1977: 211-230.
McElroy, Joseph. "Daughter Of the Revolution." 1985: 132-147.
  "The Future." 1982: 32-51.
McKenzie, Miriam. "Déjà Vu." 1962: 227-237.
McKeon, J. M. "The Gladiators." 1937: 151-161.
McKinley, Georgia. "The Mighty Distance." 1966: 245-290.
McPherson, James Alan. "The Faithful." 1974: 229-241.
  "Of Cabbages and Kings." 1970: 237-251.
  "The Silver Bullet." 1973: 80-95.
  "The Story Of a Scar." 1975: 283-296.
Maddow, Ben. "In a Cold Hotel." 1963: 67-94.
  "You, Johann Sebastian Bach." 1969: 209-236.

Mahoney, James. "The Hat Of Eight Reflections." 1923: 134-158.
Malamud, Bernard. "The Jewbird." 1964: 60-69.
   "Man In the Drawer." 1969: 1-42.
   "The Model." 1984: 134-138.
   "My Son the Murderer." 1970: 127-133.
   "Talking Horse." 1973: 35-54.
Malkin, Richard. "Pico Never Forgets." 1948: 157-172.
Malone, John. "The Fugitives." 1973: 96-106.
Malone, Michael. "Fast Love." 1982: 196-205.
Maltz, Albert. "Afternoon In the Jungle." 1941: 223-231.
   "The Happiest Man On Earth." 1938: 3-15.
Mamet, Louis. "A Writer Interviews a Banker." 1935: 141-149.
Manoff, Eva. "Mama and the Spy." 1965: 81-92.
March, William. "Fifteen From Company K." 1931: 225-236.
   "The Last Meeting." 1937: 123-135.
   "The Little Wife." 1930: 205-216.
   "Nine Prisoners." 1932: 203-213.
   "A Sum In Addition." 1936: 35-38.
Marquand, J. P. "Deep Water." 1932: 217-242.
Marquis, Don. "Country Doctor." 1935: 153-167.
   "O'Meara, The 'Mayflower'—And Mrs. MacLirr." 1928: 211-224.
   "Two Red-Haired Women." 1929: 205-229.
Marsh, Willard. "Last Tag." 1957: 68-82.
Marshall, Edison. "The Elephant Remembers." 1919: 78-104.
   "The Heart Of Little Shikara." 1921: 1-28.
Martin, Charles. "Hobogenesis." 1937: 139-147.
Martin, Hansford. "The Thousand-Yard Stare." 1945: 172-182.
Mason, Bobbie Ann. "Big Bertha Stories." 1986: 80-94.
Mason, Grace Sartwell. "Home-Brew." 1923: 159-181.
Matthews, Jack. "The Last Abandonment." 1981: 138-153.
   "On the Shore Of Chad Creek." 1972: 166-176.
Matthiessen, Peter. "Travelin Man." 1958: 293-309.
Maxwell, James A. "Fighter." 1954: 180-193.
Maxwell, William. "Over By the River." 1975: 185-222.
Mayer, Tom. "Homecoming." 1965: 71-79.
Mayhall, Jane. "The Enemy." 1973: 156-167.
Mazor, Julian. "The Skylark." 1971: 94-136.
Meinke, Peter. "The Ponoes." 1983: 216-226.
   "Uncle George and Uncle Stefan." 1986: 70-79.
Menaker, Daniel. "The Old Left." 1984: 106-117.
Meyer, Cord, Jr. "Waves Of Darkness." 1946: 48-64.
Michaels, Leonard. "Manikin." 1969: 115-120.
   "The Men's Club." 1980: 57-80.
   "Robinson Crusoe Liebowitz." 1971: 321-329.
   "Sticks and Stones." 1966: 75-86.
Miller, Alice Duer. "Slow Poison." 1920: 148-159.
Miller, Arthur. "I Don't Need You Any More." 1961: 246-287.
   "Monte Saint Angelo." 1951: 202-216.
Miller, Nolan. "A New Life." 1957: 236-244.

Miller, Warren. "Chaos, Disorder and the Late Show." 1965: 287-292.
Minot, Stephen. "Mars Revisited." 1971: 284-299.
    "A Passion For History." 1977: 105-117.
Minot, Susan. "Lust." 1985: 63-70.
Mirrielees, Edith R. "Professor Boynton Rereads History." 1924: 113-125.
Moll, Elick. "Memoir Of Spring." 1938: 233-252.
    "To Those Who Wait." 1937: 21-31.
Molyneux, Thomas W. " Visiting the Point." 1979: 133-149.
Montague, Margaret Prescott. "England To America." 1919: 3-20.
Morris, Edita. "Caput Mortuum." 1941: 235-243.
Morris, Gouverneur. "Derrick's Return." 1923: 182-192.
    "Ig's Amok." 1922: 196-209.
Morris, Wright. "Glimpse Into Another Country." 1985: 89-102.
    "Victrola." 1983: 80-89.
Morse, Robert. "The Professor and the Puli." 1948: 173-185.
Mosley, Jefferson. "The Secret At the Crossroads." 1924: 126-141.
Mountzoures, H. L. "The Empire Of Things." 1969: 253-257.
Mudrick, Marvin. "Cleopatra." 1967: 59-69.
Mumford, Ethel Watts. "'Aurore.'" 1921: 243-257.

Nemerov, Howard. "Tradition." 1956: 221-236.
Neugeboren, Jay. "Ebbets Field." 1968: 195-210.
Newhouse, Edward. "The Ambassador." 1958: 229-248.
    "Seventy Thousand Dollars." 1950: 196-208.
Newman, Frances. "Rachel and Her Children." 1924: 45-52.
Norris, Gloria. "Holding On." 1985: 206-221.
    "Revive Us Again." 1984: 37-49.
    "When the Lord Calls." 1983: 157-174.
Norris, Helen. "The Love Child." 1984: 241-254.
    "The Quarry." 1985: 51-62.
    "The Singing Well." 1987: 208-231.
Norris, Kathleen. "Sinners." 1929: 233-250.
Novick, Marian. "Advent." 1981: 154-173.

Oates, Joyce Carol. "Accomplished Desires." 1969: 43-61.
    "Ancient Airs, Voices." 1987: 274-299.
    "Blood-Swollen Landscape." 1976: 186-200.
    "The Children." 1971: 208-225.
    "The Dead." 1973: 1-34.
    "The Fine White Mist Of Winter." 1963: 216-229.
    "First Views Of the Enemy." 1965: 165-175.
    "How I Contemplated the World From the Detroit House Of Correction and Began My Life Over Again." 1970: 275-291.
    "In the Autumn Of the Year." 1979: 150-172.
    "In the Region Of Ice." 1967: 1-17.
    "The Man Whom Women Adored." 1982: 229-253.
    "Master Race." 1986: 245-268.
    "Mutilated Woman." 1981: 191-211.

"My Warszawa." 1983: 26-79.
"Saul Bird Says: Relate! Communicate! Liberate!" 1972: 16-43.
"The Seasons," 1985: 254-270.
"Stigmata." 1964: 30-48.
"The Tattoo." 1978: 129-147.
"Unmailed, Unwritten Letters." 1970: 253-274.
"Where Are You Going, Where Have You Been?" 1968: 296-313.

O'Brien, Tim. "The Ghost Soldiers." 1982: 206-228.
"Night Watch." 1976: 211-219.
"Speaking Of Courage." 1978: 159-168.
O'Connor, Flannery. "A Circle In the Fire." 1955: 35-52.
"Everything That Rises Must Converge." 1963: 1-16.
"Greenleaf." 1957: 15-36.
"The Life You Save May Be Your Own." 1954: 194-204.
"Revelation." 1965: 1-20.
"A View Of the Woods." 1959: 234-256.
O'Donnell, E. P. "Jesus Knew." 1935: 171-186.
Ogden, Maurice. "Freeway To Wherever." 1960: 221-227.
O'Hara, John. "My Girls." 1937: 165-168.
O'Hara, Mary. "My Friend Flicka." 1941: 247-269.
Oliver, Diane. "Neighbors." 1967: 131-146.
Olsen, Tillie. "Tell Me a Riddle." 1961: 21-57.
Osborn, Margaret. "Maine." 1944: 135-150.
Overbeck, Alicia O'Reardon. "Encarnatión." 1930: 219-232.
Owen, Janet Curren. "Afternoon Of a Young Girl." 1936: 273-284.
Ozick, Cynthia. "Rosa." 1984: 1-36.
"The Shawl." 1981: 15-19.
"Usurpation (Other People's Stories)." 1975: 61-98.

Packer, Nancy Huddleston. "Early Morning, Lonely Ride." 1969: 87-99.
"The Women Who Walk." 1981: 67-80.
Paley, Grace. "Distance." 1969: 199-208.
"Midrash On Happiness." 1987: 232-234.
"The Story Hearer." 1984: 233-240.
Parker, Dorothy. "Big Blonde." 1929: 3-25.
Parker, Thomas. "Troop Withdrawal—The Initial Step." 1971: 148-167.
Parsons, Elizabeth. "The Nightingales Sing." 1947: 22-36.
"Not a Soul Will Come Along." 1950: 209-219.
"Welcome Home." 1948: 186-193.
"Patch, Stephen." [See Hemenway, Robert.]
Patt, Esther. "The Butcherbirds." 1951: 217-226.
Patten, Katharine. "Man Among Men." 1937: 171-184.
Patterson, Elizabeth Gregg. "Homecoming." 1951: 227-245.
Patterson, Pernet. "Buttin' Board." 1929: 253-269.
Patton, Frances Gray. "A Piece Of Bread." 1945: 183-192.
Pattullo, George. "The Tie That Binds." 1924: 142-154.

Paul, Louis. "Lay Me Low!" 1935: 189-202.
　　"No More Trouble For Jedwick." 1934: 3-15.
Pearlman, Edith. "Conveniences." 1984: 86-95.
　　"Hanging Fire." 1978: 253-264.
Pelley, William Dudley. "The Continental Angle." 1930: 235-249.
　　"The Face In the Window." 1920: 160-183.
Pereda, Prudencio De. "The Spaniard." 1937: 187-196.
Perry, Lawrence. "A Matter Of Loyalty." 1920: 184-209.
Peterkin, Julia. "The Diamond Ring." 1930: 253-268.
　　"Maum Lou." 1925: 203-217.
Peterson, Mary. "Travelling." 1979: 299-308.
Petrakis, Harry Mark. "The Prison." 1966: 113-120.
Pfeil, Fred. "The Quality Of Light In Maine." 1979: 101-116.
Phillips, Jayne Anne. "Snow." 1980: 209-223.
Phillips, Thomas Hal. "The Shadow Of an Arm." 1951: 246-255.
Pierce, Phoebe. "The Season Of Miss Maggie Reginald." 1949:
　　198-211.
Pitzen, Jim. "The Village." 1987: 132-143.
Plagemann, Bentz. "The Best Bread." 1949: 212-224.
Plante, David. "Work." 1983: 320-336.
Porter, Katherine Anne. "The Downward Path To
　　Wisdom." 1940: 209-235.
　　"Holiday." 1962: 19-47.
Portugal, Ruth. "Call a Solemn Assembly." 1945: 193-201.
Post, Melville Davisson. "Five Thousand Dollars Reward." 1919:
　　120-134.
Potter, Nancy A. J. "Sunday's Children." 1965: 93-101.
Powers, J. F. "Lions, Harts, Leaping Does." 1944: 151-175.
　　"The Presence Of Grace." 1955: 226-247.
　　"The Trouble." 1945: 202-214.
　　"The Valiant Woman." 1947: 194-203.
Price, Reynolds. "One Sunday In Late July." 1961: 101-144.
　　"Waiting At Dachau." 1971: 67-93.
　　"The Warrior Princess Ozimba." 1962: 251-257.
Pritchard, Melissa Brown. "A Private Landscape." 1984: 127-133.
Purdy, James. "Encore." 1960: 228-236.
Putman, Clay. "The News From Troy." 1954: 40-46.
　　"The Wounded." 1950: 220-232.
Pynchon, Thomas. "Under the Rose." 1962: 49-78.

Randal, Vera. "Alice Blaine." 1966: 121-148.
Rascoe, Judith. "A Line Of Order." 1973: 125-146.
　　"Small Sounds and Tilting Shadows." 1972: 44-64.
Ravenel, Beatrice. "The High Cost Of Conscience." 1919: 228-252.
Rawlings, Marjorie Kinnan. "Black Secret." 1946: 226-232.
　　"Gal Young Un." 1933: 3-44.
　　"The Pelican's Shadow." 1940: 239-248.
Raymond, Ilene. "Taking a Chance On Jack." 1985: 229-237.
Reid, Barbara. "The Waltz Dream." 1981: 217-238.

Reid, Randall. "Detritus." 1973: 266-290.
Rice, John Andrew. "You Can Get Just So Much Justice." 1949: 225-248.
Rice, Laverne. "Wings For Janie." 1931: 239-251.
Rice, Louise. "The Lubbeny Kiss." 1919: 180-191.
Rich, Cynthia Marshall. "My Sister's Marriage." 1957: 55-67.
Rindfleisch, Norval. "A Cliff Of Fall." 1970: 29-49.
Roane, Marianne. "Quitter." 1944: 176-182.
Robbins, L. H. "Mr. Downey Sits Down." 1921: 258-272.
    "Professor Todd's Used Car." 1920: 210-222.
Roberts, Elizabeth Madox. "The Sacrifice Of the Maidens." 1930: 35-44.
Robinson, Leonard Wallace. "The Ruin Of Soul." 1950: 233-243.
Robinson, Mabel L. "Called For." 1940: 251-254.
Robinson, Selma. "The Departure." 1933: 217-223.
Robison, Mary. "I Get By." 1987: 308-315.
Rooke, Leon. "If Lost Return To the Swiss Arms." 1965: 109-123.
Rooney, Frank. "Cyclists' Raid." 1951: 256-274.
Rose, Daniel Asa. "The Goodbye Present." 1980: 189-207.
Ross, Lillian. "Night and Day, Day and Night." 1964: 81-103.
Roth, Philip. "Defender Of the Faith." 1960: 39-69.
    "Novotny's Pain." 1964: 249-269.
Rottenberg, Annette T. "The Separation." 1981: 273-288.
Rubin, Michael. "Service." 1969: 191-198.
Rugel, Miriam. "The Flower." 1954: 205-215.
Rushfeldt, Elise M. "A Coffin For Anna." 1929: 273-283.
Russ, Joanna. "Autobiography Of My Mother." 1977: 199-210.
"Rutledge, Marice" [pseud.]. "The Thing They Loved." 1920: 223-247.
Ryerson, Florence, and Colin Clements. "Lobster John's Annie." 1930: 271-279.
    "Useless." 1931: 255-275.
Ryley, Courtney, and Leo F. Creagan. "Martin Gerrity Gets Even." 1921: 113-126.

Sadoff, Ira. "An Enemy Of the People." 1976: 158-170.
St. Joseph, Ellis. "A Knocking At the Gate." 1939: 207-224.
Salinger, J. D. "For Esmé—With Love and Squalor." 1950: 244-264.
    "Just Before the War With the Eskimos." 1949: 249-261.
Salter, James. "Am Strande Von Tanger." 1970: 113-125.
    "The Destruction Of the Goetheanum." 1972: 127-140.
    "Lost Sons." 1984: 161-169.
    "Via Negativa." 1974: 117-125.
Sanborn, Ruth Burr. "Professional Pride." 1929: 287-305.
Sandburg, Helga. "Witch Chicken." 1959: 178-193.
Santee, Ross. "Water." 1935: 205-208.
"Sara" [pseud.]. "So I'm Not Lady Chatterly So Better I Should Know It Now." 1964: 213-225.
Saroyan, William. "The Daring Young Man On the Flying Trapeze." 1934: 45-51.

"Five Ripe Pears." 1935: 211-216.
"Gaston." 1963: 60-66.
"Knife-Like, Flower-Like, Like Nothing At All In the World." 1943: 235-242.
"The Summer Of the Beautiful White Horse." 1938: 255-263.
"The Three Swimmers and the Educated Grocer." 1940: 257-268.
Savler, David S. "The Beggar Boy." 1946: 233-241.
Sawyer, Ruth. "Four Dreams Of Gram Perkins." 1927: 208-219.
Saxon, Lyle. "Cane River." 1926: 213-228.
Sayles, John. "Breed." 1977: 243-267.
"I-80 Nebraska, M. 490-M.205." 1976: 33-51.
Schaeffler, Susan Fromberg. "The Exact Nature Of Plot." 1978: 292-300.
Schell, Jessie. "Alvira, Lettie, and Pip." 1975: 324-342.
"Undeveloped Photographs." 1978: 169-185.
Schevill, James. "A Hero In the Highway." 1978: 245-252.
Schmitt, Gladys. "All Souls'." 1944: 183-196.
Schoonover, Shirley W. "Old and Country Tale." 1964: 226-248.
"The Star Blanket." 1962: 99-120.
"What We Don't Know Hurts Us." 1947: 204-217.
Schorer, Mark. "Blockbuster." 1944: 197-204.
"A Lamp." 1978: 26-40.
Schramm, Wilbur L. "Windwagon Smith." 1942: 51-71.
Schwartz, Lynne Sharon. "Rough Strife." 1979: 255-274.
Schwartz, Steven. "Slow-Motion." 1983: 256-269.
Seager, Allan. "The Conqueror." 1945: 215-233.
"Pro Arte." 1937: 199-210.
Seltz, Thalia. "The Education Of a Queen." 1963: 23-59.
Settle, Mary Lee. "The Old Wives' Tale." 1957: 281-291.
Shaber, David. "A Nous La Liberté." 1961: 288-297.
"Professorio Collegio." 1962: 121-136.
"Scotch Sour." 1973: 216-230.
Shattuck, Katharine. "The Answer." 1948: 194-207.
"Subway System." 1945: 234-241.
Shaw, Irwin. "Act Of Faith." 1946: 242-258.
"God On Friday Night." 1939: 227-234.
"Gunners' Passage." 1945: 15-32.
"The Inhabitants Of Venus." 1964: 114-140.
"Then We Were Three." 1957: 199-221.
"Walking Wounded." 1944: 1-18.
Shedd, Margaret. "The Everlasting Witness." 1964: 49-59.
"The Great Fire Of 1945." 1947: 218-226.
"The Innocent Bystander." 1946: 18-30.
Sheean, Vincent. "The Conqueror." 1941: 273-286.
Shefner, Evelyn. "The Invitations." 1969: 131-146.
Shelnutt, Eve. "Angel." 1975: 142-150.
Shelton, William R. "The Snow Girl." 1948: 208-220.
Shenton, Edward. "When Spring Brings Back. . . .'" 1935: 219-226.
Sherman, Richard. "First Day." 1935: 229-234.

"First Flight." 1934: 195-198.
Shirley, Sylvia. "Slow Journey." 1951: 275-288.
Shore, Wilma. "A Cow On the Roof." 1958: 203-212.
Shreve, Anita. "Past the Island, Drifting." 1976: 220-229.
Shultz, William Henry. "The Shirts Off Their Backs." 1955: 248-261.
Shuman, John Rogers. "Yankee Odyssey." 1942: 241-256.
"Sidney, Rose" [pseud.]. "Butterflies." 1920: 248-267.
Sikes, Shirley. "The Death Of Cousin Stanley." 1973: 252-265.
Simmons, Charles. "Certain Changes." 1977: 153-178.
Singmaster, Elsie. "The Courier Of the Czar." 1924: 155-171.
Skinner, Constance Lindsay. "The Dew On the Fleece." 1926: 229-244.
Slade, Caroline. "Mrs. Susan." 1929: 309-320.
Smiley, Jane. "Lily." 1985: 1-19.
"The Pleasure Of Her Company." 1982: 62-79.
Smith, Edgar Valentine. "'Cock-a-Doodle-*Done!*'" 1931: 279-298.
"Lijah." 1924: 172-189.
"Prelude." 1923: 1-18.
Smith, Gordon Arthur. "No Flowers." 1920: 268-279.
Smith, John Campbell. "Who Too Was a Soldier." 1951: 289-298.
Smith, John Caswell, Jr. "Fighter." 1947: 227-239.
Smith, Lee. "Between the Lines." 1981: 81-93.
"Mrs. Darcy Meets the Blue-Eyed Stranger At the Beach." 1979: 227-241.
Smith, Louise Reinhardt. "The Hour Of Knowing." 1945: 242-265.
Smith, Margarita G. "White For the Living." 1943: 245-250.
Smith, Robert. "Love Story." 1933: 227-245.
Sorenson, Virginia. "The Talking Stick." 1948: 221-235.
Southern, Terry. "The Road Out Of Axotle." 1963: 120-138.
Spears, Raymond S. "A River Combine—Professional." 1924: 190-204.
Spencer, Elizabeth. "The Cousins." 1986: 175-207.
"First Dark." 1960: 237-256.
"Jean-Pierre." 1983: 108-127.
"Ship Island." 1966: 87-112.
Springer, Thomas Grant. "The Blood Of the Dragon." 1919: 135-147.
Stacton, David. "Little Brother Nun." 1968: 230-245.
"The Metamorphosis Of Kenko." 1964: 104-113.
Stafford, Jean. "Beatrice Trueblood's Story." 1956: 237-257.
"A Country Love Story." 1951: 299-311.
"The Hope Chest." 1947: 240-245.
"In the Zoo." 1955: 15-34.
"An Influx Of Poets." 1980: 423-477.
"My Blithe, Sad Bird." 1958: 79-97.
"A Reasonable Facsimile." 1959: 105-128.
"The Shorn Lamb." 1954: 216-227.
"A Summer Day." 1949: 262-275.
"The Warlock." 1957: 83-106.
Steele, Max. "Color the Daydream Yellow." 1969: 237-251.
"The Wanton Troopers." 1955: 262-277.
Steele, Wilbur Daniel. "The Anglo-Saxon." 1922: 210-233.

"Blue Murder." 1925: 237-258.
"Bubbles." 1926: 1-22.
"Can't Cross Jordan By Myself." 1931: 3-23.
"Conjuh." 1930: 283-303.
"Footfalls." 1920: 280-301.
"'For They Know Not What They Do.'" 1919: 21-41.
"Lightning." 1928: 225-239.
"The Man Who Saw Through Heaven." 1925: 218-236.
"The Marriage In Kairwan." 1921: 273-292.
"The Silver Sword." 1929: 323-339.
"What Do You Mean—Americans?" 1924: 205-224.
Stegner, Wallace. "Beyond the Glass Mountain." 1948: 15-25.
"The Blue-Winged Teal." 1950: 1-17.
"Carrion Spring." 1964: 270-286.
"The City Of the Living." 1955: 278-290.
"Two Rivers." 1942: 33-48.
Steinbeck, John. "The Affair At 7, Rue de M——." 1956: 258-265.
"How Edith McGillcuddy Met R. L. Stevenson." 1942: 259-272.
"The Murder." 1934: 179-192.
"The Promise." 1938: 85-105.
Steiner, George. "The Deeps Of the Sea." 1958: 63-78.
Sterling, Thomas. "Bedlam's Rent." 1969: 179-189.
Stern, Daniel. "The Interpretation Of Dreams By Sigmund Freud: A
Story." 1987: 300-307.
Stern, Richard G. "The Sorrows Of Captain Schreiber." 1954: 228-241.
Stern, Steve. "Isaac and the Undertaker's Daughter." 1981: 258-272.
Still, James. "Bat Flight." 1939: 33-48.
"Job's Tears." 1937: 213-221.
"The Proud Walkers." 1941: 289-304.
"So Large a Thing As Seven." 1938: 267-276.
Stone, Alma. "The Bible Salesman." 1959: 277-288.
Stone, Elinore Cowan. "One Uses the Handkerchief." 1924: 225-237.
Street, Julian. "A Matter Of Standards." 1930: 307-322
"Mr. Bisbee's Princess." 1925: 1-39.
Stribling, T. S. "Guileford." 1934: 201-215.
Strong, Austin. "'She Shall Have Music.'" 1943: 253-262.
Strong, Jonathan. "Patients." 1970: 83-91.
"Supperburger." 1967: 31-50.
Stuart, Alison. "Death and My Uncle Felix." 1943: 265-273.
"Sunday Liberty." 1944: 205-213.
"The Yoodler." 1942: 275-297.
Stuart, Jesse. "Whip-Poor-Willie." 1937: 225-240.
Suckow, Ruth. "The Little Girl From Town." 1927: 220-238.
Sulkin, Sidney. "The Plan." 1948: 236-249.
Sullivan, Richard. "Feathers." 1942: 301-312.
Sullivan, Walter. "Elizabeth." 1980: 163-188.
Summers, Hollis. "A Hundred Paths." 1977: 130-143.
Sunwall, Betty. "Things Changed." 1957: 222-235.
Svendsen, Linda. "Heartbeat." 1983: 270-284.

Swain, John D. "One Head Well Done." 1931: 27-49.
Swarthout, Glendon. "A Glass Of Blessings." 1960: 257-265.
Switzer, Robert. "Death Of a Prize Fighter." 1950: 265-272.
Sylvester, Harry. "A Boxer: Old." 1934: 219-233.
Synon, Mary. "Shadowed." 1923: 193-210.

Tabor, James. "The Runner." 1981: 52-58.
Taggart, Shirley Ann. "Ghosts Like Them." 1980: 81-95.
Tallent, Elizabeth. "The Evolution Of Birds Of Paradise." 1984: 214-225.
Targan, Barry. "Old Light." 1980: 295-307.
Tarkington, Booth. "Cider Of Normandy." 1931: 301-327.
    "Cornelia's Mountain." 1925: 259-282.
    "The One Hundred Dollar Bill." 1923: 211-228.
    "She Was Right Once." 1932: 245-268.
    "Stella Crozier." 1926: 245-268.
Tarleton, Fiswoode. "Curtains." 1928: 240-254.
Taylor, Eleanor Ross. "Jujitsu." 1971: 261-266.
Taylor, Ellen Du Pois. "Shades Of George Sand!" 1927: 239-260.
Taylor, Peter. "First Heat." 1969: 169-177.
    "The Gift Of the Prodigal." 1982: 166-185.
    "Heads Of Houses." 1961: 298-325.
    "The Old Forest." 1980: 97-151.
    "Their Losses." 1950: 273-286.
    "There." 1965: 125-148.
Taylor, Robert, Jr. "Lady Of Spain." 1987: 188-207.
    "Venus, Cupid, Folly and Time." 1959: 15-45.
Terhune, Albert Payson. "On Strike." 1919: 56-77.
    "'The Writer-Upward.'" 1922: 234-249.
Terrell, Upton. "Long Distance." 1935: 237-256.
Terrett, Courtenay. "The Saddle." 1948: 250-262.
Theroux, Paul. "The Autumn Dog." 1977: 118-129.
    "World's End." 1981: 289-300.
Thibault, David. "A Woman Like Dilsie." 1937: 243-265.
Thielen, Benedict. "The Empty Sky." 1946: 259-271.
    "Old Boy—New Boy." 1947: 246-256.
    "Silver Virgin." 1939: 237-254.
Thomas, Annabel. "Coon Hunt." 1979: 125-132.
    "The Phototropic Woman." 1981: 239-246.
Thomas, Dorothy. "The Consecrated Coal Scuttle." 1933: 249-256.
    "The Home Place." 1935: 23-53.
    "My Pigeon Pair." 1941: 307-319.
Thomason, Capt. John W., Jr. "Born On an Iceberg." 1930: 325-335.
Thompson, R. E. "It's a Nice Day—Sunday." 1951: 312-322.
Thorne, Crichton Alston. "Chimney City." 1931: 331-343.
Thurber, James. "The Cane In the Corridor." 1943: 277-282.
Thurman, Richard Young. "The Credit Line." 1957: 141-151.
Tracy, Tom. "Homecoming." 1940: 271-286.
Trefethen, Florence. "Infidelities." 1982: 260-270.

Tupper, Tristram. "Grit." 1921: 293-312.
Turner, Thomas C. "Something To Explain." 1959: 73-104.
Tyler, Anne. "The Common Courtesies." 1969: 121-130.
   "With All Flags Flying." 1972: 116-126.
Tyner, Paul. "How You Play the Game." 1968: 267-283.

Ullman, Victor. "Sometimes You Break Even." 1946: 31-47.
Updike, John. "Bech Takes Pot Luck." 1970: 185-203.
   "The Bulgarian Poetess." 1966: 1-15.
   "The City." 1983: 141-156.
   "The Doctor's Wife." 1962: 275-284.
   "Marching Through Boston." 1967: 105-113.
   "Nakedness." 1975: 316-323.
   "The Other." 1985: 299-313.
   "Separating." 1976: 296-307.
   "Wife-Wooing." 1961: 326-330.
   "Your Lover Just Called." 1968: 259-266.

Van Doren, Mark. "The Watchman." 1949: 17-29.
Van Dyke, Henry. "Du Côté De Chez Britz." 1979: 213-226.
Van Ness, Lillian. "Give My Love To Maggie." 1950: 287-305.
Van Wert, William F. "Putting & Gardening." 1983: 227-245.
Vaughn, Stephanie. "Kid MacArthur." 1986: 226-244.
   "Sweet Talk." 1980: 309-319.
Von Der Goltz, Peggy. "The Old She 'Gator." 1943: 285-292.
Vorse, Mary Heaton. "The 'Madelaine.'" 1926: 269-292.
   "Twilight Of the God." 1922: 250-260.

Walker, Alice. "The Abortion." 1981: 127-137.
   "Kindred Spirits." 1986: 1-11.
Walker, Augusta. "The Day Of the Cipher." 1954: 242-253.
Wallace, Robert. "The Secret Weapon Of Joe Smith." 1954: 254-260.
Wallace, Warren. "Up Home." 1987: 251-273.
Walter, Eugene. "I Love You Batty Sisters." 1957: 262-271.
Warren, Robert Penn. "Christmas Gift." 1937: 269-280.
Watson, John. "The Gun On the Table." 1948: 263-273.
Watts, Mary S. "Nice Neighbours." 1923: 229-246.
Weaver, Gordon. "Getting Serious." 1979: 15-34.
Weaver, John D. "Meeting Time." 1949: 276-287.
Weidman, Jerome. "Basket Carry." 1942: 315-330.
   "My Father Sits In the Dark." 1935: 259-263.
   "Thomas Hardy's Meat." 1937: 283-291.
Wells, Harriet. "Progress." 1924: 238-256.
Welty, Eudora. "The Burning." 1951: 17-31.
   "The Demonstrators." 1968: 1-17.
   "Livvie Is Back." 1943: 3-16.
   "Petrified Man." 1939: 257-275.
   "A Sketching Trip." 1946: 272-293.
   "The Whole World Knows." 1947: 257-275.

"The Wide Net." 1942: 3-30.

"A Worn Path." 1941: 17-27.

Wescott, Glenway. "Prohibition." 1928: 255-268.

West, Jessamyn. "The Blackboard." 1946: 294-303.

"Breach Of Promise." 1954: 261-280.

"Horace Chooney, M.D." 1947: 276-285.

"Lead Her Like a Pigeon." 1945: 266-274.

"The Picnickers." 1963: 139-158.

"Public Address System." 1949: 288-305.

West, Ray B., Jr. "The Ascent." 1948: 274-282.

Weston, Christine. "Raziya." 1944: 214-224.

Wetherell, W. D. "If a Woodchuck Could Chuck Wood." 1983: 128-140.

"The Man Who Loved Levittown." 1981: 174-190.

Wetjen, Albert Richard. "Command." 1926: 36-46.

Wexley, John. "Southern Highway 51." 1934: 237-242.

Wheeler, Kate. "La Victoire." 1982: 136-151.

Wheelis, Allen. "Sea-Girls." 1967: 189-202.

Whelan, Gloria. "The Dogs In Renoir's Garden." 1983: 310-319.

Whitbread, Thomas. "The Rememberer." 1962: 259-274.

White, Robin. "First Voice." 1958: 213-227.

"Shower Of Ashes." 1960: 70-85.

White, William C. "Pecos Bill and the Willful Coyote." 1943: 295-309.

Whitehand, Robert. "The Fragile Bud." 1938: 279-292.

Whitehill, Joseph. "Able Baker." 1956: 266-278.

Whitlock, Brand. "The Sofa." 1925: 283-296.

Whitman, Stephen French. "The Last Room Of All." 1920: 302-322.

Whitmore, Stanford. "Lost Soldier." 1954: 281-286.

Whittemore, Reed. "The Stutz and the Tub." 1954: 287-293.

Wilbur, Richard. "A Game Of Catch." 1954: 47-50.

Wilcox, Wendell. "The Pleasures Of Travel." 1944: 225-233.

Wilde, Hagar. "Little Boat." 1933: 259-266.

Willard, Nancy. "Theo's Girl." 1970: 219-235.

Williams, Ben Ames. "The Nurse." 1926: 293-308.

"They Grind Exceeding Small." 1919: 42-55.

Williams, Jesse Lynch. "Not Wanted." 1923: 247-277.

Williams, Joy. "The Roomer." 1966: 171-179.

Williams, Thomas. "Goose Pond." 1959: 150-164.

Williams, Wythe. "Splendid With Swords." 1925: 40-72.

Wilmot, Jeanne. "Dirt Angel." 1986: 162-174.

Wilner, Herbert. "The Passion For Silver's Arm." 1958: 249-272.

"Whistle and the Heroes." 1954: 294-307.

Wilson, Eric. "The Axe, the Axe, the Axe." 1985: 238-253.

Wilson, Leon. "Six Months Is No Long Time." 1949: 306-323.

Wilson, Michael. "Come Away Home." 1945: 275-285.

Winslow, Anne Goodwin. "Seasmiles." 1950: 306-325.

Wolf, Leonard. "Fifty-Fifty." 1965: 177-188.

Wolfe, Thomas. "Boom Town." 1934: 245-279.

"Only the Dead Know Brooklyn." 1935: 267-273.

Wolfert, Ira. "The Indomitable Blue." 1955: 291-311.

Wolff, Tobias. "In the Garden Of the North American Martyrs." 1981: 105-116.
    "Next Door." 1982: 254-259.
    "Sister." 1985: 199-205.
Wood, Frances Gilchrist. "Turkey Red." 1919: 105-119.
Worthington, Marjorie. "Hunger." 1942: 333-346.
Worthington, Rex. "A Kind Of Scandal." 1954: 308-316.
Wright, Richard. "Almos' a Man." 1940: 289-305.
    "Fire and Cloud." 1938: 19-81.
Wylie, Jeanne E. "A Long Way To Go." 1942: 75-88.

Yates, Richard. "The Best Of Everything." 1956: 279-292.
    "A Good and Gallant Woman." 1967: 203-218.
    "Oh, Joseph, I'm So Tired." 1979: 275-298.
Yerby, Frank G. "Health Card." 1944: 42-51.
Young, Marguerite. "Old James." 1944: 234-250.

Zelver, Patricia. "The Flood." 1973: 64-79.
    "The Little Pub." 1977: 144-152.
    "My Father's Jokes." 1979: 187-202.
    "Norwegians." 1975: 239-250.
    "On the Desert." 1972: 141-153.
Ziller, Eugene. "Sparrows." 1960: 266-282.
Zorn, George A. "Mr. and Mrs. McGill." 1966: 205-224.
    "Thompson." 1964: 190-212.
Zugsmith, Leane. "King Lear In Evansville." 1934: 283-293.

Index of Titles

Index Of Titles

[B = Best Stories]
[P = Prize Stories]

"A Nous La Liberté." Shaber, David.—P. 1961: 288-297.
"Able Baker." Whitehill, Joseph.—P. 1956: 266-278.
"The Abortion." Walker, Alice.—P. 1981: 127-137.
"About Boston." Just, Ward.—P. 1985: 174-198.
"Absolutely Perfect." Haardt, Sara.—P. 1933: 175-187.
"The Academy." Ely, David.—B. 1966: 59-68.
"The Accident." Stuart, Jesse.—B. 1967: 279-290.
"Accomplished Desires." Oates, Joyce Carol.—P. 1969: 43-61.
"Acme Rooms and Sweet Marjorie Russell." Hunt, Hugh Allyn.—B.
    1967: 135-150.
"Act Of Faith." Shaw, Irwin.—B. 1947: 382-400; P. 1946: 242-258.
"The Actes and Monuments." Corrington, John William.—B. 1976:
    68-97; P. 1976: 107-140.
"The Actor." Johnson, Nunnally.—P. 1928: 196-210.
"Advent." Novick, Marian.—P. 1981: 154-173.
"Adventure." Hahn, Emily.—B. 1930: 87-90.
"Adventures Of Andrew Lang. Finger, Charles J.—B. 1924: 74-94.
"The Æsculapians." Mandell, Marvin.—B. 1972: 235-255.
"The Affair At 7, Rue De M——." Steinbeck, John.—P. 1956: 258-265.
"An Afternoon." Warner, Elizabeth.—B. 1944: 423-429.
"Afternoon In the Jungle." Maltz, Albert.—P. 1941: 223-231.
"Afternoon Of a Young Girl." Owen, Janet Curren.—P. 1936: 273-284.
"Alabama Sketches." Tartt, Ruby Pickens.—B. 1945: 272-282.
"Alaska." Adams, Alice.—P. 1984: 96-105.
"Alcantara." Jenkins, MacGregor.—B. 1929: 130-145.
"Alexander To the Park." Johnson, Josephine.—P. 1942: 207-215.
"Alice." Anderson, Sherwood.—P. 1929: 65-71.
"Alice Blaine." Randal, Vera.—P. 1966: 121-148.
"All Around the Town." Benét, Stephen Vincent.—B. 1941: 14-27.
"All My Relations." McIlroy, Christopher.—B. 1986: 155-179.
"All Prisoners Here." Pfeffer, Irving.—B. 1949: 219-237.
"All Right." Fuller, Blair.—P. 1978: 106-128.
"All Souls'." Schmitt, Gladys.—B. 1944: 332-344; P. 1944: 183-196.
"All the Pelageyas." Dillon, Millicent G.—P. 1980: 409-422.
"Allonym." McClatchy, J. D.—P. 1972: 219-234.
"Alma Mater." Lewis, O. F.—P. 1920: 141-147.
"Almos' a Man." Wright, Richard.—B. 1941: 356-370; P. 1940: 289-305.
"Along a Sandy Road." Bishop, Ellen.—B. 1930: 1-5.

Index Of Titles

"Alternatives." Adams, Alice.—P. 1974: 54-67.

"Alvira, Lettie, and Pip." Schell, Jessie.—P. 1975: 324-342.

"Always Afternoon." Hale, Nancy.—P. 1938: 203-212.

"Always Good For a Belly Laugh." Glen, Emilie.—B. 1952: 181-189.

"Am Strande Von Tanger." Salter, James.—P. 1970: 113-125.

"Amanuensis: A Tale Of the Creative Life." Godwin, Gail.—P. 1980: 321-344.

"The Amateurs." Swados, Harvey B.—B. 1978: 306-308.

"Amazement." Whitman, Stephen French.—B. 1920: 320-347.

"The Amazing Mystery At Storick, Dorschi, Pflaumer, Inc." Fuchs, Daniel.—P. 1938: 171-189.

"The Ambassador." Newhouse, Edward.—P. 1958: 229-248.

"The Ambassador." Spingarn, Lawrence P.—B. 1968: 315-322.

"An American Home." Eustis, Helen.—P. 1947: 143-155.

"American Nocturne." Whitehand, Robert.—B. 1936: 305-311.

"The American Sickness." Yglesias, Jose.—B. 1975: 278-290.

"An American Student In Paris." Farrell, James T.—B. 1968: 43-74.

"Amethyst." Corle, Edwin.—B. 1934: 67-80.

"Amid a Place Of Stone." Butler, Frank.—B. 1959: 26-38.

"Among the Dangs." Elliott, George P.—P. 1959: 46-72.

"The Analyst." Hunter, Evan.—B. 1975: 124-136.

"Ancestral Home." Canfield, Dorothy.—P. 1932: 87-106.

"Ancient Airs, Voices." Oates, Joyce Carol.—P. 1987: 274-299.

"Andrew." Morgan, Berry.—B. 1967: 187-192.

"Angel." Shelnutt, Eve.—P. 1975: 142-150.

"Angela." Mukherjee, Bharati.—B. 1985: 157-167.

"The Anglo-Saxon." Steele, Wilbur Daniel.—P. 1922: 210-233.

"The Animals' Fair." Miller, Warren.—B. 1945: 143-153.

"Annunciation." LeSueur, Meridel.—B. 1936: 210-220.

"Another Story." Matthews, Jack.—B. 1970: 161-173.

"Another Wife." Anderson, Sherwood.—B. 1927: 50-58.

"Anschluss." Boyle, Kay.—B. 1940: 1-19; P. 1939: 79-102.

"Answer." Furniss, Ruth Pine.—B. 1930: 54-58.

"The Answer." Shattuck, Katharine.—P. 1948: 194-207.

"Antæus." Deal, Borden.—B. 1962: 41-50.

"Anthropology: What Is Lost In Rotation." Wilson, William S.—B. 1977: 338-348.

"The Apartment Hunter." Moore, Brian.—B. 1967: 175-186.

"The Apostate." Milburn, George.—B. 1973: 202-207.

"The Apothecary." Bromfield, Louis.—P. 1929: 93-119.

"An Apple, an Orange." Johnson, Diane.—P. 1973: 168-183.

"Apple Seed and Apple Thorn." Enright, Elizabeth.—B. 1954: 79-85.

"The Application." Neugeboren, Jay.—B. 1965: 251-258.

"The Apprentice." Canfield, Dorothy.—B. 1948: 36-45.

"April 25th, As Usual." Ferber, Edna.—P. 1919: 274-298.

"Arcturus." Connell, Evan S., Jr.—B. 1957: 93-127.

"Are You a Doctor?" Carver, Raymond.—P. 1975: 111-118.

"The Argosies." Hull, Alexander.—P. 1920: 123-140.

"An Argument In 1934." Schwartz, Delmore.—B. 1943: 279-291.

"An Arm Upraised." MacDonald, Alan.—B. 1939: 183-188.
"An Army With Banners." Gerould, Katharine Fullerton.—B. 1925: 122-147.
"Around the Dear Ruin." Berriault, Gina.—B. 1957: 8-18.
"An Arrival At Carthage." Lockwood, Scammon.—B. 1932: 153-164.
"Arrival On a Holiday." Wright, Wilson.—B. 1937: 380-387.
"Art For Art's Sake." Barrett, Richmond Brooks.—P. 1922: 56-70.
"Art History." Arensberg, Ann.—P. 1975: 151-168.
"The Artificial Moonlight." Justice, Donald.—B. 1984: 123-139; P. 1984: 199-213.
"The Artificial Nigger." O'Connor, Flannery.—B. 1956: 264-284.
"The Artist." Kaplan, Ralph.—B. 1950: 234-249.
"As a Dog Should." Alexander, Charles.—P. 1922: 44-55.
"As I Was Going Up the Stair." Chester, Alfred.—B. 1958: 96-118.
"The Ascent." West, Ray B., Jr.—P. 1948: 274-282.
"The Ascent Of Ariel Goodbody." Clark, Walter Van Tilburg.—P. 1943: 129-139.
"Asphodel." Welty, Eudora.—B. 1943: 400-411.
"The Assembly." Gallant, Mavis.—B. 1981: 150-157.
"At Isham's." Venable, Edward C.—B. 1918: 293-304.
"At Mrs. Farrelly's." Carroll, Joseph.—B. 1953: 53-61.
"At Peace." Copeland, Ann.—B. 1977: 43-65.
"At Sallygap." Lavin, Mary.—B. 1942: 385-409.
"At the Anarchists' Convention." Sayles, John.—B. 1980: 302-311.
"At the Drugstore." Taylor, Peter.—B. 1963: 327-353.
"At the End Of the Road." Muilenburg, Walter J.—B. 1916: 262-271.
"At the Sign Of the Three Daughters." Canfield, Dorothy.—B. 1928: 60-76.
"At the Swamp." Lewis, Janet.—B. 1930: 135-141.
"Athens, Greece, 1942." Gregory, Vahan Krikorian.—B. 1953: 148-153.
"August." Gallant, Mavis.—B. 1960: 64-101.
"Aunt Mary." Hermann, John.—B. 1963: 185-195.
"'Aurore.'" Mumford, Ethel Watts.—P. 1921: 243-257.
"The Author." Johnson, Josephine W.—B. 1950: 215-233.
"Autobiography Of My Mother." Russ, Joanna.—P. 1977: 199-210.
"The Autumn Dog." Theroux, Paul.—P. 1977: 118-129.
"Autumn Full Of Apples." Wakefield, Dan.—B. 1966: 283-287.
"An Awakening." Anderson, Sherwood.—B. 1919: 24-33.
"Awakening and the Destination." Krantz, David E.—B. 1937: 170-178.
"Awroopdedoop!" Appel, Benjamin.—P. 1937: 45-52.
"The Axe, the Axe, the Axe." Wilson, Eric.—P. 1985: 238-253.
"The Aztec Dog." Graves, John.—P. 1962: 201-216.

"Baby." Goodman, Ivy.—P. 1981: 212-216.
"Babylon Revisited." Fitzgerald, F. Scott.—B. 1931: 122-142.
"Bachelor Of Arts." Chaikin, Nancy G.—B. 1955: 25-38.
"Bad Boy From Brooklyn." Seide, Michael.—B. 1939: 244-258.
"Bad Company." Gallagher, Tess.—B. 1986: 100-112.

"The Ballad Of Jesse Neighbours." Humphrey, William.—P. 1965: 53-70.

"The Ballad Of the Sad Café." McCullers, Carson.—B. 1944: 205-264.

"Bambi Meets the Furies." Busch, Frederick.—B. 1975: 37-46.

"The Bamboo Trap." Lemmon, Robert S.—P. 1923: 120-133.

"The Banks Of the Ohio." Bingham, Sallie.—P. 1964: 70-80.

"The Banquet Of Crow." Parker, Dorothy.—B. 1958: 225-235.

"Barbed Wire." Canzoneri, Robert.—B. 1971: 74-85.

"Bare Bones." Bingham, Sallie.—P. 1966: 235-243.

"Barn Burning." Faulkner, William.—P. 1939: 3-29.

"Basil From Her Garden." Barthelme, Donald.—B. 1986: 1-9; P. 1987: 115-123.

"Basket Carry." Weidman, Jerome.—P. 1942: 315-330.

"Basquerie." Kelly, Eleanor Mercein.—P. 1926: 173-212.

"Bat Flight." Still, James.—P. 1939: 33-48.

"Battered Armor." McKenna, Edward L.—B. 1928: 211-221.

"Be Heavy." Hagopian, Richard.—B. 1945: 90-98.

"Be Nice To Mr. Campbell." Lowry, Robert.—P. 1950: 37-51.

"The Beach Party." Grau, Shirley Ann.—B. 1966: 83-94.

"Beachhead In Bohemia." Marsh, Willard.—B. 1953: 207-213.

"The Bear." Faulkner, William.—B. 1943: 70-86.

"Beasts Of the Wild." Algren, Nelson.—B. 1957: 1-7.

"Beatrice Trueblood's Story." Stafford, Jean.—P. 1956: 237-257.

"The Beautiful Fire." Morris, I. V.—B. 1940: 229-243.

"Beautiful Girl." Adams, Alice.—P. 1978: 67-75.

"Beautiful, Helpless Animals." Chaikin, Nancy.—B. 1976: 54-67.

"A Beautiful Night For Orion." Clay, Richard.—B. 1954: 14-47.

"Beautifully and Bravely." Sylvester, Harry.—B. 1940: 433-449.

"Because I Was Flesh." Dahlberg, Edward.—B. 1962: 32-40.

"Bech Takes Pot Luck." Updike, John.—P. 1970: 185-203.

"Bedlam's Rent." Sterling, Thomas.—P. 1969: 179-189.

"Beebee." Vreuls, Diane.—B. 1983: 269-284.

"The Bees." Vatsek, Joan.—B. 1942: 372-384.

"The Beggar Boy." Savler, David S.—P. 1946: 233-241.

"The Beggar Of Alcazar." Bercovici, Konrad.—B. 1925: 64-80.

"Beggarman, Rich Man, Or Thief." Loeser, Katinka.—B. 1963: 196-199.

"Beginning Of Wisdom." Field, Rachel.—B. 1943: 87-104.

"Beginnings." Bumpus, Jerry.—B. 1974: 6-15.

"The Bella Lingua." Cheever, John.—B. 1959: 39-58.

"Belshazzar's Letter." Gerould, Katharine Fullerton.—B. 1922: 171-194.

"Ben." Hill, Pati.—B. 1958: 134-149.

"Benjamin Burning." Winslow, Joyce Madelon.—B. 1969: 287-303.

"Berceuse." Chester, Alfred.—B. 1961: 45-57.

"Berkshire Comedy." Seager, Allan.—B. 1939: 233-243.

"The Best Bread." Plagemann, Bentz.—P. 1949: 212-224.

"The Best Of Everything." Yates, Richard.—P. 1956: 279-292.

"Best Quality Glass Company, New York." Stark, Sharon Sheehe.—B. 1983: 210-221.

"The Betrayal." Sassoon, Babette.—B. 1963: 280-314.

"Between the Lines." Smith, Lee.—P. 1981: 81-93.

"Beyond." Faulkner, William.—B. 1934: 91-104.

"Beyond the Cross." Burnet, Dana.—B. 1923: 98-124.

"Beyond the Glass Mountain." Stegner, Wallace.—B. 1948: 294-304; P. 1948: 15-25.

"The Bible Salesman." Stone, Alma.—P. 1959: 277-288.

"Biceps." Algren, Nelson.—B. 1942: 1-18.

"Big Bertha Stories." Mason, Bobbie Ann.—P. 1986: 80-94.

"The Big Black and White Game." Bradbury, Ray.—B. 1946: 40-55.

"Big, Black, Good Man." Wright, Richard.—B. 1958: 337-347.

"Big Blonde." Parker, Dorothy.—P. 1929: 3-25.

"Big Boy." Ford, Jesse Hill.—B. 1975: 100-110.

"The Big Brown Trout." Travers, Robert.—B. 1967: 303-314.

"Big Buick To the Pyramids." Liberman, M. M.—P. 1957: 272-280.

"Big Days Beginning." Heth, Edward Harris.—P. 1936: 227-242.

"Big Dog." Lavers, Norman.—P. 1987: 170-187.

"Big Jules." Callaghan, Morley.—B. 1941: 35-42.

"Big Singing." Boone, Jack H., and Merle Costiner.—P. 1932: 49-68.

"The Big Stranger On Dorchester Heights." Pentz, Albert Duverney.—B. 1916: 272-274.

"The Biggest Thing Since Custer." Eastlake, William.—P. 1970: 17-28.

"Billy." Cram, Mildred.—B. 1924: 19-38.

"The Biography Of Blade." Gale, Zona.—B. 1924: 95-99.

"Bird Man." Stuart, David.—B. 1955: 295-303.

"The Bird Of Serbia." Street, Julian.—B. 1918: 268-292.

"Bird Song." Goss, John Mayo.—B. 1946: 1-17; P. 1947: 95-113.

"Birds, Clouds, Frogs." Phelan, R. C.—B. 1963: 235-245.

"The Birthday Party." Berriault, Gina.—P. 1966: 197-204.

"Birthday Party." Jackson, Shirley.—B. 1964: 161-171.

"A Birthday Present." Sayre, Anne.—B. 1959: 259-273.

"The Bitter Bread." Ford, Jesse Hill.—P. 1967: 51-58.

"Black Art and Ambrose." Gilpatric, Guy.—P. 1920: 81-93.

"The Black Beach." Carr, Archie.—P. 1956: 121-132.

"Black Boy's Good Time." Grossberg, Elmer.—P. 1943: 167-177.

"The Black Laugh." Shiffrin, A. B.—B. 1924: 191-197.

"Black Secret." Rawlings, Marjorie Kinnan.—P. 1946: 226-232.

"Black Snowflakes." Horgan, Paul.—B. 1964: 137-151.

"Black Tobias and the Empire." Werner, Heinz.—B. 1939: 327-335.

"Black Troubadour." Cohn, David L.—B. 1939: 60-67.

"Black Water Blues." Culver, Monty.—P. 1951: 87-97.

"Black Wind and Lightning." Fessier, Michael.—B. 1938: 141-145.

"Black Wolf." Edmonds, Walter D.—B. 1933: 91-107.

"The Blackboard." West, Jessamyn.—P. 1946: 294-303.

"The Blacktop Champion Of Ickey Honey." Sorrells, Robert T.—B. 1978: 136-162.

"A Blade Of Grass." Morris, Edita.—B. 1937: 226-244.

Index Of Titles

"Bleat Blodgette." Phillips, John.—B. 1968: 283-314.

"Blight." Dybek, Stuart.—P. 1987: 81-102.

"Blind Man's Buff." Benedict, Libby.—B. 1938: 54-58.

"Blind Vision." Freedley, Mary Mitchell.—B. 1918: 85-91.

"Blinker Was a Good Dog." Lampman, Ben Hur.—P. 1943: 215-219.

"Blockbuster." Schorer, Mark.—P. 1944: 197-204.

"Blood Letting." Gerald, John Bart.—B. 1970: 108-114.

"The Blood Of the Dragon." Springer, Thomas Grant.—P. 1919: 135-147.

"Blood-Burning Moon." Toomer, Jean.—B. 1923: 385-393.

"The Blood-Red One." Burt, Maxwell Struthers.—B. 1919: 96-107.

"Blood-Swollen Landscape." Oates, Joyce Carol.—P. 1976: 186-200.

"Bloodflowers." Valgardson, W. D.—B. 1971: 329-346.

"A Blue Blonde In the Sky Over Pennsylvania." Lynds, Dennis.—B. 1965: 223-239.

"The Blue Kimono." Callaghan, Morley.—B. 1936: 16-22.

"Blue Murder." Steele, Wilbur Daniel.—P. 1925: 237-258.

"The Blue Sash." Beck, Warren.—B. 1939: 1-15.

"The Blue Serge Suit." Langdon, John.—B. 1957: 171-184; P. 57: 107-120.

"Blue Sky." Gilkyson, Walter.—B. 1930: 59-73.

"The Blue-Winged Teal." Stegner, Wallace.—P. 1950: 1-17.

"The Boat." McLeod, Alistair.—B. 1969: 99-116.

"Bodies Like Mouths." Clayton, John J.—P. 1978: 186-204.

"The Bookseller." Hardwick, Elizabeth.—B. 1981: 158-170.

"Boom Town." Wolfe, Thomas.—P. 1934: 245-279.

"Born On an Iceberg." Thomason, Capt. John W., Jr.—P. 1930: 325-335.

"A Bottle Of Milk For Mother." Algren, Nelson.—P. 1941: 71-89.

"The Bottomless Well." Terry, Walter S.—B. 1966: 269-282.

"Bound For Rio Grande." Dingle, A. E.—B. 1926: 71-89.

"Boundary Line." Beck, Warren.—B. 1943: 10-22.

"The Bounty-Jumper." Synon, Mary.—B. 1915: 257-274.

"A Boxer: Old." Sylvester, Harry.—B. 1935: 285-297; P. 1934: 219-233.

"The Boy In the Green Hat." Klein, Norma.—B. 1969: 69-80.

"Boy In the Summer Sun." Schorer, Mark.—B. 1938: 254-264.

"The Boy Next Door." Cramer, Alice Carver.—P. 1949: 123-134.

"The Boy Who Was Astrid's Mother." Briskin, Mae Seidman.—B. 1976: 34-53.

"Boys Will Be Boys." Cobb, Irvin S.—B. 1917: 86-127.

"Brahmin Beachhead." Hale, Nancy.—B. 1952: 190-203.

"Breach Of Promise." West, Jessamyn.—P. 1954: 261-280.

"Bread and Butter Questions." Koch, Claude.—P. 1985: 71-88.

"Bread and Games." Weaver, John D.—B. 1947: 476-489.

"The Breadman." Heath, Mary.—B. 1972: 93-112.

"Break-Neck Hill." Forbes, Esther.—P. 1920: 71-80.

"Breathe Upon These Slain." LeSueur, Meridel.—P. 1946: 177-194.

"Breed." Sayles, John.—B. 1977: 293-316; P. 1977: 243-267.

"Bremen's." Coatsworth, Elizabeth.—P. 1949: 89-99.

"Bridal Pond." Gale, Zona.—P. 1928: 49-54.

"The Bridge." Stark, Irwin.—B. 1946: 355-399.

"Bridge Of Music, River Of Sand." Goyen, William.—P. 1976: 153-157.

"Bridgeport Bus." Howard, Maureen.—P. 1962: 239-250.

"Brief Lives In California." L'Heureux, John.—P. 1981: 247-257.

"Bright and Morning." Parker, Glidden.—B. 1950: 337-348.

"Bright and Morning Star." Wright, Richard.—B. 1939: 374-414.

"Broad Day." Price, Reynolds.—B. 1976: 209-219.

"The Broken Globe." Kreisel, Henry.—B. 1966: 155-165.

"The Broken Wheel." Goryan, Sirak.—B. 1934: 152-163.

"The Broken Wings." Lardas, Konstantinos.—B. 1973: 195-205.

"Bromeliads." Williams, Joy.—B. 1978: 303-309.

"The Broomstick On the Porch." Arkin, Frieda.—P. 1964: 1-14.

"Brother Quintillian and Dick the Chemist." Elliott, George P.—B. 1955: 107-122.

"Brothers." Anderson, Sherwood.—B. 1921: 3-12.

"The Brothers." Cheever, John.—B. 1938: 86-99.

"The Brothers' House." Algren, Nelson.—P. 1935: 63-67.

"Brownstone." Adler, Renata.—P. 1974: 13-25.

"Bruns." Rush, Norman.—B. 1984: 243-254.

"Bubbles." Steele, Wilbur Daniel.—P. 1926: 1-22.

"The Buck In the Hills." Clark, Walter Van Tilburg.—P. 1944: 52-62.

"The Buck in Trotevale's." Williams, Thomas.—B. 1959: 359-380.

"The Buffalo Wallow." Jackson, Charles.—B. 1953: 165-175.

"The Bulgarian Poetess." Updike, John.—P. 1966: 1-15.

"Bulldog." Daniels, Roger.—P. 1927: 126-148.

"The Bunker Mouse." Greene, Frederick Stuart.—B. 1917: 283-306.

"The Burden." Lynch, John A.—B. 1948: 200-212; P. 1947: 181-193.

"The Burglar." Klein, Norma.—P. 1963: 108-119.

"The Burial." Matthews, Jack.—B. 1975: 162-177.

"Burial In the Desert." Fenton, Edward.—B. 1945: 49-63; P. 1945: 90-104.

"The Burning." Cady, Jack.—B. 1966: 1-11.

"The Burning." Welty, Eudora.—P. 1951: 17-31.

"Burns." Just, Ward.—B. 1973: 150-165.

"Bury Your Own Dead." Breuer, Bessie.—B. 1946: 56-73; P. 1945: 61-74.

"The Bus." Jackson, Shirley.—B. 1966: 125-137.

"Bus To Biarritz." Cole, Madelene.—B. 1935: 115-124; P. 1934: 89-100.

"Buster." Brown, Katharine Holland.—B. 1918: 43-60.

"The Butcher." Shore, Wilma.—B. 1941: 293-301.

"The Butcherbirds." Patt, Esther.—B. 1951: 259-267; P.1951: 217-226.

"Butterflies." "Sidney, Rose" [pseud.].—B. 1920: 214-235; P. 1920: 248-267.

"Buttin' Board." Patterson, Pernet.—P. 1929: 253-269.

"The Button." Goodman, Henry.—B. 1923: 240-262.

"By Due Process Of Law." Stimson, F. J.—B. 1923: 339-361.

"By the People." Faulkner, William.—P. 1957: 121-140.

"By the River." Oates, Joyce Carol.—B. 1969: 195-212.

Index Of Titles

"By the Yellow Lake." Marsh, Peter.—B. 1978: 212-222.

"Caddies' Day." Schinto, Jeanne.—B. 1984: 271-278.
"Cadence." Dubus, Andre.—B. 1975: 80-99.
"The Café De Paris." Gupta, Roberta.—B. 1982: 151-181.
"The Call." Laurence, Bethel.—B. 1925: 225-236.
"Call a Solemn Assembly." Portugal, Ruth.—B. 1945: 170-179; P. 1945: 193-201.
"Called For." Robinson, Mabel L.—P. 1940: 251-254.
"The Caller." Liben, Meyer.—B. 1946: 243-254.
"The Caller In the Night." Kline, Burton.—B. 1917: 365-382.
"Calloway's Climb." Sandberg, Peter L.—B. 1974: 219-243.
"Calves." DeJong, David Cornel.—P. 1939: 51-62.
"Cambridge Is Sinking!" Clayton, John J.—B. 1973: 38-56; P. 1974: 87-104.
"The Camel's Back." Fitzgerald, F. Scott.—P. 1920: 43-70.
"The Canals Of Mars." Boyle, Kay.—P. 1943: 79-88.
"The Cane In the Corridor." Thurber, James.—P. 1943: 277-282.
"Cane River." Saxon, Lyle.—B. 1927: 240-254; P. 1926: 213-228.
"Can't Cross Jordan By Myself." Steele, Wilbur Daniel.—P. 1931: 3-23.
"The Cape." McCoy, Esther.—B. 1950: 308-316.
"The Captain Is Impaled." Algren, Nelson.—P. 1950: 52-67.
"Caput Mortuum." Morris, Edita.—B. 1942: 201-209; P. 1941: 235-243.
"Careless Love." Bradford, Roark.—P. 1930: 55-68.
"Carmencita." Root, Waverley.—B. 1948: 266-273.
"Carrie Snyder." Benefield, Barry.—B. 1926: 1-18.
"Carrion Spring." Stegner, Wallace.—P. 1964: 270-286.
"The Case Of the Missing Photographs." Eaton, Charles Edward.—P. 1972: 192-208.
"Cass Mastern's Wedding Ring." Warren, Robert Penn.—B. 1945: 303-343.
"Castle Of Snow." Heller, Joseph.—B. 1949: 127-134.
"The Cat Of the Cane-Brake." Greene, Frederick Stuart.—B. 1916: 149-161.
"The Cat That Lived At the Ritz." Bromfield, Louis.—B. 1928: 13-30.
"Catafalque." Cooke, Charles.—B. 1936: 70-79.
"The Catbird Seat." Thurber, James.—B. 1943: 360-369.
"Cathedral." Carver, Raymond.—B. 1982: 3-17.
"The Cats Which Cried." Burnett, Whit.—B. 1934: 25-39.
"Cayetano the Perfect." Conrad, Barnaby.—P. 1949: 110-122.
"A Celebration For Joe." Gold, Herbert.—P. 1956: 194-202.
"Célestine." Hopper, James.—P. 1923: 92-103.
"Celtic Twilight." Ostrow, Joanna.—B. 1968: 247-268.
"The Centenarian." Ingersoll, Will E.—B. 1919: 225-236.
"Center Of Gravity." Amster, L. J.—B. 1965: 1-44.
"Certain Changes." Simmons, Charles.—P. 1977: 153-178.
"Certain Hard Places." Arking, Linda.—P. 1975: 251-282.
"'A Certain Rich Man——.'" Perry, Lawrence.—B. 1917: 391-411.
"Chains." Godschaux, Elma.—B. 1937: 78-94; P. 1936: 203-223.

"The Chamber Music Evening." Lopate, Phillip.—B. 1974: 142-166.
"Champlin." Burke, Morgan.—B. 1924: 3-18.
"Change." Woiwode, Larry.—B. 1981: 317-330.
"A Change Of Air." Gold, Ivan.—B. 1954: 123-144.
"Change Of Plan." Purdy, Ken.—B. 1953: 257-262.
"A Change Of Season." Bond, James.—B. 1983: 48-67.
"Chaos, Disorder and the Late Show." Miller, Warren.—P. 1965: 287-292.
"Char On Raven's Bench." Holwerda, Frank.—B. 1954: 174-184.
"Charybdis." Holt, T. E.—P. 1982: 80-98.
"Chautonville." Comfort, Will Levington.—B. 1915: 46-54.
"The Cheat's Remorse." Callaghan, Morley.—B. 1938: 81-85.
"The Chevigny Man." Macauley, Robie.—P. 1956: 203-220.
"Chicken On the Wind." King, Mary.—P. 1940: 147-166.
"The Chicken Which Became a Rat." Drake, Albert.—B. 1971: 86-106.
"Chico." Dickerson, George.—B. 1963: 109-124.
"The Chicory Neighbors." DeJong, David Cornel.—P. 1937: 65-73.
"Child Of God." Bradford, Roark.—B. 1927: 72-85; P. 1927: 1-14.
"Child Of God." Janeway, Elizabeth.—P. 1948: 136-147.
"The Children." Oates, Joyce Carol.—P. 1971: 208-225.
"Children Are Bored On Sunday." Stafford, Jean.—B. 1949: 295-304.
"Children Of Ruth." Elliott, George P.—B. 1952: 118-147.
"The Children's Wing." Johnson, Joyce.—P. 1987: 15-24.
"Chimney City." Thorne, Crichton Alston.—P. 1931: 331-343.
"Ching, Ching, Chinaman." Steele, Wilbur Daniel.—B. 1917: 441-467.
"The Chink and the Clock People." Robbins, Tom.—B. 1977: 275-290.
"Chips Off the Old Block." Stegner, Wallace.—B. 1943: 310-326.
"The Chocolate Hyena." Cobb, Irvin S.—B. 1923: 144-169.
"Christ In Concrete." DiDonato, Pietro.—B. 1938: 127-140.
"The Christian Bite." Komroff, Manuel.—B. 1926: 156-170.
"A Christmas Carillon." Calisher, Hortense.—P. 1955: 68-84.
"Christmas Gift." Warren, Robert Penn.—B. 1938: 309-319; P. 1937: 269-280.
"A Chronicle Of Love." Francis, H. E.—B. 1976: 98-115; P. 1976: 277-295.
"The Chrysanthemums." Steinbeck, John.—B. 1938: 277-287.
"Cider Of Normandy." Tarkington, Booth.—P. 1931: 301-327.
"The Cinderella Waltz." Beattie, Ann.—P. 1980: 389-407.
"A Circle In the Fire." O'Connor, Flannery.—B. 1955: 230-248; P. 1955: 35-52.
"The Citizen." Dwyer, James Francis.—B. 1915: 57-76.
"The City." Updike, John.—P. 1983: 141-156.
"City Of Boys." Nugent, Beth.—B. 1985: 168-182.
"A City Of Churches." Barthelme, Donald.—B. 1973: 1-5.
"The City Of Refuge." Fisher, Rudolph.—B. 1925: 105-121.
"The City Of the Living." Stegner, Wallace.—P. 1955: 278-290.
"Claustrophobia." Goodloe, Abbie Carter.—P. 1926: 125-138.
"Cleopatra." Mudrick, Marvin.—P. 1967: 59-69.
"A Cliff Of Fall." Rindfleisch, Norval.—P. 1970: 29-49.

"The Climate Of the Family." Chaikin, Nancy G.—B. 1952: 86-96.
"Clothing." L'Heureux, John.—B. 1985: 126-138.
"Coach." Robison, Mary.—B. 1982: 93-107.
"'Cock-a-Doodle-*Done!*'" Smith, Edgar Valentine.—P. 1931: 279-298.
"The Cocoon." Goodwin, John B. L.—B. 1947: 76-94.
"The Coffin." Wood, Clement.—B. 1922: 293-301.
"A Coffin For Anna." Rushfeldt, Elise M.—P. 1929: 273-283.
"The Cold Room." Pei, Lowry.—B. 1984: 223-237.
"The Cold Winter." Caldwell, Erskine.—B. 1935: 98-102.
"The Colleagues Of Mr. Chips." Sandmel, Samuel.—B. 1961: 314-339.
"A Colonel Of Kentucky." Cobb, Irvin S.—P. 1932: 109-133.
"The Colony." Singer, Isaac Bashevis.—B. 1969: 275-286.
"Color the Daydream Yellow." Steele, Max.—P. 1969: 237-251.
"'Color Trouble.'" Garfinkle, Harold.—B. 1941: 97-119.
"Colorado." Taylor, Robert, Jr.—B. 1983: 222-235.
"Come Away Home." Wilson, Michael.—P. 1945: 275-285.
"Come Away, Oh Human Child." Sandberg-Diment, Erik.—B. 1973: 248-261.
"Come Dance With Me In Ireland." Jackson, Shirley.—B. 1944: 135-140.
"Come Lady Death." Beagle, Peter S.—P. 1965: 149-164.
"Come Out the Wilderness." Baldwin, James.—P. 1959: 208-233.
"The Comedian." L'Heureux, John.—P. 1986: 31-43.
"Comes a Day." Lamkin, Speed.—B. 1950: 259-273; P. 1950: 181-195.
"Comet." Derieux, Samuel A.—P. 1921: 156-168.
"The Coming Of Age." Jaynes, Clare.—P. 1942: 195-203.
"Coming Over." Milton, Edith.—B. 1982: 233-250.
"Command." Wetjen, Albert Richard.—P. 1926: 36-46.
"The Common Courtesies." Tyler, Anne.—P. 1969: 121-130.
"Communist." Ford, Richard.—B. 1986: 83-99.
"Confusions." Ludwig, Jack.—B. 1961: 207-225.
"Conjuh." Steele, Wilbur Daniel.—P. 1930: 283-303.
"'Conjur.'" Patterson, Pernet.—B. 1929: 206-238.
"The Conqueror." Seager, Allan.—P. 1945: 215-233.
"The Conqueror." Sheean, Vincent.—P. 1941: 273-286.
"The Conqueror." Wincelberg, Simon.—B. 1953: 384-397.
"The Consecrated Coal Scuttle." Thomas, Dorothy.—P. 1933: 249-256.
"'Contact!'" Hart, Frances Noyes.—P. 1920: 23-42.
"The Contest For Aaron Gold." Roth, Philip.—B. 1956: 285-299.
"The Continental Angle." Pelley, William Dudley.—P. 1930: 235-249.
"The Continental Heart." McLaughlin, Lissa.—B. 1982: 144-150.
"The Contract Of Corporal Twing." Stewart, Solon K.—B. 1923: 322-338.
"Conveniences." Pearlman, Edith.—P. 1984: 86-95.
"The Conventional Wisdom." Elkin, Stanley.—B. 1978: 223-247.
"The Conversion Of the Jews." Roth, Philip.—B. 1959: 244-258.
"The Conversion Of Willie Heaps." Garner, Hugh.—B. 1952: 151-159.
"The Convict." Burke, James Lee.—B. 1986: 34-47.
"Coon Hunt." Thomas, Annabel.—P. 1979: 125-132.

Index Of Titles

"Cora Unashamed." Hughes, Langston.—B. 1934: 188-197.
"Cornelia's Mountain." Tarkington, Booth.—P. 1925: 259-282.
"Coroner's Inquest." Connelly, Mark.—P. 1930: 47-52.
"Corporal Hardy." Danielson, Richard Ely.—B. 1939: 68-81.
"Corputt." Greenwald, Tupper.—B. 1924: 100-109.
"The Costa Brava, 1959." Just, Ward.—P. 1986: 55-69.
"The Count and the Princess." Epstein, Joseph.—B. 1983: 117-140.
"Counterclockwise." Young, Elisabeth Larsh.—B. 1960: 354-377.
"Counting Months." Leavitt, David.—P. 1984: 66-85.
"The Country Doctor." Beede, Ivan.—B. 1929: 26-37.
"Country Doctor." Marquis, Don.—P. 1935: 153-167.
"Country Full Of Swedes." Caldwell, Erskine.—P. 1933: 119-136.
"The Country Husband." Cheever, John.—B. 1955: 39-63; P. 1956: 15-40.
"A Country Love Story." Stafford, Jean.—P. 1951: 299-311.
"Country Of the Painted Freaks." Sheltzline, David.—B. 1973: 262-275.
"A Country Passion." Callaghan, Morley.—B. 1928: 51-59.
"The Courier Of the Czar." Singmaster, Elsie.—P. 1924: 155-171.
"A Courtship." Faulkner, William.—P. 1949: 1-16.
"The Courtship Of Widow Sobcek." Higgins, Joanna.—B. 1982: 37-53.
"The Cousins." Spencer, Elizabeth.—P. 1986: 175-207.
"Covenant." Cherry, Kelly.—B. 1972: 20-47.
"A Cow On the Roof." Shore, Wilma.—P. 1958: 203-212.
"Coward's Castle." Gilkyson, Walter.—B. 1925: 148-166.
"The Cracked Looking-Glass." Porter, Katherine Anne.—B. 1933: 223-253.
"The Cracked Teapot." Dobie, Charles Caldwell.—B. 1924: 53-69.
"The Cradle Of Civilization." Parker, Dorothy.—B. 1930: 154-157.
"The Crazy Guy." Sylvester, Harry.—B. 1939: 274-282.
"Crazy Ladies." Johnson, Greg.—P. 1986: 17-30.
"Crazy Sunday." Fitzgerald, F. Scott.—B. 1933: 115-132.
"The Credit Line." Thurman, Richard Young.—P. 1957: 141-151.
"Creole Love Song." LaMar, Nathaniel.—B. 1956: 226-241.
"Criers and Kibbitzers, Kibbitzers and Criers." Elkin, Stanley.—B. 1962: 51-80.
"Crime Passionnel." Bromfield, Louis.—B. 1945: 19-29.
"Crisis." Gale, Zona.—P. 1936: 195-200.
"Crispin's Way." Downey, Harris.—B. 1953: 101-111.
"Crossroads Woman." Corning, Howard McKinley.—B. 1934: 81-90.
"The Crow Woman." Heller, Steve.—P. 1985: 148-173.
"Crown's Bess." Heyward, Du Bose.—P. 1925: 192-202.
"Cruelties." Babcock, Edwina Stanton.—B. 1918: 24-42.
"The Cruise Of the Cashalot." Edmonds, Walter D.—P. 1932: 149-161.
"The Crusader." Saroyan, William.—B. 1937: 316-324.
"A Cup Of Tea." Burt, Maxwell Struthers.—B. 1917: 45-69.
"The Cure." Brown, Mary Ward.—B. 1984: 45-55.
"A Curtain Of Green." Welty, Eudora.—B. 1939: 319-326.
"Curtains." Tarleton, Fiswoode.—P. 1928: 240-254.
"Cyclists' Raid." Rooney, Frank.—B. 1952: 237-253; P. 1951: 256-274.

"The Czech Dog." Hardy, W. G.—B. 1945: 109-114.

"Da Vinci Is Dead." Hamilton, R. C.—P. 1985: 116-131.
"The Dancing Boy." Eastlake, William.—B. 1971: 107-117.
"Dancing Ducks and Talking Anus." Ferry, James.—B. 1982: 18-36.
"Daphne's Lover." Taylor, Peter.—B. 1970: 344-366.
"The Daring Young Man On the Flying Trapeze." Saroyan,
    William.—P. 1934: 45-51.
"Dark." Johnson, Josephine W.—P. 1934: 171-175.
"The Dark City." Aiken, Conrad.—B. 1922: 3-12.
"The Dark Days Of Christmas." Branda, Eldon.—P. 1968: 246-258.
"The Dark Hour." Steele, Wilbur Daniel.—B. 1918: 258-267.
"The Dark Roots Of the Rose." Clemons, Walter.—B. 1957: 70-92.
"Darkness." Cobb, Irvin S.—B. 1921: 52-81.
"The Darkness." Mayhall, Jane.—B. 1947: 282-292.
"The Darkness Of Love." Boswell, Robert.—P. 1987: 25-64.
"Daughter Of the Revolution." McElroy, Joseph.—P. 1985: 132-147.
"Dawn Of Remembered Spring." Stuart, Jesse.—B. 1943: 337-344.
"The Dawn Swings In." Jeffers, Lance.—B. 1948: 157-171.
"A Day For Fishing." Fowler, Janet.—P. 1960: 133-145.
"A Day In Operations." Grinstead, David.—P. 1970: 205-217.
"A Day In the Country." Burnett, Whit.—B. 1931: 70-80.
"A Day In the Life Of the Boss." Geeslin, Hugh, Jr.—B. 1959: 121-136.
"Day Of Gold and Darkness." Fontaine, Robert.—B. 1947: 56-61.
"The Day Of the Bullet." Ellin, Stanley.—B. 1960: 11-28.
"The Day Of the Cipher." Walker, Augusta.—P. 1954: 242-253.
"The Day Of the Equinox." Curley, Daniel.—B. 1955: 84-95.
"A Day On Ragged." Hall, Donald.—B. 1962: 181-199.
"The Day That It Rained Forever." Bradbury, Ray.—B. 1958: 73-83.
"The Day the Flowers Came." Madden, David.—B. 1969: 117-128.
"The Dead." Oates, Joyce Carol.—P. 1973: 1-34.
"Dead Center." Merril, Judith.—B. 1955: 176-201.
"Dead Man." Cain, James M.—P. 1936: 91-104.
"The Dear Little Ones." Green, Eleanor.—P. 1942: 161-168.
"Dear Mr. Flessheimer." Cook, Whitfield.—B. 1938: 110-117.
"Death and My Uncle Felix." Stuart, Alison.—B. 1943: 327-336; P.
    1943: 265-273.
"Death and Transfiguration." Marshall, Alan.—B. 1934: 267-281.
"Death In a Cathedral." Woods, Glennyth.—B. 1946: 540-561.
"A Death In the Family." Frosher, Wingate.—B. 1953: 137-147.
"Death In the Woods." Anderson, Sherwood.—P. 1926: 23-35.
"Death Of a Country Doctor." Medearis, Mary.—B. 1942: 174-200.
"Death Of a Favorite." Powers, J. F.—B. 1951: 268-285.
"Death Of a Prize Fighter." Switzer, Robert.—P. 1950: 265-272.
"Death Of an Outcast." Komroff, Manuel.—B. 1940: 145-154.
"The Death Of Cousin Stanley." Sikes, Shirley.—P. 1973: 252-265.
"The Death Of Murdo." Bercovici, Konrad.—B. 1922: 25-41.
"Death Of Red Peril." Edmonds, Walter D.—B. 1929: 92-103.

"The Death Of Sun." Eastlake, William.—B. 1973: 99-118; P. 1974: 242-260.

"A Death On Eight' Avenue." Graeve, Oscar.—P. 1926: 139-152.

"A Death On the East Side." Gold, Herbert.—B. 1972: 48-74; P. 1972: 235-264.

"Death Under the Hawthorns." Bennett, Peggy.—B. 1950: 67-79; P. 1950: 68-80.

"Deaths Of Distant Friends." Updike, John.—B. 1983: 249-254.

"Decades." Sorrentino, Gilbert.—B. 1978: 316-328.

"The Decline and Fall Of Augie Sheean." Coogan, Joe.—B. 1955: 74-83.

"The Decline and Fall Of Officer Fergerson." Montgomery, Marion.—B. 1971: 176-201.

"Deep Water." Marquand, J. P.—P. 1932: 217-242.

"The Deeps Of the Sea." Steiner, George.—P. 1958: 63-78.

"Defeat." Boyle, Kay.—P. 1941: 3-14.

"Defender Of the Faith." Roth, Philip.—B. 1960: 278-306; P. 1960: 39-69.

"Déjà Vu." McKenzie, Miriam.—B. 1962: 246-256; P. 1962: 227-237.

"A Delayed Hearing." Nemerov, Howard.—B. 1958: 179-191.

"The Demonstrators." Welty, Eudora.—P. 1968: 1-17.

"Department Store." Bayer, Ann.—P. 1975: 343-349.

"The Departure." Robinson, Selma.—P. 1933: 217-223.

"Departure Of Husband." Gibbons, Robert.—B. 1949: 100-105.

"The Derby Hopeful." Caputi, Anthony.—P. 1979: 242-254.

"Derrick's Return." Morris, Gouverneur.—P. 1923: 182-192.

"The Desert In the Oasis." Tucci, Niccolò.—B. 1963: 354-379.

"Desert Matinee." Bumpus, Jerry.—B. 1975: 26-36.

"The Deserter." Boyer, Agnes.—B. 1974: 1-5.

"Design In Plaster." Fitzgerald, F. Scott.—B. 1940: 82-88.

"The Destruction Of the Goetheanum." Salter, James.—P. 1972: 127-140.

"Detritus." Reid, Randall.—P. 1973: 266-290.

"The Devil and Daniel Webster." Benét, Stephen Vincent.—P. 1937: 3-17.

"The Devil Drum." Willoughby, Barrett.—B. 1925: 287-310.

"The Devil On a Hot Afternoon." Dorrance, Ward.—B. 1956: 90-104.

"DeVilmarte's Luck." Vorse, Mary Heaton.—B. 1918: 305-324.

"The Dew On the Fleece." Skinner, Constance Lindsay.—P. 1926: 229-244.

"The Diamond Ring." Peterkin, Julia.—P. 1930: 253-268.

"The Dichotomy." Greene, Philip L.—P. 1971: 267-283.

"Did You Once See Shelley?" Cardwell, Guy A.—P. 1971: 28-57.

"Diesel." Mitchell, Don.—B. 1971: 156-175.

"Dietz At War." Just, Ward.—B. 1976: 133-144.

"The Dignity Of Life." Bly, Carol.—B. 1983: 25-47.

"Dirt Angel." Wilmot, Jeanne.—P. 1986: 162-174.

"Diseases Of the Heart." Knickerbocker, Conrad.—P. 1967: 159-168.

"Dishes." Brownell, Agnes Mary.—B. 1919: 82-95.

"Distance." Paley, Grace.—P. 1969: 199-208.

"A Distant Episode." Bowles, Paul.—B. 1948: 20-31.
"A Distant Harbour." Horgan, Paul.—B. 1935: 217-227.
"A Distant Street." Faragoh, Francis Edward.—1923: 59-74.
"Division." Burnett, Whit.—B. 1935: 41-97.
"The Dock-Witch." Ozick, Cynthia.—B. 1972: 256-289.
"Dr. Cahn's Visit." Stern, Richard.—B. 1980: 325-329.
"The Doctor's Wife." Updike, John.—P. 1962: 275-284.
"Doe Season." Kaplan, David Michael.—B. 1986: 120-135.
"Dog Days." Jones, Madison P., Jr.—B. 1953: 189-206.
"Dog In the Manger." Rothschild, Michael.—B. 1974: 194-218.
"The Dogs In Renoir's Garden." Whelan, Gloria.—P. 1983: 310-319.
"Dogs' Lives." Bishop, Michael.—B. 1985: 24-43.
"The Dolphin Story." Renwick, Joyce.—B. 1982: 124-143.
"Done Got Over.'" Ellerbe, Alma, and Paul Ellerbe.—P. 1927: 175-191.
"Don't Get Me Wrong." Lull, Roderick.—B. 1941: 231-244; P. 1940:
     25-41.
"Don't Scrub Off These Names." McNulty, John.—B. 1945: 133-142.
"The Doorstop." Flannagan, Roy.—B. 1936: 134-141.
"Dorothy." Caldwell, Erskine.—B. 1931: 81-87.
"Dotson Gerber Resurrected." Bennett, Hal.—B. 1971: 10-23.
"Double Birthday." Cather, Willa.—B. 1929: 60-85.
"The Double House." Hale, Nancy.—B. 1935: 210-216.
"Dovisch In the Wilderness." Wilner, Herbert.—B. 1966: 327-357.
"Down In the Reeds By the River." Lincoln, Victoria.—B. 1947:
     238-250.
"Down On Their Knees." Steele, Wilbur Daniel.—B. 1916: 322-348.
"Down the American River." Ignatow, Rose Graubart.—B. 1974:
     67-86.
"The Downward Path To Wisdom." Porter, Katherine Anne.—B.
     1940: 311-332; P. 1940: 209-235.
"The Dream Of Angelo Zara." D'Agostino, Guido.—B. 1943: 47-55.
"Dressed In Shade." Macauley, Robie.—P. 1967: 169-188.
"Dressing Up." Burnett, W. R.—P. 1930: 3-13.
"Dried Rose Petals In a Silver Bowl." Winn, Janet Bruce.—B. 1968:
     331-341.
"A Drink Of Water." Brown, T. K., III.—P. 1958: 179-201.
"Drums Again." Holmes, Edward M.—B. 1972: 113-122.
"Du Côté De Chez Britz." Van Dyke, Henry.—P. 1979: 213-226.
"The Dummy-Chucker." Roche, Arthur Somers.—B. 1920: 198-213.
"Dunelight." Babcock, Edwina Stanton.—P. 1925: 94-111.
"Dust." Griffith, Patricia.—P. 1976: 89-106.

"Each In His Generation." Burt, Maxwell Struthers.—P. 1920: 3-22.
"Early Morning, Lonely Ride." Parker, Nancy Huddleston.—B. 1968:
     269-282; P. 1969: 87-99.
"Ebbets Field." Neugeboren, Jay.—P. 1968: 195-210.
"The Echo." Bowles, Paul.—P. 1947: 61-75.
"The Eclipse." Enright, Elizabeth.—P. 1958: 111-118.
"Edge Of Doom." Beck, Warren.—B. 1950: 42-58.

"The Education Of a Queen." Selz, Thalia.—B. 1962: 340-377; P. 1963: 23-59.
"Eight O'Clock One Morning." Grau, Shirley Ann.—P. 1962: 153-159.
"Eighteenth Summer." Abbett, Hallie Southgate.—P. 1941: 31-46.
"The Eldest Child." Brennan, Maeve.—B. 1969: 1-8.
"The Elephant Forgets." Cooper, Courtney Ryley.—P. 1930: 113-128.
"The Elephant Remembers." Marshall, Edison.—P. 1919: 78-104.
"Elephants Through the Country." Johnston, Mary.—P. 1929: 165-186.
"Elizabeth." Sullivan, Walter.—P. 1980: 163-188.
"Ellen Craig." Berkman, Sylvia.—P. 1960: 86-107.
"Elmer." Boyd, Albert Truman.—B. 1933: 30-41.
"The Embarkment For Cythera." Cheever, John.—P. 1964: 1-29.
"The Emerald." Barthelme, Donald.—B. 1980: 1-26.
"The Emperor Of Elam." Dwight, H. G.—B. 1917: 147-207.
"Emperor Of the Air." Canin, Ethan.—B. 1985: 44-57.
"The Empire Of Things." Mountzoures, H. L.—P. 1969: 253-257.
"The Empty Sky." Thielen, Benedict.—P. 1946: 259-271.
"Encarnatión." Overbeck, Alicia O'Reardon.—P. 1930: 219-232.
"The Enchanted." Knight, Laurette MacDuffie.—B. 1943: 187-217.
"Encore." Purdy, James.—P. 1960: 228-236.
"Encounter In Haiti." Gold, Herbert.—P. 1957: 37-47.
"The End Of the Depression." Bolté, Mary.—B. 1951: 37-44.
"The End Of the Party." Gerould, Christopher.—P. 1932: 195-199.
"The End Of the Path." Noyes, Newbold.—B. 1915: 184-188.
"An End To Dreams." Benét, Stephen Vincent.—P. 1932: 3-15.
"The Enemy." Buck, Pearl.—P. 1943: 107-126.
"The Enemy." Gordon, Caroline.—P. 1938: 193-199.
"The Enemy." Mayhall, Jane.—P. 1973: 156-167.
"Enemy Country." Gilkyson, Walter.—B. 1936: 152-168.
"An Enemy Of the People." Sadoff, Ira.—P. 1976: 158-170.
"England To America." Montague, Margaret Prescott.—P. 1919: 3-20.
"The English Gardens." Jackson, David.—P. 1962: 161-199.
"The Enigma." Adamic, Louis.—B. 1931: 3-23.
"The Enormous Radio." Cheever, John—B. 1948: 46-56.
"Enter Daisy; To Her, Alexandra." Cooke, Charles.—B. 1937: 29-37.
"Entropy." Pynchon, Thomas.—B. 1961: 300-313.
"An Episode At Pintail Lake." Cobb, Irvin S.—P. 1928: 148-168.
"Episode At the Pawpaws." Reed, Louis.—B. 1933: 254-265.
"Episode From Life." Mamet, Louis.—B. 1935: 246-250.
"Episode In a Machine Age." Brown, Cambray.—P. 1928: 134-147.
"Episode Of a House Remembered." Rogers, John.—B. 1949: 238-247.
"Escape From the Mine." Edmonds, Walter D.—P. 1936: 143-168.
"Escape To the City." Woodward, Gordon.—B. 1957: 331-345.
"Eskimo Pies." Somerlott, Robert.—B. 1965: 291-298.
"Estate and Trespass: A Gothic Story." Hall, James B.—P. 1954: 142-150.
"Eustacia." Stuart, Jesse.—B. 1939: 259-273.
"Evening." Gale, Zona.—B. 1926: 114-119.

"Evening and Morning Prayer." Goss, John Mayo.—P. 1949: 162-171.
"An Evening Performance." Garrett, George.—B. 1960: 102-111.
"Evenings At Home." Hartwick, Elizabeth.—B. 1949: 117-126.
"Evensong." Waldron, Daniel.—B. 1952: 336-346.
"The Everlasting Witness." Shedd, Margaret.—P. 1964: 49-59.
"Everything That Rises Must Converge." O'Connor, Flannery.—B. 1962: 324-339; P. 1963: 1-16.
"The Evolution Of Birds Of Paradise." Tallent, Elizabeth.—P. 1984: 214-225.
"The Exact Nature Of Plot." Schaeffer, Susan Fromberg.—P. 1978: 292-300.
"Excerpts From Swan Lake." Cameron, Peter.—P. 1986: 110-117.
"Exchange Value." Johnson, Charles.—B. 1982: 108-115.
"The Excursion." Babcock, Edwina Stanton.—B. 1917: 1-19.
"The Excursionists." Cardozo, Nancy.—B. 1955: 13-24.
"An Exile In the East." O'Connor, Flannery.—B. 1979: 28-38.
"Exiles From the Creuse." Mian, Mary.—B. 1944: 273-279.
"Exodus." Deal, Borden.—B. 1949: 60-71.
"Experiment." Burt, Maxwell Struthers.—B. 1921: 28-51.
"'Extra! Extra!'" Sherwood, Robert E.—B. 1926: 237-243.
"Extra Men." Rhodes, Harrison.—B. 1918: 223-231.
"The Eye." Bowles, Paul.—B. 1979: 214-221.

"The Face In the Window." Pelley, William Dudley.—P. 1920: 160-183.
"Facing Front." Kenney, Susan.—P. 1982: 1-31.
"The Facts In the Case." Leenhouts, Grant.—B. 1933: 187-201.
"Faith, Hope and Charity." Cobb, Irvin S.—P. 1930: 91-109.
"The Faithful." Hardwick, Elizabeth.—B. 1980: 196-209.
"The Faithful." McPherson, James Alan.—P. 1974: 229-241.
"The Faithful Wife." Callaghan, Morley.—B. 1930: 34-38.
"Falconer." Cheever, John.—B. 1977: 24-42.
"The Fall Of Machine Gun McGurk." Farrell, James T.—B. 1940: 53-64.
"Falling Off the Scaffold." Coffin, Lyn.—B. 1979: 131-149.
"The False Talisman." Dobie, Charles Caldwell.—P. 1931: 131-149.
"Fame For Mr. Beatty." Hall, James Norman.—B. 1929: 112-122.
"Fame Takes the J Car." Albee, George.—B. 1933: 3-13.
"Familiar Usage In Leningrad." Cole, Tom.—B. 1962: 79-98.
"A Family Affair." L'Heureux, John.—B. 1974: 112-141.
"The Family Chronicle." Tüting, Bernhard Johann.—B. 1932: 243-252.
"Family History." Pasinetti, P. M.—B. 1940: 244-284.
"Family In the Wind." Fitzgerald, F. Scott.—P. 1933: 139-161.
"A Family Man." Hutter, Donald.—B. 1965: 167-185.
"A Family Matter." Elliott, George P.—P. 1954: 92-132.
"The Fancy Woman." Taylor, Peter.—B. 1942: 313-342.
"Fanutza." Bercovici, Konrad.—B. 1921: 13-27.
"Faq'." Elliott, George P.—B. 1953: 127-136.
"Farewell, Sweet Love." Heath, Priscilla.—B. 1954: 145-162.

"Farewell To Cuba." Cozzens, James Gould.—P. 1932: 19-36.

"The Farlow Express." Robinson, Anthony.—B. 1957: 272-291.

"The Farmer's Children." Bishop, Elizabeth.—B. 1949: 39-47.

"Fast Love." Malone, Michael.—P. 1982: 196-205.

"Fat Girl." Gill, Brendan.—P. 1972: 94-115.

"'The Fat Of the Land.'" Yezierska, Anzia.—B. 1919: 326-349.

"Fatal." Chasin, Helen.—P. 1980: 239-247.

"Father and Son." Callaghan, Morley.—B. 1935: 103-114.

"Father Delacroix." Martenet, May Davies.—B. 1947: 269-281.

"The Father's Hand." Humphrey, G.—B. 1918: 125-130.

"A Father's Story." Dubus, Andre.—B. 1984: 72-94.

"The Fawn." Burt, Struthers.—P. 1939: 121-130.

"Fear." Bellah, James Warner.—P. 1927: 53-83.

"The Fear Of Innocence." Fiedler, Leslie A.—B. 1950: 143-190.

"Feasting." Benedict, Elizabeth.—P. 1983: 246-255.

"Feathers." Sullivan, Richard.—P. 1942: 301-312.

"Feet Of Gold." Smith, Gordon Arthur.—B. 1916: 294-321.

"Fellow-Creatures." Morris, Wright.—B. 1985: 150-156.

"The Female Of the Fruit Fly." March, William.—B. 1944: 197-204.

"The Fence." Villa, José Garcia.—B. 1933: 314-320.

"Fences." "Paul, L." [pseud.]—B. 1928: 228-245.

"Fever Flower." Johnson, Josephine.—B. 1945: 115-122.

"Fiddlers Of Moon Mountain." Gowen, Emmett.—B. 1931: 164-178.

"Fifteen From Company K." March, William.—B. 1931: 202-213; P. 1931: 225-236.

"Fifty-Fifty." Wolf, Leonard.—P. 1965: 177-188.

"Fifty-Two Weeks For Florette.— Heermann, Elizabeth Alexander.—P. 1921: 169-192.

"Fighter." Maxwell, James A.—P. 1954: 180-193.

"Fighter." Smith, John Caswell, Jr.—P. 1947: 227-239.

"Figure Over the Town." Goyen, William.—B. 1964: 125-135.

"The Final Fate Of the Alligators." Hoagland, Edward.—P. 1971: 330-340.

"The Final Proof Of Fate and Circumstance." Abbott, Lee K.—B. 1984: 1-12.

"The Fine White Mist Of Winter." Oates, Joyce Carol.—B. 1963: 220-234; P. 1963: 216-229.

"Finisterre." Rubin, Louis D., Jr.—B. 1979: 243-269.

"Fire and Cloud." Wright, Richard.—P. 1938: 19-81.

"Fire and Water." Wescott, Glenway.—B. 1925: 270-286.

"The Firebird." Doughty, LeGarde S.—B. 1954: 72-78.

"Fireflies." Goldman, Miriam.—P. 1967: 71-76.

"The Fireflies." McKelway, St. Clair.—B. 1963: 200-210.

"The First Autumn." Caldwell, Erskine.—B. 1933: 54-59.

"The First Clean Fact." Heinemann, Larry.—B. 1980: 210-220.

"First Dark." Spencer, Elizabeth.—P. 1960: 237-256.

"First Day." Sherman, Richard.—P. 1935: 229-234.

"First Day Finish." West, Jessamyn.—B. 1945: 344-355.

"The First Face." Enright, Elizabeth.—B. 1952: 148-150.

Index Of Titles

"The First Fish." Beck, Warren.—B. 1945: 8-18.
"First Flight." Sherman, Richard.—P. 1934: 195-198.
"The First Flower." Lyons, Augusta Wallace.—B. 1956: 242-248.
"First Heat." Taylor, Peter.—P. 1969: 169-177.
"The First Lover." Boyle, Kay.—P. 1932: 71-76.
"First Marriage." McKelway, St. Clair.—B. 1961: 238-244.
"First Oboe." Glover, James Webber.—B. 1929: 104-111.
"The First Of Mr. Blue." Connolly, Myles.—B. 1928: 113-124.
"The First Stone." Mason, Grace Sartwell.—B. 1926: 197-209.
"First Views Of the Enemy." Oates, Joyce Carol.—B. 1965: 259-270; P. 1965: 165-175.
"First Voice." White, Robin.—P. 1958: 213-227.
"Firstborn." Woiwode, Larry.—B. 1983: 285-316.
"The Fish Trap." Leach, Peter.—P. 1974: 167-174.
"Fisherman's Luck." Gowen, Emmett.—B. 1933: 145-156.
"The Fishermen From Chihuahua." Connell, Evan S., Jr.—B. 1955: 64-73.
"The Fishermen Of Patzcuaro." Fifield, William.—P. 1944: 101-116; P. 1943: 43-59.
"5135 Kensington: August, 1903." Benson, Sally.—B. 1942: 28-40.
"Five Ripe Pears." Saroyan, William.—P. 1935: 211-216.
"Five Thousand Dollars Reward." Post, Melville Davisson.—P. 1919: 120-134.
"The Five-Forty-Eight." Cheever, John.—P. 1955: 103-116.
"The Five-Minute Girl." Bradley, Mary Hastings.—P. 1931: 53-67.
"The Flag Is Down." Olsen, Paul.—B. 1970: 223-235.
"The Flaming Chariot." Gilpatric, Guy.—B. 1931: 151-163.
"The Flashlight." Cleaver, Eldridge.—B. 1970: 20-52; P. 1971: 226-260.
"Flesh and Blood." Critchell, Laurence.—B. 1946: 128-146; P. 1945: 47-60.
"Fleur." Erdrich, Louise.—P. 1987: 1-14.
"Flight Of the Circle Heart." Eastlake, William.—P. 1959: 194-207.
"Flight Through the Dark." Angell, Roger.—B. 1951: 1-9.
"Flights." Adams, Alice.—P. 1977: 186-198.
"The Flood." Zelver, Patricia.—P. 1973: 64-79.
"Flora and Fauna." Wilson, Harry Leon.—B. 1923: 414-439.
"The Flower." Rugel, Miriam.—P. 1954: 205-215.
"Fly Away Home." Jackson, Roberts.—B. 1953: 176-188.
"'Fly, Fly, Little Dove.'" Garrigan, Philip.—B. 1948: 99-105.
"Fog." Burnet, Dana.—B. 1916: 58-74.
"Fogbound In Avalon." McGrath, Elizabeth.—B. 1981: 203-219.
"Fool About a Horse." Faulkner, William.—B. 1937: 38-54.
"Football Girl." Brush, Katharine.—P. 1932: 79-83.
"Footfalls." Steele, Wilbur Daniel.—P. 1920: 280-301.
"Footnote To a Life." Morris, Lloyd.—B. 1933: 210-222.
"Footnote To American History." Lull, Roderick.—B. 1949: 166-178.
"For a Beautiful Relationship." Ruml, Wentzle, III.—B. 1946: 316-336.
"For Each Of Us." Bryan, Jack Y.—B. 1942: 50-66.

136

"For Esmé—With Love and Squalor." Salinger, J. D.—P. 1950: 244-264.

"For I Have Wept." Stein, Gerald.—B. 1965: 325-343.

"For Jeromé—With Love and Kisses." Lish, Gordon.—P. 1984: 255-292.

"For My Sister." Driftmier, Lucile.—P. 1936: 129-139.

"For Nancy's Sake." Bird, Virginia.—P. 1937: 55-61.

"'For They Know Not What They Do.'" Steele, Wilbur Daniel.—P. 1919: 21-41.

"Foreign Shores." Salter, James.—B. 1984: 255-270.

"The Foreigner." Adams, Bill.—B. 1932: 3-15.

"The Foreigner In the Blood." Hughes, Mary Gray.—B. 1969: 49-68.

"The Forest." Leffland, Ella.—B. 1970: 138-160.

"Forest Cover." Bryner, Edna.—B. 1922: 70-82.

"The Forest Of the Night." Weston, Christine.—B. 1953: 353-362.

"Forgiveness." Reese, Lizette Woodworth.—B. 1924: 167-174.

"Forrester." Hume, Cyril.—P. 1931: 173-191.

"Four Annas." Weston, Christine.—B. 1956: 324-335.

"Four Dreams Of Gram Perkins." Sawyer, Ruth.—P. 1927: 208-219.

"Four Generations." Suckow, Ruth.—B. 1924: 198-210.

"Four Worms Turning." Stern, Morton.—B. 1940: 381-386.

"Fox and Swan." L'Heureux, John.—B. 1972: 212-225.

"The Fragile Bud." Whitehand, Robert.—P. 1938: 279-292.

"Frankie and Thomas and Bud Asbury." Gordon, Caroline.—B. 1940: 89-108; P. 1939: 181-204.

"Free the Canaries From Their Cages!" Granit, Arthur.—B. 1956: 167-183; P. 1957: 182-198.

"Freedom's a Hard-Bought Thing." Benét, Stephen Vincent.—P. 1940: 3-21.

"Freeway To Wherever." Ogden, Maurice.—P. 1960: 221-227.

"French Eva." Gerould, Katharine Fullerton.—B. 1921: 142-167.

"Frenchman's Ship." Boyle, Kay.—B. 1943: 23-40.

"Frère Jacques." Cheever, John.—B. 1939: 32-38.

"A Fresno Fable." Saroyan, William.—B. 1977: 291-292.

"A Friend Of Napoleon." Connell, Richard.—P. 1923: 19-37.

"Friends." Paley, Grace.—B. 1980: 250-261.

"The Frill." Buck, Pearl S.—P. 1933: 47-59.

"From the Other Side Of the South." Steele, Wilbur Daniel.—B. 1922: 273-292.

"The Frozen Fields." Bowles, Paul.—B. 1958: 54-72.

"Frozen Stillness." Morang, Alfred.—B. 1935: 251-253.

"Fru Holm." Karmel, Ilona.—B. 1951: 168-186.

"A Fugitive From the Mind." Bennett, Peggy.—B. 1951: 24-36.

"The Fugitives." Malone, John.—P. 1973: 96-106.

"Fugue For Harmonica." Seager, Allan.—B. 1936: 264-269.

"The Fugue Of the Fig Tree." Sultan, Stanley.—B. 1953: 321-331.

"The Fur Coat." Loveridge, George.—P. 1944: 124-134.

"The Further Adventures Of Brunhild." Kavaler, Rebecca.—B. 1972: 193-211.

"Further Tales About Men and Women." Maxwell, William.—B. 1966: 219-233.

"The Fury." Coates, Robert M.—P. 1937: 35-42.

"The Future." McElroy, Joseph.—B. 1981: 185-202; P. 1982: 32-51.

"Gal Young Un." Rawlings, Marjorie Kinnan.—P. 1933: 3-44.

"The Game." Patton, Frances Gray.—B. 1954: 232-251.

"Game Chicken." Seager, Allan.—B. 1947: 366-381.

"A Game Of Chess." Wilbur, Richard.—P. 1954: 47-50.

"The Games That We Played." Weathers, Winston.—B. 1968: 323-330.

"The Garden Of Redemption." DiFranco, Anthony.—P. 1986: 152-161.

"The Gardens Of Mont-Saint Michel." Maxwell, William.—B. 1970: 174-193.

"Gargoyle." Babcock, Edwina Stanton.—B. 1920: 12-35.

"Gaston." Saroyan, William.—P. 1963: 60-66.

"Gay." Oates, Joyce Carol.—B. 1977: 235-255.

"The Gay Old Dog." Ferber, Edna.—B. 1917: 208-233.

"Gent." DeMarinis, Rick.—B. 1984: 56-71.

"Gentleman In Blue." Stallings, Laurence.—B. 1932: 231-242.

"The German Refugee." Malamud, Bernard.—B. 1964: 203-215.

"Gertrude and Sidney." Jarrell, Randall.—B. 1954: 185-205.

"Gertrude Donovan." Asch, Nathan.—B. 1925: 39-52.

"The Gesture." Groshong, James W.—B. 1965: 99-112.

"Gesturing." Updike, John.—B. 1980: 409-419.

"Get Ready the Wreaths." Hurst, Fannie.—B. 1917: 326-360.

"The Get-Away." Lewis, O. F.—P. 1921: 234-242.

"Getaway." Coates, Robert M.—B. 1959: 59-75.

"Getting Into Death." Disch, Thomas M.—P. 1975: 223-238.

"Getting On In the World." Callaghan, Morley.—B. 1940: 30-36.

"Getting Serious." Weaver, Gordon.—P. 1979: 15-34.

"Getting To Williamstown." Hood, Hugh.—B. 1966: 113-124.

"Ghitza." Bercovici, Konrad.—B. 1920: 36-48.

"The Ghost Soldiers." O'Brien, Tim.—P. 1982: 206-228.

"Ghosts Like Them." Taggart, Shirley Ann.—P. 1980: 81-95.

"The Giant's Thunder." Tracy, Virginia.—B. 1926: 282-310.

"Gideon." Foster, Joseph O'Kane.—P. 1939: 163-177.

"Gideon's Revenge." Wylie, Elinor.—B. 1925: 311-321.

"The Gift." Alexander, Sandra.—B. 1925: 1-20.

"The Gift Bearer." O'Connor, Philip F.—B. 1971: 217-236.

"A Gift From the City." Updike, John.—B. 1959: 340-358.

"The Gift Horse's Mouth." Smith, R. E.—B. 1982: 193-209.

"Gift Of Grass." Adams, Alice.—P. 1971: 58-66.

"A Gift Of Light." Enright, Elizabeth.—P. 1960: 119-132.

"The Gift Of the Prodigal." Taylor, Peter.—P. 1982: 166-185.

"The Girl." LeSueur, Meridel.—B. 1938: 160-170.

"The Girl Across the Room." Adams, Alice.—P. 1979: 319-327.

"A Girl For Walter." Jacobs, Theodore.—B. 1961: 183-190.

"The Girl From the River Barge." Schoenstedt, Walter.—B. 1939: 225-232.

"A Girl I Knew." Salinger, J. D.—B. 1949: 248-260.
"The Girl Who Sang With the Beatles." Hemenway, Robert [pseud. "Patch, Stephen"].—P. 1970: 1-16.
"The Girl Who Was No Kin To the Marshalls." Freeman, Anne Hobson.—B. 1982: 251-279.
"The Girl With the Flaxen Hair." Komroff, Manuel.—B. 1937: 160-169.
"The Gittel." Sandor, Marjorie.—B. 1985: 220-234.
"Give My Love To Maggie." Van Ness, Lillian.—P. 1950: 287-305.
"Give This Little Girl a Hand." Hurst, Fannie.—B. 1928: 180-210.
"The Gladiator." McKeon, J. M.—P. 1937: 151-161.
"A Glance In the Mirror." Swados, Harvey.—B. 1960: 318-333.
"The Glass Eye Of Throgmorton." Corley, Donald.—B. 1926: 36-55.
"The Glass House." Livesay, Dorothy.—B. 1951: 218-227.
"Glass Houses." Colby, Nathalie.—P. 1936: 113-125.
"A Glass Of Blessings." Swarthout, Glendon.—P. 1960: 257-265.
"The Glass Pigeon." Johnson, Josephine.—P. 1943: 203-212.
"The Glass Wall." Lincoln, Victoria.—B. 1950: 274-300.
"Glimpse Into Another Country." Morris, Wright.—B. 1984: 161-176; P. 1985: 89-102.
"Glory, Glory, Hallelujah!" Foley, Martha.—B. 1937: 67-77.
"God On Friday Night." Shaw, Irwin.—P. 1939: 227-234.
"Gods Of Darkness." Hilton, Charles.—P. 1937: 101-108.
"God's Agents Have Beards." Winters, Emmanuel.—B. 1944: 443-451.
"God's Wrath." Malamud, Bernard.—B. 1973: 221-227.
"Goin' To Town." Stegner, Wallace.—B. 1941: 302-314.
"Going After Cacciato." O'Brien, Tim.—B. 1977: 256-274.
"Going Home." Kenary, James S.—B. 1973: 166-179.
"Going To Market." Halper, Albert.—B. 1953: 161-169.
"Going To Naples." Welty, Eudora.—B. 1955: 349-385.
"Gold." Beal, M. F.—B. 1972: 1-15.
"Gold Coast." McPherson, James Alan.—B. 1969: 165-182.
"Gold Is Not Always." Faulkner, William.—B. 1941: 83-96.
"The Golden Honeymoon." Lardner, Ring W.—B. 1922: 242-259.
"The Golden Stallion." Hardwick, Elizabeth.—B. 1947: 141-170.
"Gold-Mounted Guns." Buckley, F. R.—P. 1922: 36-43.
"The Gonzaga Manuscripts." Bellow, Saul.—P. 1956: 76-102.
"A Good and Gallant Woman." Yates, Richard.—P. 1967: 203-218.
"The Good Days and the Bad." Eustis, Helen.—B. 1944: 81-100.
"A Good Loser." Cullinan, Elizabeth.—B. 1978: 46-64.
"Good Morning, Major." Marquand, J. P.—B. 1927: 213-239.
"Good Rockin' Tonight." Hauptman, William.—B. 1982: 54-74.
"Good Wednesday." Brush, Katharine.—P. 1931: 101-117.
"The Goodbye Present." Rose, Daniel Asa.—P. 1980: 189-207.
"Goodbye To Cap'm John." Field, S. S.—B. 1937: 55-66.
"Goose Pond." Williams, Thomas.—P. 1959: 150-164.
"Gossip." Conroy, Frank.—B. 1986: 66-82.
"'Government Goat.'" Glaspell, Susan.—B. 1919: 147-166.
"The Grave." Porter, Katherine Anne.—B. 1936: 245-250.
"Graveyard Day." Mason, Bobbie Ann.—B. 1983: 178-190.

Index Of Titles

"The Gray." Schneider, Philip H.—B. 1974: 252-265.
"Greased Samba." Deck, John.—B. 1968: 29-42.
"The Great Auk." Cobb, Irvin S.—B. 1916: 85-114.
"The Great Fire of 1945." Shedd, Margaret.—P. 1947: 218-226.
"The Great Hunter Of the Woods." Stevens, James.—B. 1931: 258-266.
"A Great Reckoning In a Little Room." Bush, Geoffrey.—B. 1954: 1-13.
"The Greatest Idea In the World." Raphaelson, Samson.—B. 1947: 336-349.
"The Greatest Slump Of All Time." Carkeet, David.—P. 1982: 271-288.
"The Green Fly." Graves, John.—P. 1955: 215-225.
"Green Gardens." Hart, Frances Noyes.—B. 1921: 240-252.
"Green Grass, Blue Sky, White House." Morris, Wright.—B. 1970: 194-206.
"The Green Village." Peattie, Margaret Rhodes.—B. 1942: 231-244.
"Greenleaf." O'Connor, Flannery.—B. 1957: 241-263; P. 1957: 15-36.
"Greyhound People." Adams, Alice.—P. 1982: 289-300.
"Grimaldi." Meriwether, Susan.—B. 1926: 210-219.
"Grit." Tupper, Tristram.—P. 1921: 293-312.
"Group Sex." Arensberg, Ann.—P. 1980: 271-294.
"Growing Up In No Time." Damon, Philip.—B. 1977: 102-110.
"Grubbing For Roots." Minot, Stephen.—B. 1976: 156-169.
"Grudges." Hughes, Rupert.—B. 1924: 137-154.
"Gryphon." Baxter, Charles.—B. 1986: 10-27.
"Guard Of Honor." Benefield, Barry.—B. 1925: 53-63.
"The Guardeen Angel." Brennan, Frederick Hazlitt.—B. 1928: 1-12.
"The Guest." Morton, Frederic.—B. 1965: 241-249.
"The Guide." Lytle, Andrew.—P. 1946: 195-217.
"Guileford." Stribling, T. S.—P. 1934: 201-215.
"A Guilty Woman." Wescott, Glenway.—B. 1929: 239-255.
"The Gun On the Table." Watson, John.—P. 1948: 263-273.
"Gunners' Passage." Shaw, Irwin.—B. 1945: 238-256; P. 1945: 15-32.
"The Guns In the Closet." Yglesias, Jose.—B. 1972: 373-389.
"The Guy In Ward 4." Rosten, Leo.—B. 1959: 228-243.

"Habakkuk." Gerould, Katharine Fullerton.—B. 1920: 90-115.
"The Habits Of the Animals: The Progress Of the Seasons." Higgins, George V.—B. 1973: 142-149.
"Hail Brother and Farewell.'" Karchmer, Sylvan.—B. 1950: 250-258.
"Hair." Stuart, Jesse.—B. 1937: 325-339.
"Haircut." Lardner, Ring.—B. 1925: 174-185.
"The Half Pint Flask." Heyward, DuBose.—B. 1927: 142-157.
"Half-Past Ten." Tildesley, Alice L.—B. 1916: 349-356.
"Hamlet's Dagger." Komroff, Manuel.—B. 1934: 210-217.
"The Hand Of Emmagene." Taylor, Peter.—B. 1976: 314-332.
"The Hand That Fed Me." Rosenfeld, Isaac.—B. 1945: 188-204.
"Hand Upon the Waters." Faulkner, William.—B. 1940: 65-81; P. 1940: 97-116.
"The Hands Of the Enemy." Dobie, Charles Caldwell.—B. 1925: 85-104.

"Handy." Caldwell, Erskine.—B. 1941: 28-34.

"Hanging Fire." Pearlman, Edith.—P. 1978: 253-264.

"Hanging Hair." Leahy, Jack Thomas.—B. 1962: 221-234.

"Hansel." Diefenthaler, Andra.—B. 1932: 101-107.

"The Happiest Man On Earth." Maltz, Albert.—B. 1939: 189-201; P. 1938: 3-15.

"Happiness." Lavin, Mary.—B. 1969: 81-98.

"Happiness Up the River." Hartwick, Harry.—B. 1930: 91-103.

"Happy August the 10th." Williams, Tennessee.—B. 1973: 276-288.

"The Harbor Master." Hallet, Richard Matthews.—B. 1921: 207-239.

"Hard To Be Good." Barich, Bill.—B. 1983: 1-24.

"The Hardys." Humphrey, William.—P. 1950: 138-151.

"Harmony Of the World." Baxter, Charles.—B. 1982: 210-232.

"Harvest." Deasy, Mary.—B. 1945: 38-48.

"The Hat Of Eight Reflections." Mahoney, James.—P. 1923: 134-158.

"Haunted Ground." LaFarge, Oliver.—P. 1931: 71-75.

"The Haunted Palace." Roberts, Elizabeth Madox.—B. 1938: 237-253.

"Have You Seen Sukie?" Warren, Robert Penn.—B. 1964: 325-336.

"Havoc Is a Circle." Bird, Virginia.—P. 1936: 55-63.

"He Laughed At the Gods." Oppenheim, James.—B. 1922: 260-269.

"He Man." Douglas, Marjory Stoneman.—P. 1927: 149-174.

"The Head Of a Sad Angel." Chester, Alfred.—P. 1956: 133-164.

"The Headless Hawk." Capote, Truman.—B. 1947: 31-55.

"Heads Of Houses." Taylor, Peter.—P. 1961: 298-325.

"Health." Williams, Joy.—B. 1986: 279-288.

"Health Card." Yerby, Frank G.—P. 1944: 42-51.

"The Healthiest Girl In Town." Stafford, Jean.—B. 1952: 271-288.

"The Heart Being Perished." Frost, Frances M.—P. 1933: 165-171.

"A Heart Of Furious Fancies." McClintic, Winona.—B. 1957: 234-240.

"Heart Of Gold." Lavin, Mary.—B. 1965: 199-222.

"The Heart Of Little Shikara." Marshall, Edison.—P. 1921: 1-28.

"Heart Of Marzipan." Morris, Edita.—B. 1944: 280-284.

"The Heart Of This Or That Man." Gropman, Donald.—B. 1968: 137-148.

"Heart Of Youth." Muilenburg, Walter J.—B. 1915: 172-183.

"Heartbeat." Svendsen, Linda.—P. 1983: 270-284.

"Heel, Toe, and a 1, 2, 3, 4." Milburn, George.—B. 1932: 177-186.

"The Heifer." Morgan, Patrick.—B. 1949: 212-218.

"Helen, I Love You!" Farrell, James T.—B. 1933: 108-114.

"Hello, Tib." Aiken, Conrad.—P. 1941: 61-67.

"The Helpless Ones." Booth, Frederick.—B. 1922: 49-69.

"The Hemlock Tree." Sheean, Vincent.—B. 1934: 292-305.

"Her Breath Upon the Windowpane." Goyen, William.—B. 1951: 139-143.

"Her Own Sweet Simplicity." Foley, Martha.—B. 1936: 142-151.

"Here We Are." Parker, Dorothy.—B. 1931: 243-252.

"Herman's Day." Swados, Harvey.—B. 1955: 304-330.

"Hero." Roberts, Phyllis.—B. 1960: 262-277.

"A Hero In the Highway." Schevill, James.—P. 1978: 245-252.

"The Heroic Journey." Lee, Lawrence.—B. 1967: 151-160.
"The Heroine." Highsmith, Patricia.—P. 1946: 133-148.
"Herself." Burt, Katherine Newlin.—P. 1930: 71-88.
"Herself." Pooler, James.—B. 1940: 296-310.
"The Hidden Room." Williams, Lawrence.—B. 1947: 490-504.
"The High Cost Of Conscience." Ravenel, Beatrice.—P. 1919: 228-252.
"High Diver." Ashworth, John.—P. 1949: 43-57.
"The Hill People." Marshall, Elizabeth.—B. 1953: 214-226.
"Him and Her." Brush, Katharine.—P. 1929: 55-62.
"The Hired Man." Strong, Joan.—B. 1950: 399-406.
"His Day Out." Kalechofsky, Roberta.—B. 1972: 180-192.
"His Friend the Pig." McCarthy, Wilson.—B. 1929: 169-180.
"His Job." Mason, Grace Sartwell.—B. 1920: 169-186.
"His Sacred Family." Hull, Helen R.—P. 1922: 139-158.
"His Smile." Glaspel, Susan.—B. 1921: 194-206.
"His Son, In His Arms, In Light, Aloft." Brodkey, Harold.—P. 1976: 15-32.
"The Hitch-Hikers." Welty, Eudora.—B. 1940: 459-475.
"The Hobo." Downey, Harris.—B. 1956: 105-122.
"Hobogenesis." Martin, Charles.—P. 1937: 139-147.
"Hog's Heart." Weaver, Gordon.—B. 1980: 439-454.
"Holding On." Norris, Gloria.—P. 1985: 206-221.
"The Holiday." Deasy, Mary.—P. 1947: 111-123.
"Holiday." Porter, Katherine Anne.—P. 1962: 19-47.
"The Hollow Heart." Fisher, M. F. K.—B. 1948: 93-98.
"Home." Robison, James.—B. 1980: 262-271.
"Home and Native Land." Virgo, Seán.—B. 1979: 39-43.
"Home From Camp." Van Scoyk, Bob.—B. 1958: 317-320.
"Home Girl." Ferber, Edna.—B. 1923: 216-239.
"Home Is a Place." Breuer, Bessie.—P. 1944: 19-28.
"Home Is the Hero." Malamud, Bernard.—B. 1979: 284-311.
"Home Is the Sailor." Adams, Bill.—P. 1928: 55-72.
"Home Is Where You Hang Your Childhood." Zugsmith, Leane.—B. 1934: 336-346.
"The Home Place." Thomas, Dorothy.—P. 1935: 23-53.
"Home To Mother's." Harris, Eleanor E.—B. 1928: 150-165.
"The Home Town." Waldman, Milton.—B. 1925: 253-269.
"Home-Brew." Mason, Grace Sartwell.—P. 1923: 159-181.
"Homecoming." Bradbury, Ray.—P. 1947: 76-88.
"Homecoming." Heth, Edward Harris.—B. 1937: 127-141.
"Homecoming." Mayer, Tom.—P. 1965: 71-79.
"Homecoming." Patterson, Elizabeth Gregg.—P. 1951: 227-245.
"Homecoming." Tracy, Tom.—P. 1940: 271-286.
"Homecoming." Treichler, Jessie.—B. 1943: 370-390.
"Home-Coming." DeJong, David Cornel.—B. 1935: 135-149.
"The Homesick Ladies." Howard, Sidney.—P. 1929: 29-51.
"Homework." Cameron, Peter.—P. 1985: 222-228.
"The Honest Wine Merchant." Caperton, Helena Lefroy.—B. 1932: 76-79.

"The Honey House." King, Mary.—B. 1940: 123-144.

"The Honey Pot." Dobie, Charles Caldwell.—B. 1933: 77-90.

"Honeymoon." Vivante, Arturo.—B. 1974: 312-317.

"Honor Of the County." Edmonds, Walter D.—P. 1940: 113-140.

"Hook." Clark, Walter Van Tilburg.—P. 1941: 113-136.

"The Hope Chest." Stafford, Jean.—B. 1947: 240-245.

"Hope Of Zion." Flowers, Sandra Hollin.—P. 1981: 117-126.

"Hopeless Acts Performed Properly, With Grace." Dunn, Robert.—P. 1980: 225-237.

"Horace Chooney, M. D." West, Jessamyn.—P. 1947: 276-285.

"Horizon." Besslie, Alvah C.—B. 1932: 16-24.

"Horse and Horse." Dobie, Charles Caldwell.—P. 1924: 93-112.

"The Horse Like September." Griffith, Paul.—B. 1947: 114-124.

"The Horse Of Hurricane Reef." Jackson, Charles Tenney.—P. 1922: 159-176.

"Horse Thief." Caldwell, Erskine.—B. 1934: 40-45.

"Hot Copy." Blackman, M. C.—P. 1928: 98-114.

"The Hot Dog." Cobb, Jane.—P. 1947: 98-110.

"Hot Ice." Dybek, Stuart.—P. 1985: 20-45.

"Houdini." Weidman, Jerome.—B. 1941: 332-340.

"'Hound Of Heaven.'" Addington, Sarah.—B. 1929: 1-19.

"The Hounds Of Summer." McCarthy, Mary.—P. 1965: 249-285.

"The Hound-Tuner Of Callaway." Weeks, Raymond.—B. 1927: 289-307.

"The Hour Of Knowing." Smith, Louise Reinhardt.—P. 1945: 242-265.

"The House Of Flowers." Capote, Truman.—P. 1951: 32-45.

"House Of Many Rooms." White, Robin.—B. 1958: 321-336.

"House Of the Blues." Wiser, William.—B. 1967: 315-331.

"The House On the Esplanade." Hébert, Anne.—B. 1954: 163-173.

"How Beautiful With Shoes." Steele, Wilbur Daniel.—B. 1933: 280-300.

"How Does It Feel To Be Free?" Komroff, Manuel.—B. 1925: 167-173.

"How Edith McGillcuddy Met R. L. Stevenson." Steinbeck, John.—B. 1942: 291-302; P. 1942: 259-272.

"How I Contemplated the World From the Detroit House Of Correction and Began My Life Over Again." Oates, Joyce Carol.—B. 1970: 207-222; P. 1970: 275-291.

"How Jerem Came Home." Kaser, Paul.—B. 1975: 137-143.

"How Levon Dai Was Surrendered To the Edemuses." Housepian, Marjorie Anaïs.—B. 1956: 184-194.

"How the Devil Came Down Division Street." Algren, Nelson.—B. 1945: 1-7.

"How the Mountains Are." Ford, Jesse Hill.—P. 1961: 181-190.

"How To Win." Brown, Rosellen.—B. 1975: 12-25.

"How Willie Proudfit Came Home." Warren, Robert Penn.—B. 1939: 292-318.

"How You Play the Game." Tyner, Paul.—P. 1968: 267-283.

"The Howard Parker Montcrief Hoax." McNamara, Eugene.—B. 1975: 178-196.

"How's Your Vacuum Cleaner Working?" McCully, Emily Arnold.—P. 1977: 211-230.

"Huey, the Engineer." Stuart, Jesse.—B. 1938: 288-305.

"The Human Fly." Gustafson, Ralph.—B. 1948: 139-147.

"The Hummingbird That Lived Through Winter." Saroyan, William.—B. 1942: 245-249.

"'Humoresque.'" Hurst, Fanny.—P. 1919: 148-179.

"The Hunch." Carr, A. H. Z.—B. 1936: 57-69.

"A Hundred Paths." Summers, Hollis.—P. 1977: 130-143.

"The Hundredth Centennial." Hyman, Mac.—B. 1955: 123-146.

"Hunger." Worthington, Marjorie.—B. 1942: 410-422; P. 1942: 333-346.

"The Hunt." Kuehn, Susan.—P. 1950: 167-180.

"The Hunter." MacDonald, Lachlan.—B. 1960: 165-190.

"The Hunters." Downey, Harris.—B. 1951: 100-114; P. 1951: 1-16.

"Hunter's Home." Grau, Shirley Ann.—B. 1958: 119-133.

"I Came From Yonder Mountain." Connell, Evan S., Jr.—P. 1951: 78-86.

"'I Don't Believe This.'" Gerber, Merrill Joan.—P. 1986: 95-104.

"I Don't Need You Any More." Miller, Arthur.—B. 1960: 204-244; P. 1961: 246-287.

"I Forgot Where I Was." Enright, Elizabeth.—P. 1946: 115-122.

"I Get By." Robison, Mary.—P. 1987: 308-315.

"I Got a Friend." Van Doren, Mark.—B. 1955: 331-337.

"I Have Letters For Marjorie." McKenna, Edward L.—B. 1929: 181-192.

"I Hear You, Mr. and Mrs. Brown." Herbst, Josephine.—B. 1931: 179-188.

"I Look Out For Ed Wolfe." Elkin, Stanley. —B. 1963: 140-165.

"I Love You Batty Sisters." Walter, Eugene.—P. 1957: 262-271.

"I See You Never." Bradbury, Ray.—B. 1948: 32-35.

"I Stand Here Ironing." Olsen, Tillie.—B. 1957: 264-271.

"I Take Care Of Things." Cady, Jack.—B. 1971: 67-73.

"I Thought Of Chatterton, the Marvelous Boy." Gewertz, Kenneth.—P. 1982: 114-135.

"I Want You, I Need You, I Love You." Hecht, Julie.—P. 1979: 57-73.

"Icarus Again." Harris, Marilyn.—P. 1968: 284-295.

"Ice." Tallent, Elizabeth.—B. 1981: 303-311.

"Ice Water, Pl——." Hurst, Fannie.—B. 1916: 181-211.

"I'd Give It All Up For Tahiti." Kunasz, Paul.—P. 1941: 213-219.

"The Idea Of Switzerland." Abish, Walter.—B. 1981: 1-28.

"The Idols Of Afternoon." Bumpus, Jerry.—P. 1976: 201-210.

"I-80 Nebraska, M. 490-M. 205." Sayles, John.—P. 1976: 33-51.

"If a Woodchuck Could Chuck Wood." Wetherell, W. D.—P. 1983: 128-140.

"If Lost Return To the Swiss Arms." Rooke, Leon.—P. 1965: 109-123.

"If They Knew Yvonne." Dubus, Andre.—B. 1970: 84-107.

"Ignition." Clark, Valma.—B. 1923: 125-143.

"Ig's Amok." Morris, Gouverneur.—P. 1922: 196-209.

"Ike and Us Moons." Shumway, Naomi.—B. 1933: 266-279.
"I'll Call You." Inman, Robert.—P. 1971: 168-196.
"I'll Take You To Tennessee." Connell, Evan S., Jr.—P. 1949: 100-109.
"The Ill Wind." Robinson, Robert.—B. 1925: 186-194.
"The Illumination." West, Jessamyn.—B. 1944: 430-442.
"Ill-Winds From the Wide World." Neagoe, Peter.—B. 1941: 255-268.
"I'm a Fool." Anderson, Sherwood.—B. 1922: 13-24.
"I'm Going To Asia." Cheever, John.—P. 1941: 105-110.
"I'm Really Fine." Schulberg, Stuart.—B. 1952: 264-270.
"The Imaginary Jew." Berryman, John.—P. 1946: 65-73.
"Imagination." Gerould, Gordon Hall.—B. 1918: 92-108.
"The Immortal Woman." Tate, Allen.—B. 1934: 312-326.
"Immortality." Henderson, Robert.—P. 1960: 191-202.
"The Impossible He." Robinson, Rosanne Smith.—B. 1957: 292-304.
"Impulse." Aiken, Conrad.—P. 1933: 95-109.
"In a Cold Hotel." Maddow, Ben.—P. 1963: 67-94.
"In a Foreign City." Coates, Robert M.—B. 1956: 64-75; P. 1956: 165-177.
"In a Military Manner." Elkin, Samuel.—B. 1946: 165-183.
"In a Park." Sabsay, Nahum.—B. 1934: 285-291.
"In a Thicket." Wescott, Glenway.—B. 1924: 240-247.
"In a Tropical Minor Key." Holwerda, Frank.—B. 1959: 172-189.
"In an Early Winter." Angell, Roger.—B. 1956: 1-17.
"In Berlin." O'Reilly, Mary Boyle.—B. 1915: 196.
"In Black and White." Jones, Ann.—B. 1972: 138-152.
"In Case Of Survival." Gertler, T.—B. 1980: 176-195; P. 1980: 249-270.
"In Greenwich There Are Many Gravelled Walks." Calisher, Hortense.—B. 1951: 45-59.
"In Late Youth." Rush, Norman.—B. 1971: 275-290.
"In Maulmain Fever-Ward." Gilbert, George.—B. 1918: 109-124.
"In Miami, Last Winter." Kaplan, James.—B. 1978: 329-353.
"In Portofino." Sullivan, Alan.—B. 1927: 279-288.
"In Shock." Litwak, Leo E.—B. 1968: 201-214; P. 1969: 101-113.
"In Sickness As In Health." Gellhorn, Martha.—P. 1958: 15-45.
"In the Autumn Of the Year." Oates, Joyce Carol.—P. 1979: 150-172.
"In the Cage." Burlingame, Roger.—B. 1936: 1-15.
"In the Caldron." Kentfield, Calvin.—P. 1960: 203-220.
"In the Flow Of Time." Griffith, Beatrice.—B. 1949: 106-116.
"In the Forests Of Riga the Beasts Are Very Wild Indeed." Brown, Margery Finn.—P. 1972: 209-218.
"In the French Style." Shaw, Irwin.—B. 1954: 278-292.
"In the Garden Of the North American Martyrs." Wolff, Tobias.—P. 1981: 105-116.
"In the Heart Of the Heart Of the Country." Gass, William H.—B. 1968: 101-124.
"In the Land Of the Morning Calm, Déjà Vu." Siegel, Jules.—B. 1970: 288-307.
"In the Metropolis." Rosenblatt, Benjamin.—B. 1922: 270-272.
"In the Middle Of the Fields." Lavin, Mary.—B. 1962: 205-220.

"In the Miro District." Taylor, Peter.—B. 1978: 98-135.
"In the Open Code." Kline, Burton.—B. 1918: 149-153.
"In the Park." Joffe, Eugene.—B. 1933: 170-172.
"In the Red Room." Bowles, Paul.—B. 1984: 35-44.
"In the Region Of Ice." Oates, Joyce Carol.—P. 1967: 1-17.
"In the Time Of Demonstrations." Hall, James B.—P. 1951: 116-129.
"In the Twilight." Stegner, Wallace.—B. 1942: 279-290.
"In the White Night." Beattie, Ann.—P. 1985: 46-50.
"In the Words Of." Hayden, Julie.—B. 1973: 132-141.
"In the Zoo." Stafford, Jean.—P. 1955: 15-34.
"The Indian Feather." Mabry, Thomas.—P. 1954: 21-39.
"Indian On the Road." Clark, Gean.—B. 1939: 39-51.
"The Indomitable Blue." Wolfert, Ira.—B. 1954: 373-395; P. 1955: 291-311.
"Inexorable Progress." Hood, Mary.—B. 1984: 106-122.
"Infidelities." Trefethen, Florence.—P. 1982: 260-270.
"An Influx Of Poets." Stafford, Jean.—P. 1980: 423-477.
"The Inhabitants Of Venus." Shaw, Irwin.—P. 1964: 114-140.
"The Inheritance Of Emmy One Horse." Milton, John R.—B. 1969: 183-194.
"Inland, Western Sea." Asch, Nathan.—B. 1951: 10-23.
"The Inland Years." Cassill, R. V.—P. 1955: 85-102.
"Innocence." Lane, Rose Wilder.—B. 1922: 23-35.
"The Innocent Bystander." Shedd, Margaret.—P. 1946: 18-30.
"Innocents." Hutchins, M. P.—P. 1946: 149-176.
"An Instrument Of the Gods." Colcord, Lincoln.—B. 1921: 82-108.
"Instruments of Seduction." Rush, Norman.—B. 1985: 192-205.
"The Insufficient Rope." Molinaro, Ursule.—B. 1963: 211-219.
"The Interior Castle." Stafford, Jean.—B. 1947: 416-432.
"Interior Space." Irving, John.—P. 1981: 20-51.
"The Interpretation Of Dreams By Sigmund Freud: A Story." Stern, Daniel.—P. 1987: 300-307.
"The Interval." O'Sullivan, Vincent.—B. 1917: 383-390.
"An Interval Like This." Davis, Robert Gorham.—P. 1942: 117-124.
"Intimacy." Maloney, Ralph.—B. 1972: 226-234.
"The Intrigue Of Mr. S. Yamamoto." Linn, R. H.—B. 1937: 195-199.
"Into the Wind." Henderson, Robert.—B. 1980: 221-230.
"The Invaders." Macauley, Robie.—P. 1951: 182-191.
"The Investigator." Finney, Ernest J.—B. 1967; 115-129.
"Invisible Life." Nelson, Kent.—B. 1986: 219-240.
"The Invitations." Shefner, Evelyn.—P. 1969: 131-146.
"The Iowan's Curse." Finney, Charles G.—B. 1959: 76-90.
"The Iron City." Thompson, Lovell.—B. 1937: 354-379.
"Is Anyone Left This Time Of Year?" Busch, Frederick.—P. 1974: 77-86.
"Is He Dead?" Elliott, George P.—B. 1956: 134-166.
"Isaac and the Undertaker's Daughter." Stern, Steve.—P. 1981: 258-272.
"An Island For My Friends." Shapiro, Madelon.—B. 1949: 285-294.

"The Island Of Ven." Berriault, Gina.—P. 1987: 124-131.
"Isn't Today the Day?" Saroyan, William.—B. 1974: 244-251.
"It Had To Be Done." Callaghan, Morley.—B. 1939: 25-31.
"It Never Happened." Hahn, Emily.—B. 1945: 99-108.
"It's a Nice Day—Sunday." Thompson, R. E.—P. 1951: 312-322.
"It's Cold Out There." Buchan, Perdita.—P. 1970: 51-70.
"The Ivory Tower." Burnett, W. R.—B. 1946: 87-109.

"Jack Frost." Jacobsen, Josephine.—P. 1978: 148-158.
"The Janeites." Lott, James.—P. 1987: 103-114.
"Janus." Beattie, Ann.—B. 1986: 28-33.
"Jawaharlal and the Three Cadavers." Berry, John.—B. 1959: 1-14.
"Jean-Pierre." Spencer, Elizabeth.—P. 1983: 108-127.
"Jerry." Angoff, Charles.—B. 1946: 1-12.
"Jerry." Hunter, Laura.—B. 1949: 149-156.
"The Jersey Heifer." Love, Peggy Harding.—P. 1951: 170-181.
"Jesus Knew." O'Donnell, E. P.—P. 1935: 171-186.
"The Jew." Seaver, Edwin.—B. 1928: 258-261.
"The Jewbird." Malamud, Bernard.—B. 1964: 60-69.
"The Jewels Of the Cabots." Cheever, John.—B. 1973: 23-37; P. 1973: 184-200.
"The Jinx Of the 'Shandon Belle.'" Horn, R. DeS.—P. 1922: 124-138.
"Jishin." Christopher, Robert.—B. 1950: 102-108.
"Job's Tears." Still, James.—P. 1937: 213-221.
"The Jockey." McCullers, Carson.—P. 1942: 231-237.
"Joe College." Donohue, H. E. F.—P. 1970: 93-112.
"Joe, the Vanishing American." Swados, Harvey.—B. 1958: 281-298.
"John Henry's Home." McCluskey, John.—B. 1976: 145-155.
"John Of God, the Water Carrier." Chambers, María Cristina.—B. 1928: 77-93.
"John the Baptist." Frank, Waldo.—B. 1922: 132-150.
"John the Six." Johnson, Josephine W.—P. 1935: 57-59.
"Johnny Panic and the Bible Of Dreams." Plath, Sylvia.—B. 1969: 233-248.
"Johnny Pye and the Fool-Killer." Benét, Stephen Vincent.—P. 1938: 109-134.
"The Johnstown Polka." Stark, Sharon Sheehe.—B. 1985: 256-272.
"Joshua." Grau, Shirley Ann.—P. 1955: 190-214.
"The Journal Of an Old Gent." Cheever, John.—P. 1957: 159-181.
"The Joybell." Thomas, Dorothy.—B. 1933: 301-313.
"The Judge." Hughes, Mary Gray.—B. 1972: 123-137.
"The Judgment Of Vulcan." Hartman, Lee Foster.—B. 1920: 116-147: P. 1920: 94-122.
"Jujitsu." Taylor, Eleanor Ross.—P. 1971: 261-266.
"Jukes." Adams, Bill.—P. 1927: 34-52.
"The Jungle Of Injustice." Johnson, Nora.—P. 1982: 99-113.
"The Jungle Of Lord Lion." Jacobsen, Josephine.—P. 1971: 197-207.
"A Jury Of Her Peers." Glaspell, Susan.—B. 1917: 256-282.

"Just Before the War With the Eskimos." Salinger, J. D.—P. 1949: 249-261.
"Justice Has No Number." Segre, Alfredo.—B. 1949: 261-284.

"K. 590." Baker, Nicholson.—B. 1982: 116-123.
"Keeley Street Blues." Baker, Dorothy.—P. 1939: 65-76.
"The Key." Singer, Isaac Bashevis.—B. 1970: 308-317.
"The Keyhole Eye." Carter, John Stewart.—B. 1963: 57-82.
"Kid MacArthur." Vaughn, Stephanie.—P. 1986: 226-244.
"The Kid Who Fractioned." Sturm, Carol.—B. 1967: 291-302.
"The Kill." Havill, Edward.—P. 1940: 45-56.
"The Killers." Hemingway, Ernest.—B. 1927: 40-49; P. 1927: 15-24.
"The Kimono." Morris, Ira V.—B. 1932: 187-197.
"A Kind Of a Sunset." Larsen, Erling.—B. 1936: 203-209.
"A Kind Of Savage." Hall, James Baker.—P. 1968: 211-229.
"A Kind Of Scandal."—P. 1954: 308-316.
"Kindred." Thayer, Harriet Maxon.—B. 1921: 362-385.
"Kindred Spirits." Walker, Alice.—P. 1986: 1-11.
"King Lear In Evansville." Zugsmith, Leane.—P. 1934: 283-293.
"The King Of the Cats." Benét, Stephen Vincent.—P. 1929: 73-89.
"The Kingdom Of Gordon." Goodman, J. Carol.—B. 1951: 121-127.
"The King's Daughter." Schmitt, Gladys.—B. 1946: 337-354.
"The Kiss Of the Accolade." Bennett, James W.—P. 1922: 91-112.
"The Kitchen Gods." Alsop, G. F.—B. 1919: 3-23; P. 1919: 253-273.
"Kittens Have Fathers." Coombes, Evan.—P. 1932: 137-146.
"The Klausners." Tushnet, Leonard.—B. 1971: 316-328.
"Knife-Like, Flower-Like, Like Nothing At All In the World." Saroyan, William.—B. 1943: 271-278; P. 1943: 235-242.
"The Knight's Move." Gerould, Katharine Fullerton.—B. 1917: 234-255.
"A Knocking At the Gate." St. Joseph, Ellis.—P. 1939: 207-224.
"The Knot Hole." Canfield, Dorothy.—B. 1944: 41-61; P. 1943: 19-39.
"The Kugelmass Episode." Allen, Woody.—P. 1978: 15-25.
"Kullan." Morris, Edita.—B. 1940: 214-228.

"La Bataille Des Fleurs." Ostroff, Anthony.—B. 1958: 213-224.
"La Dernière Mobilisation." Dwiggins, W. A.—B. 1915: 55-56.
"La Victoire." Wheeler, Kate.—P. 1982: 136-151.
"Ladies and Gentlemen, the Original Music Of the Hebrew Alphabet." Leviant, Curt.—P. 1978: 205-237.
"The Lady." Justice, Donald.—P. 1950: 152-166.
"Lady Of Spain." Taylor, Robert, Jr.—P. 1987: 188-207.
"Lady Wipers—Of Ypres." Hughes, Llewellyn.—B. 1928: 166-179.
"Ladybug, Fly Away Home." Heden, Mary.—P. 1977: 179-185.
"Lamb Says." Coggeshall, Rosanne.—B. 1982: 299-310.
"Lambing Out." Clearman, Mary.—P. 1972: 65-82.
"Lambs Of God." Engberg, Susan.—P. 1969: 261-290.
"A Lamp." Schorer, Mark.—P. 1978: 26-40.

"The Land Of Plenty." Cantwell, Robert.—B. 1933: 68-76.
"Larchmoor Is Not the World." Cassill, R. V.—B. 1951: 73-88.
"The Last Abandonment." Matthews, Jack.—P. 1981: 138-153.
"Last Courtesies." Leffland, Ella.—P. 1977: 17-41.
"The Last Day." Karmel-Wolfe, Henia.—B. 1962: 200-204.
"The Last Dive." Drake, Carlos.—B. 1924: 70-73.
"The Last Equation." Burlingame, Roger.—B. 1937: 15-22.
"The Last Meeting." March, William.—B. 1938: 186-197; P. 1937: 123-135.
"The Last Mohican." Malamud, Bernard.—B. 1959: 190-211.
"The Last Of the Grizzly Bears." West, Ray B., Jr.—B. 1951: 312-337.
"The Last Rite." Yu-Hwa, Lee.—B. 1965: 371-384.
"The Last Room Of All." Whitman, Stephen French.—P. 1920: 302-322.
"The Last Running." Graves, John.—B. 1960: 112-125.
"Last Tag." Marsh, Willard.—P. 1957: 68-82.
"The Last Voyage." Filer, Tom.—P. 1959: 257-276.
"The Latter End." Loveridge, George.—B. 1954: 219-231.
"The Laugh." Cohen, Bella.—B. 1925: 81-84.
"Laughter." Dobie, Charles Caldwell.—B. 1917: 128-146.
"The Law Beaters." Connell, Richard.—P. 1928: 169-179.
"Lawns." Simpson, Mona.—B. 1986: 258-278.
"Lay Me Low!" Paul, Louis.—P. 1935: 189-202.
"Layaways." Dixon, Stephen.—P. 1982: 152-165.
"Lead Her Like a Pigeon." West, Jessamyn.—P. 1945: 266-274.
"Leaf Unfolding." Beems, Griffith.—P. 1931: 79-98.
"The Leather Man." Doctorow, E. L.—B. 1985: 58-66.
"Leaving the Church." Helprin, Mark.—P. 1976: 171-185.
"The Ledge." Hall, Lawrence Sargent.—B. 1960: 126-142; P. 1960: 21-38.
"Legend Of Two Swimmers." Macauley, Robey.—B. 1958: 150-167.
"Lemon Tree." Johnson, Curt.—B. 1980: 231-249.
"Lena." Gallant, Mavis.—B. 1984: 95-105.
"Leora's Father." Hamill, Katharine.—P. 1935: 87-100.
"The Lesser Gift." Hess, Leonard L.—B. 1924: 119-136.
"Let Nothing You Dismay." McGinnis, Allen.—B. 1937: 207-218.
"Let's Not Talk About It Now." Coates, Robert M.—P. 1940: 87-94.
"Letter From Sakaye." Mitchell, Beverly.—B. 1974: 179-193.
"A Letter To Ismael In the Grave." Brown, Rosellen.—P. 1972: 186-191.
"A Letter To Mr. Priest." Cousins, Margaret.—B. 1948: 78-92.
"The Letters." Swados, Harvey.—B. 1952: 305-330.
"Leviathan." St. Joseph, Ellis.—B. 1939: 202-220.
"Li Chang's Million." Felsen, Henry Gregor.—B. 1949: 94-99.
"The Lie." Banks, Russell.—B. 1975: 1-7.
"Lieutenant Pearson." Thielen, Benedict.—B. 1937: 340-353.
"Life." Hecht, Ben.—B. 1915: 80-83.
"The Life and Times Of Major Fiction." Baumbach, Jonathan.—P.

1984: 186-198.
"A Life In the Day Of a Writer." Slesinger, Tess.—B. 1936: 270-281.
"The Life Of Five Points." Bryner, Edna Clare.—B. 1920: 49-65.
"The Life Of the Mind." Kees, Weldon.—B. 1941: 161-173.
"The Life Of the Party." Bradley, Mary Hastings.—P. 1938: 137-150.
"The Life Of the Sleeping Beauty." Cassill, R. V.—B. 1952: 62-80.
"The Life You Save May Be Your Own." O'Connor, Flannery.—P. 1954: 194-204.
"The Light Of Morning." Fineman, Morton.—B. 1945: 64-70.
"The Light Of the Sea." Arkin, Frieda.—B. 1962: 1-15.
"Light Without Heat." Mullen, Robert.—B. 1929: 193-205.
"Lightning." Steele, Wilbur Daniel.—P. 1928: 225-239.
"'Lijah." Smith, Edgar Valentine.—P. 1924: 172-189.
"Like a Field Mouse Over the Heart." Eastman, Elizabeth.—B. 1944: 62-80; P. 1944: 63-82.
"Like a Winding Sheet." Petry, Ann.—B. 1946: 302-315.
"Lily." Smiley, Jane.—B. 1985: 235-255; P. 1985: 1-19.
"Lily Daw and the Three Ladies." Welty, Eudora.—B. 1938: 320-329.
"A Line Of Order." Rascoe, Judith.—P. 1973: 125-146.
"A Lingering Death." Tennenbaum, Silvia.—B. 1979: 270-283.
"Lion." Faulkner, William.—P. 1936: 171-191.
"Lions, Harts, Leaping Does." Powers, J. F.—B. 1944: 309-331; P. 1944: 151-175.
"The Listener." Berry, John.—B. 1961: 41-44.
"Little Baseball World." Lowry, Robert.—B. 1947: 252-268.
"The Little Black Boys." Laidlaw, Clara.—B. 1943: 218-231; P. 1943: 63-75.
"Little Brat." Wilde, Hagar.—P. 1933: 259-266.
"Little Bride." McCleary, Dorothy.—B. 1938: 177-185.
"Little Brother Nun." Stacton, David.—P. 1968: 230-245.
"Little Dombey." Shay, Frank.—B. 1927: 259-278.
"Little Elise." McCleary, Dorothy.—P. 1935: 125-138.
"The Little Girl From Town." Suckow, Ruth.—P. 1927: 220-238.
"Little Joe." Eastlake, William.—B. 1955: 96-106.
"The Little Master Of the Sky." Komroff, Manuel.—B. 1921: 288-299.
"The Little Pub." Zelver, Patricia.—P. 1977: 144-152.
"Little Selves." Lerner, Mary.—B. 1916: 212-225.
"Little Victor." Lewis, Robert.—P. 1947: 37-60.
"A Little Walk." Bessie, Alvah C.—B. 1933: 14-20.
"Little White Girl." Haardt, Sara.—B. 1935: 182-190.
"The Little Wife." March, William.—B. 1930: 142-153; P. 1930: 205-216.
"Living Alone." Wilson, Robley, Jr.—B. 1979: 167-171.
"Living Alone In Iota." Abbott, Lee K., Jr.—P. 1984: 118-126.
"Livvie Is Back." Welty, Eudora.—P. 1943: 3-16.
"The Lizard." Gottlieb, Elaine.—P. 1972: 154-165.
"The Lizard God." Finger, Charles J.—B. 1921: 109-129.
"Lizzie Borden In the P.M." Henson, Robert.—P. 1974: 26-53.
"Lo!" Faulkner, William.—B. 1935: 150-167.

"Load." Schnable, Dudley.—B. 1932: 216-230.
"A Loaf Of Bread." Gibbons, Robert.—B. 1942: 116-128.
"Lobster John's Annie." Ryerson, Florence, and Colin Clements.—P. 1930: 271-279.
"A Local Skirmish." Houston, Noel.—B. 1944: 128-134.
"The Lone Pilgrim." Colwin, Laurie.—P. 1977: 231-242.
"The Lone Pioneer." Wilson, William E.—B. 1936: 316-326.
"Lonely Places." Buzzell, Francis.—B. 1917: 70-85.
"Long Calls." Busch, Frederick.—B. 1980: 27-43.
"A Long Day's Dying." Eastlake, William.—B. 1964: 109-123.
"Long Distance." Terrell, Upton.—P. 1935: 237-256.
"Long, Long Ago." Bartlett, Frederick Orin.—B. 1919: 74-81.
"The Long Night." Blanton, Lowell D.—P. 1958: 155-165.
"Long Shadow On the Lawn." Deasy, Mary.—P. 1945: 75-89.
"A Long Story Short." Hazzard, Shirley.—P. 1977: 42-65.
"A Long Way To Go." Wylie, Jeanne E.—P. 1942: 75-88.
"Longing For America." Rubin, David.—B. 1967: 257-278.
"Look At a Teacup." Hampl, Patricia.—B. 1977: 181-187.
"Looking For Mother." Krysl, Marilyn.—P. 1980: 153-162.
"Looking Into Nothing." Nelson, Kent.—B. 1976: 170-180.
"Lord Of Marutea." Hall, James Norman.—B. 1934: 164-187.
"The Lost." Boyle, Kay.—B. 1952: 31-48.
"Lost In the Funhouse." Barth, John.—P. 1969: 63-85.
"The Lost Novel." Anderson, Sherwood.—B. 1929: 20-25.
"The Lost Phoebe." Dreiser, Theodore.—B. 1916: 115-132.
"The Lost Salt Gift Of Blood." MacLeod, Alistair.—B. 1975: 144-161.
"Lost Soldier." Whitmore, Stanford.—P. 1954: 281-286.
"Lost Sons." Salter, James.—P. 1984: 161-169.
"The Lottery." Jackson, Shirley.—P. 1949: 172-180.
"Loud Sing Cuckoo." Weston, Christine.—B. 1952: 347-360.
"Love." Stuart, Jesse.—B. 1941: 315-318.
"Love Affair." Weigel, Henietta.—B. 1946: 497-524.
"Love and Like." Gold, Herbert.—B. 1959: 137-171; P. 1960: 146-182.
"The Love and Sorrow Of Henry Pimber." Gass, W. H.—B. 1961: 58-88.
"The Love Child." Norris, Helen.—P. 1984: 241-254.
"Love In the Winter." Curley, Daniel.—P. 1965: 199-212.
"Love Is For Lovers." Lavin, Mary.—B. 1943: 232-255.
"Love On a Dark Street." Shaw, Irwin.—B. 1962: 378-399.
"Love Story." Smith, Robert.—P. 1933: 227-245.
"The Lover." Garber, Eugene K.—B. 1977: 161-180.
"The Lovers." Berryman, John.—B. 1946: 26-39.
"Love's So Many Things." Bragdon, Clifford.—B. 1932: 25-33.
"The Lubbeny Kiss." Rice, Louise.—P. 1919: 180-191.
"The Lubber." Adams, Bill.—P. 1933: 75-92.
"Lula Borrow." Mabry, Thomas.—B. 1957: 185-233.
"Lullaby." Silko, Leslie.—B. 1975: 254-263.
"Lust." Minot, Susan.—P. 1985: 63-70.

"Mac In Love." Dixon, Stephen.—P. 1977: 268-278.

"The Machine." Shepley, John.—B. 1956: 300-323.

"The 'Madelaine.'" Vorse, Mary Heaton.—P. 1926: 269-292.

"Mademoiselle." Finley-Thomas, Elisabeth.—B. 1927: 103-117.

"Magic." Klein, Norma.—P. 1969: 145-167.

"Magic." Morris, Wright.—B. 1971: 202-216.

"Magic Apple." Street, Penelope.—B. 1972: 309-323.

"The Magic Barrel." Malamud, Bernard.—B. 1955: 159-175.

"The Magic Poker." Coover, Robert.—B. 1970: 53-73.

"The Magic Wire." Gizycka, Felicia.—B. 1941: 120-153.

"The Magician." Burgess, Jackson.—P. 1961: 145-153.

"The Magnolias." Leiper, Gudger Bart.—P. 1950: 18-36.

"Maiden In a Tower." Stegner, Wallace.—B. 1955: 282-294.

"The Maid's Shoes." Malamud, Bernard.—B. 1960: 191-203.

"Main Currents Of American Thought." Shaw, Irwin.—B. 1940: 357-367.

"Main Street Morning." Petesch, Natalie L. M.—B. 1978: 163-176.

"Maine." Osborn, Margaret.—P. 1944: 135-150.

"Mainlanders." Brown, Rosellen.—P. 1973: 55-63.

"The Making Of a Clerk." Litwak, Leo.—P. 1958: 119-143.

"Making Port." Hallet, Richard Matthews.—B. 1916: 162-180.

"Mama and the Spy." Manoff, Eva.—P. 1965: 81-92.

"Mama Is a Lady." DeJong, David Cornel.—B. 1941: 54-58.

"Mama Tuddi Done Over." Rooke, Leon.—B. 1980: 272-301.

"Man Among Men." Patten, Katharine.—P. 1937: 171-184.

"Man and Woman." Caldwell, Erskine.—P. 1938: 153-159.

"The Man In Gray." Weston, Christine.—B. 1954: 363-372.

"Man In the Drawer." Malamud, Bernard.—P. 1969: 1-42.

"The Man In the Mirror." Gerstley, Adelaide.—B. 1947: 62-75.

"The Man In the Toolhouse." Swados, Harvey.—B. 1959: 274-310.

"A Man Of Affairs." Davis, Christopher.—P. 1966: 181-195.

"Man Of Distinction." Fowler, Mary Dewees.—P. 1955: 155-172.

"A Man Of the World." Held, John, Jr.—P. 1930: 173-181.

"Man On a Road." Maltz, Albert.—B. 1936: 237-244.

"The Man Who Caught the Weather." Aldrich, Bess Streeter.—P. 1928: 89-97.

"The Man Who Cursed the Lilies." Jackson, Charles Tenney.—P. 1921: 29-44.

"The Man Who Lived." Targan, Barry.—B. 1975: 264-277.

"The Man Who Looked Like Jesus." Fast, Howard.—B. 1960: 44-63.

"The Man Who Lost the Sea." Sturgeon, Theodore.—B. 1960: 307-317.

"The Man Who Loved Extinct Mammals." Updike, John.—B. 1974: 333-339.

"The Man Who Loved Levittown." Wetherell, W. D.—P. 1981: 174-190.

"The Man Who Saw Through Heaven." Steele, Wilbur Daniel.—P. 1925: 218-236.

"The Man Who Won the War." Buckner, Robert.—B. 1937: 1-14.

"The Man Whom Women Adored." Oates, Joyce Carol.—P. 1982: 229-253.

"The Man With the Good Face." Mott, Frank Luther.—B. 1921: 300-320.

"The Mango Community." Jacobsen, Josephine.—B. 1985: 282-298.

"The Mango Tree." Robinson, Rosanne Smith.—B. 1954: 268-277.

"Manicure." Leech, Margaret.—B. 1929: 146-158; P. 1929: 189-201.

"Manikin." Michaels, Leonard.—P. 1969: 115-120.

"Man's Courage." Blassingame, Wyatt.—B. 1957: 32-38; P. 1957: 152-158.

"The Man's Story." Anderson, Sherwood.—B. 1923: 30-49.

"Mansion, Magic, and Miracle." Horne, Lewis B.—B. 1974: 52-66.

"Marching Orders." Morris, I. V.—B. 1937: 245-269.

"Marching Through Boston." Updike, John.—P. 1967: 105-113.

"Margaret Blake." Crowell, Chester T.—P. 1924: 25-44.

"Margins." Barthelme, Donald.—P. 1965: 103-107.

"Markowitz and the Gypsies." Waksler, Norman.—B. 1980: 420-438.

"The Marne." Knight, Eric.—P. 1936: 267-269.

"The Marriage In Kairwan." Steele, Wilbur Daniel.—P. 1921: 273-292.

"Mars Revisited." Minot, Stephen.—P. 1971: 284-299.

"Martin Gerrity Gets Even." Ryley, Courtney, and Leo F. Creagan.—P. 1921: 113-126.

"Martyr." Foley, Martha.—B. 1933: 140-144.

"Ma's Pretties." Buzzell, Francis.—B. 1916: 75-84.

"Master Of Fallen Years." O'Sullivan, Vincent.—B. 1921: 321-336.

"Master Race." Oates, Joyce Carol.—P. 1986: 245-268.

"A Master Time." Still, James.—B. 1950: 390-398.

"Maternal." Eliot, Ethel Cook.—P. 1925: 170-182.

"A Matter Of Loyalty." Perry, Lawrence.—P. 1920: 184-209.

"A Matter Of Price." Bowen, Robert O.—B. 1955: 1-12.

"A Matter Of Standards." Street, Julian.—P. 1930: 307-322.

"Maud Island." Caldwell, Erskine.—P. 1934: 73-85.

"Maudie." Carver, Ada Jack.—B. 1926: 19-35.

"Maum Lou." Peterkin, Julia.—P. 1925: 203-217.

"Maybe the Sun Will Shine." March, William.—B. 1937: 219-225.

"The Meeker Ritual." Hergesheimer, Joseph.—B. 1919: 200-224.

"Meet Me In the Green Glen." Warren, Robert Penn.—B. 1972: 324-346.

"Meeting Time." Weaver, John D.—P. 1949: 276-287.

"Melanie and the Purple People Eaters." Faust, Irvin.—P. 1983: 90-107.

"Memoir Of Spring." Moll, Elick.—P. 1938: 233-252.

"The Men." Mayhall, Jane.—B. 1949: 205-211.

"Mendel Marantz—Housewife." Freedman, David.—B. 1922: 151-170.

"The Menorah." Rosenblatt, Benjamin.—B. 1916: 275-281.

"The Men's Club." Michaels, Leonard.—P. 1980: 57-80.

"A Mercenary." Ozick, Cynthia.—B. 1976: 181-208.

"Messengers." Johnston, Calvin.—B. 1919: 237-268.

"The Metamorphosis Of Kenko." Stacton, David.—P. 1964: 104-113.
"The Mexican Girl." Kerouac, Jack.—B. 1956: 205-225.
"Mexican Hayride." Marsh, Willard.—B. 1961: 226-237.
"Miami—New York." Gellhorn, Martha.—B. 1948: 106-123.
"Michael Finney and the Little Men." Humphreys, John Richard.—B. 1947: 221-237.
"The Middle Drawer." Calisher, Hortense.—P. 1945: 79-88.
"The Middle Place." Hedin, Mary.—B. 1979: 172-183.
"Midrash On Happiness." Paley, Grace.—P. 1987: 232-234.
"Midwestern Primitive." Suckow, Ruth.—B. 1928: 267-284.
"The Mighty Distance." McKinley, Georgia.—P. 1966: 245-290.
"Mighty, Mighty Pretty." Albee, George.—B. 1949: 1-18.
"Minstrels Of the Mist." Burman, Ben Lucien.—B. 1927: 86-102.
"The Miracle." Wilson, Anne Elizabeth.—B. 1931: 289-302.
"Miracle Play." Elliott, George P.—P. 1957: 48-54.
"Miriam." Capote, Truman.—P. 1946: 103-114.
"Misfortune's Isle." Hallet, Richard Matthews.—P. 1930: 145-169.
"Miss Cudahy Of Stowes Landing." Elliott, George P.—P. 1955: 117-139.
"Miss Cynthie." Fisher, Rudolph.—B. 1934: 105-117.
"Miss Leonora When Last Seen." Taylor, Peter.—B. 1961: 340-367.
"Miss Willett." Benefield, Barry.—B. 1916: 37-51.
"Miss Winters and the Wind." Goven, Christine Noble.—P. 1947: 156-161.
"The Missing Person." Kumin, Maxine.—B. 1979: 234-242.
"Mist On the Meadow." March, William.—B. 1932: 165-176.
"Mlle. Irene the Great." Johnson, Nunnally.—P. 1930: 185-202.
"The Model." Malamud, Bernard.—P. 1984: 134-138.
"The Model Chapel." Gilbert, Sister Mary.—B. 1962: 167-180.
"The Model House." Upson, William Hazlett.—B. 1931: 267-282.
"A Modern Development." Blake, George.—P. 1970: 71-82.
"The Mohammedans." Kaplan, H. J.—B. 1944: 164-189.
"Molly's Dog." Adams, Alice.—P. 1986: 118-129.
"Monday At Six." Hubbell, Catherine.—P. 1945: 151-159.
"Money At Home." Terrell, Upton.—B. 1934: 327-335.
"Monitor." Dillon, Millicent.—P. 1987: 160-169.
"Monkey Motions." Kelly, Eleanor Mercein.—P. 1927: 192-207.
"Monsieur Les Deux Chapeaux." Munro, Alice.—B. 1986: 180-206.
"Monte Saint Angelo." Miller, Arthur.—P. 1951: 202-216.
"The Month Of His Birthday." Karmel-Wolfe, Henia.—B. 1965: 187-197.
"More Like a Coffin." Hawthorne, Hazel.—B. 1944: 125-127.
"Morning, a Week Before the Crime." Lincoln, Victoria.—B. 1948: 172-188.
"Morning Sun." Deasy, Mary.—B. 1953: 90-100.
"Morrison's Reaction." Kirk, Stephen.—B. 1984: 140-149.
"The Most Dangerous Game." Connell, Richard.—P. 1924: 71-92.

"The Most Elegant Drawing Room In Europe." Hale, Nancy.—P. 1968: 97-115.

"The Moth and the Primrose." Dethier, Vincent G.—B. 1981: 110-128.

"Mother Tanner." Lineweaver, John.—B. 1934: 218-223.

"Mothers." Plath, Sylvia.—B. 1973: 238-247.

"Mother's Helper." McCleary, Dorothy.—P. 1940: 181-205.

"The Mother's Story." Johnson, Josephine W.—B. 1951: 157-167.

"A Mother's Tale." Agee, James.—B. 1953: 1-18.

"The Motion Of Forgetfulness Is Slow." Eaten, Charles Edward.—B. 1952: 108-117.

"A Mountain Summer." Ballard, James.—B. 1953: 19-40.

"The Mountains Where Cithæron Is." Moseley, Amelia.—B. 1981: 220-240.

"The Mourners." Schmitt, Gladys.—B. 1945: 222-237.

"Mourning Call." Leviant, Curt.—B. 1966: 203-218.

"The Mouse." Hauser, Marianne.—B. 1950: 201-214.

"Mr. Acarius." Faulkner, William.—B. 1966: 69-82.

"Mr. and Mrs. Fairbanks." Callaghan, Morley.—B. 1934: 46-51.

"Mr. and Mrs. McGill." Zorn, George A.—P. 1966: 205-224.

"Mr. Bisbee's Princess." Street, Julian.—P. 1925: 1-39.

"Mr. Cardeezer." Babcock, Edwina Stanton.—B. 1923: 50-80.

"Mr. Downey Sits Down." Robbins, L. H.—P. 1921: 258-272.

"Mr. Eberdeen's House." Johnson, Arthur.—B. 1915: 118-144.

"Mr. Henig's Wall." Hartley, Lodwick.—P. 1948: 97-107.

"Mr. Iscariot." Brown, Richard G.—B. 1964: 15-25.

"Mr. Mergenthwirker's Lobblies." Bond, Nelson S.—B. 1938: 74-80.

"Mr. Pruitt." Robin, Ralph.—B. 1958: 236-258.

"Mr. Smith." Hartman, Lee Foster.—P. 1928: 180-195.

"Mr. Sycamore." Ayre, Robert.—B. 1938: 1-53.

"Mrs. Darcy Meets the Blue-Eyed Stranger At the Beach." Smith, Lee.—P. 1979: 227-241.

"Mrs. Drainger's Veil." Jones, Howard Mumford.—B. 1919: 269-296.

"Mrs. Ketting and Clark Gable." Chidester, Ann.—P. 1950: 119-129.

"Mrs. Lancaster-Jones." Morris, Edita.—B. 1935: 254-264.

"Mrs. Mean." Gass, William H.—B. 1959: 91-120.

"Mrs. Razor." Still, James.—B. 1946: 419-424.

"Mrs. Schwellenbach's Receptions." Luhrs, Marie.—P. 1931: 213-221.

"Mrs. Susan." Slade, Caroline.—P. 1929: 309-320.

"Mule No. 095." Lolos, Kimon.—B. 1964: 191-201.

"The Mulhausen Girls." Downey, Harris.—P. 1949: 135-149.

"Mummery." Beer, Thomas.—P. 1921: 66-83.

"The Murder." Steinbeck, John.—P. 1934: 179-192.

"The Murder On Jefferson Street." Canfield, Dorothy.—B. 1936: 23-56.

"Murphy Jones: Pearblossom, California." Schott, Max.—B. 1978: 177-191.

"Murphy's Xmas." Costello, Mark.—B. 1969: 21-36.

"The Muse and Mr. Parkinson." Gidney, James B.—P. 1948: 62-71.

"A Mussel Named Ecclesiastes." Dickerson, George.—B. 1966: 13-33.

"The Mustydines Was Ripe." Vines, Howell.—B. 1936: 293-304.
"Mutilated Woman." Oates, Joyce Carol.—P. 1981: 191-211.
"My Apples." Granat, Robert.—P. 1958: 273-292.
"My Blithe, Sad Bird." Stafford, Jean.—P. 1958: 79-97.
"My Brother Down There." Frazee, Steve.—B. 1954: 86-122.
"My Brother Osong's Career In Politics." Bulosan, Carlos.—B. 1945: 30-37.
"My Brother's Second Funeral." Newhouse, Edward.—B. 1950: 317-327.
"My Dead Brother Comes To America." Godin, Alexander.—B. 1934: 126-132.
"My Father and the Circus." Brookhouser, Frank.—B. 1949: 55-59.
"My Father Sits In the Dark." Weidman, Jerome.—P. 1935: 259-263.
"My Father's Jokes." Zelver, Patricia.—P. 1979: 187-202.
"My Friend Flicka." O'Hara, Mary.—B. 1942: 210-230; P. 1941: 247-269.
"My Girls." O'Hara, John.—P. 1937: 165-168.
"My Life As a West African Gray Parrot." Bienen, Leigh Buchanan.—P. 1983: 175-188.
"My Mistress." Colwin, Laurie.—B. 1983: 99-116.
"My Old Man." Hemingway, Ernest.—B. 1923: 263-276.
"My Pigeon Pair." Thomas, Dorothy.—B. 1942: 343-354; 1941: 307-319.
"My Public." Shedd, Margaret.—B. 1943: 301-309.
"My Redeemer Cometh. . . ." Katz, Shlomo.—P. 1968: 50-77.
"My Russian Cap." Surmelian, Leon Z.—B. 1944: 378-384.
"My Sister's Marriage." Rich, Cynthia Marshall.—P. 1957: 55-67.
"My Son the Murderer." Malamud, Bernard.—P. 1970: 127-133.
"My Warszawa." Oates, Joyce Carol.—P. 1983: 26-79.
"The Mysteries Of Eleusis." Hardwick, Elizabeth.—B. 1946: 203-213.

"Nairobi." Oates, Joyce Carol.—B. 1984: 177-183.
"The Naked Lady." Bell, Madison Smartt.—B. 1984: 13-18.
"Nakedness." Updike, John.—P. 1975: 316-323.
"A Name For the City." Faulkner, William.—P. 1951: 98-115.
"The Names and Faces Of Heroes." Price, Reynolds.—B. 1964: 257-283.
"Napoleon's Hat Under Glass." Komroff, Manuel.—B. 1932: 134-137.
"Natalka's Portion." Cohen, Rose Gollup.—B. 1922: 83-99.
"Near the Line." Kentfield, Calvin.—P. 1968: 78-96.
"The Need." Coates, Robert M.—B. 1953: 81-89.
"Neighbors." Oliver, Diane.—P. 1967: 131-146.
"Neither Here Nor There." Portugal, Ruth.—B. 1944: 295-308.
"Neither Jew Nor Greek." John, William M.—P. 1930: 17-31.
"Nel Bagno." Jacobsen, Josephine.—P. 1976: 75-88.
"The Nemesis." Stafford, Jean.—B. 1951: 295-311.
"The Net." Coates, Robert M.—B. 1941: 43-53.
"Never In This World." Avery, Stephen Morehouse.—P. 1928: 73-88.
"The New Kid." Heyert, Murray.—P. 1945: 137-150.
"A New Life." Miller, Nolan.—P. 1957: 236-244.
"The New Music." Barthelme, Donald.—B. 1979: 312-323.

"The New Nobility." Broner, E. M.—P. 1968: 18-49.
"New Shoes." Berry, John.—P. 1950: 81-88.
"Newfoundland Night." Godfrey, Dave.—B. 1963: 166-174.
"The News From Troy." Putman, Clay.—P. 1954: 40-46.
"Next Door." Wolff, Tobias.—P. 1982: 254-259.
"Nice Neighbours." Watts, Mary S.—P. 1923: 229-246.
"The Nickel Misery Of George Washington Carver Brown." Gold,
   Ivan.—B. 1961: 89-130; P. 1961: 58-100.
"Nigger Horse." Franklin, F. K.—P. 1968: 129-144.
"Niggers Are Such Liars." Creyke, Richard Paulett.—B. 1938:
   118-126.
"A Night Among the Horses." Barnes, Djuna.—B. 1919: 65-73.
"Night and Day At Panacea." Price, Reynolds.—B. 1975: 197-211.
"Night and Day, Day and Night." Ross, Lilian.—P. 1964: 81-103.
"Night and the Lost Armies." Thielen, Benedict.—B. 1940: 450-458.
"Night Club." Brush, Katharine.—P. 1927: 84-96.
"The Night Club In the Woods." Calisher, Hortense.—P. 1956:
   103-120.
"Night Flight." Johnson, Josephine W.—P. 1944: 109-115.
"Night In Funland." Peden, William.—B. 1961: 291-299.
"Night March." O'Brien, Tim.—P. 1976: 211-219.
"Night Watch." Heggen, Thomas.—B. 1947: 189-207.
"The Nightingales Sing." Parsons, Elizabeth.—P. 1947: 22-36.
"Nights At O'Rear's." Griffith, Patricia Browning.—P. 1970: 135-148.
"Nine Prisoners." March, William.—P. 1932: 203-213.
"The Ninth Cold Day." Weisbrod, Rosine.—B. 1970: 367-378.
"No Dam' Yankee." Cobb, Irvin S.—B. 1928: 94-112.
"No Final Word." Bessie, Alvah C.—B. 1934: 15-24.
"No Flowers." Smith, Gordon Arthur.—P. 1920: 268-279.
"No More Trouble For Jedwick." Paul, Louis.—P. 1934: 3-15.
"No Trace." Madden, David.—B. 1971: 134-155.
"No Way Down." Jenks, Almet.—B. 1954: 206-218.
"Nobody Say a Word." Van Doren, Mark.—B. 1952: 331-335.
"Nocturne: A Red Shawl." Sergel, Roger.—B. 1924: 175-190.
"Noises In the City." Shaw, Irwin.—B. 1963: 315-326.
"None So Blind." Synon, Mary.—B. 1917: 468-482.
"The Norm." Gottlieb, Elaine.—B. 1946: 184-202.
"North Is Black." LaFarge, Oliver, III.—B. 1927: 169-180.
"The North Wind Doth Blow." Coombes, Evan.—B. 1936: 80-86.
"Norwegians." Zelver, Patricia.—P. 1975: 239-250.
"Not a Good Girl." Klass, Perri.—P. 1984: 226-232.
"Not a Soul Will Come Along." Parsons, Elizabeth.—P. 1950: 209-219.
"Not Another Word." Thurman, Richard.—B. 1958: 299-316.
"Not Very Close." McCleary, Dorothy.—P. 1946: 218-225.
"Not Wanted." Williams, Jesse Lynch.—P. 1923: 247-277.
"Not With Our Fathers." Rothberg, Abraham.—B. 1950: 364-377.
"Notes Of a Dangling Man." Bellow, Saul.—B. 1944: 21-40.
"Nothing Can Change It." Cooke, Charles.—P. 1939:147-160.
"Nothing Ever Breaks Except the Heart." Boyle, Kay.—B. 1942: 41-49.

"Novotny's Pain." Roth, Philip.—P. 1964: 249-269.
"Now There Is Peace." Sherman, Richard.—B. 1934: 306-311.
"The NRACP." Elliott, George P.—B. 1950: 109-142.
"A Nun No More." Fante, John.—B. 1941: 74-82.
"The Nurse." Williams, Ben Ames.—P. 1926: 293-308.

"O Lovely Appearance Of Death." Currie, Ellen.—P. 1961: 154-180.
"Ocean." Friedman, Sanford.—P. 1965: 21-51.
"Of Cabbages and Kings." McPherson, James Alan.—P. 1970: 237-251.
"Of the River and Uncle Pidcock." Kjelgaard, Jim.—B. 1949: 157-165.
"Of This Time, Of That Place." Trilling, Lionel.—B. 1944: 385-422.
"Off the Highway." Wolfert, Ira.—B. 1938: 330-340.
"Offerings." Kornblatt, Joyce R.—P. 1986: 44-54.
"Oh, Joseph, I'm So Tired." Yates, Richard.—P. 1979: 275-298.
"The Old Acrobat and the Ruined City." Putman, Clay.—B. 1950: 349-363.
"Old and Country Tale." Shoonover, Shirley W.—P. 1964: 226-248.
"The Old Army Game." Garrett, George.—B. 1962: 96-107.
"Old Bill Bent To Drink." Lampman, Ben Hur.—B. 1946: 224-242; P. 1945: 33-46.
"Old Boy—New Boy." Thielen, Benedict.—P. 1947: 246-256.
"Old Century's River." LaFarge, Oliver.—B. 1951: 187-200; P. 1951: 154-169.
"The Old Folks." Gass, William H.—B. 1980: 159-175.
"The Old Forest." Taylor, Peter.—B. 1980: 356-408; P. 1980: 97-151.
"Old James." Young, Marguerite.—P. 1944: 234-250.
"The Old Lady." Scott, Evelyn.—B. 1925: 195-206.
"The Old Left." Menaker, Daniel.—P. 1984: 106-117.
"Old Light." Targan, Barry.—P. 1980: 295-307.
"Old Maid." Lane, Rose Wilder.—P. 1933: 191-213.
"An Old Man and His Hat." Freitag, George H.—B. 1968: 75-78.
"Old Man Ledge." Stanley, May.—B. 1925: 207-227.
"Old Men Dream Dreams, Young Men See Visions." Corrington, John William.—B. 1973: 57-66.
"The Old Order." Porter, Katherine Anne.—B. 1937: 270-284.
"The Old People." Faulkner, William.—P. 1941: 155-169.
"Old Peter Takes an Afternoon Off." Lewis, O. F.—P. 1922: 177-195.
"Old Red." Gordon, Caroline.—P. 1934: 19-41.
"The Old She 'Gator." Von Der Goltz, Peggy.—P. 1943: 285-292.
"Old Turkey Neck." Lanning, George.—B. 1951: 201-209.
"Old Vemish." Targan, Barry.—B. 1974: 266-305.
"The Old Wives' Tale." Settle, Mary Lee.—P. 1957: 281-291.
"'Ollie, Oh. . . .'" Chute, Carloyn.—B. 1983: 84-98.
"O'Meara, the 'Mayflower'—and Mrs. MacLirr." Marquis, Don.—P. 1928: 211-224.
"On Strike." Terhune, Albert Payson.—P. 1919: 56-77.
"On the Desert." Zelver, Patricia.—P. 1972: 141-153.
"On the Edge Of Arcadia." Cole, Tom.—P. 1966: 57-73.

Index Of Titles

"On the Island." Jacobsen, Josephine.—B. 1966: 139-153; P. 1967: 71-91.

"On the Lake." Douglas, Ellen.—P. 1963: 230-260.

"On the Mountain-Side." Roberts, Elizabeth Madox.—B. 1928: 246-257.

"On the Shore of Chad Creek." Matthews, Jack.—P. 1972: 166-176.

"On the Sidewalk." Williams, Calvin.—B. 1936: 312-315.

"On the Way To Somewhere Else." Pennell, Joseph Stanley.—B. 1945: 164-169.

"One Head Well Done." Swain, John D.—P. 1931: 27-49.

"The One Hundred Dollar Bill." Tarkington, Booth.—P. 1923: 211-228.

"One Night For Several Samurai." Whitehill, Joseph.—B. 1966: 289-325.

"One Of the Boys." Francis, H. E.—B. 1967: 67-84.

"One Of You Must Be Wendell Corey." Green, Philip L.—P. 1966: 149-159.

"One Ordinary Day, With Peanuts." Jackson, Shirley.—B. 1956: 195-204.

"One Summer." Lavin, Mary.—B. 1966: 167-202.

"One Sunday In Late July." Price, Reynolds.—P. 1961: 101-144.

"One Uses the Handkerchief." Stone, Elinore Cowan.—P. 1924: 225-237.

"One With Shakespeare." Foley, Martha.—B. 1931: 143-150.

"The One-Star Jew." Evanier, David.—B. 1980: 44-79.

"Only By Chance Are Pioneers Made." Hunt, Hamlen.—P. 1938: 215-230.

"The Only People." Higgins, Judith.—B. 1968: 161-186.

"The Only Son Of the Doctor." Gordon, Mary.—P. 1983: 203-215.

"Only the Dead Know Brooklyn." Wolfe, Thomas.—B. 1936: 327-331; P. 1935: 267-273.

"Only We Are Barren." Bessie, Alvah C.—B. 1931: 27-46.

"Onnie." Beer, Thomas.—B. 1917: 20-44.

"The Open Window." Dobie, Charles Caldwell.—B. 1918: 61-84.

"Opening Day." Gilchrist, Jack.—B. 1965: 93-98.

"Opening the Door On Sixty-Second Street." Kumin, Maxine.—B. 1974: 87-94.

"The Operator." Enright, Elizabeth.—P. 1955: 141-154.

"Oreste." Shultz, Henry.—B. 1953: 294-320.

"The Other." Updike, John.—P. 1985: 299-313.

"The Other Child." Davis, Olivia.—B. 1970: 74-83.

"The Other Foot." Bradbury, Ray.—B. 1952: 49-60.

"The Other Margaret." Trilling, Lionel.—B. 1946: 464-496.

"The Other River." Bowen, Robert O.—B. 1952: 18-30.

"The Other Road." Strater, Edward L.—B. 1926: 264-281.

"The Other Room." Marquis, Don.—B. 1931: 214-233.

"The Other Room." Vorse, Mary Heaton.—B. 1919: 312-325.

"The Other Side Of the River." Hauser, Marianne.—P. 1948: 108-124.

"The Other Side Of the Street." Horgan, Paul.—B. 1931: 189-201.

"The Other Woman." Anderson, Sherwood.—B. 1920: 3-11.

"Our Vegetable Love." Putman, Clay.—B. 1953: 263-278.

"Out In the Garage." Hill, Richard.—P. 1974: 68-76.
"Out Of Exile." Steele, Wilbur Daniel.—B. 1920: 266-292.
"Out Of Line." Beck, Warren.—B. 1946: 13-25.
"Out Of the Wind." Steele, Wilbur Daniel.—B. 1926: 244-263.
"Outside Yuma." Appel, Benjamin.—B. 1935: 1-6.
"Over By the River." Maxwell, William.—P. 1975: 185-222.
"The Overcoat." Benson, Sally.—B. 1935: 7-10.
"The Owl and The Bens." Mitchell, W. O.—B. 1946: 277-291.
"The Owl That Kept Winking." Pratt, Theodore.—B. 1945: 180-187.

"Paddycake, Paddycake . . . A Memoir." Apple, Max.—P. 1978: 76-86.
"Pain Was My Portion." Harvor, Beth.—B. 1971: 118-133.
"A Pair Of Shoes." White, Max.—B. 1935: 306-312.
"The Pale Green Fishes." Taylor, Kressmann.—B. 1954: 306-327.
"Palo." Saroyan, William.—B. 1952: 254-263.
"Papa, Mama and Economics." Panetta, George.—B. 1945: 154-163.
"Papago Wedding." Austin, Mary.—P. 1925: 73-76.
"Paper Covers Rock." Thompson, Jean.—B. 1979: 222-233.
"Paper Poppy." Rugel, Miriam.—B. 1969: 249-264.
"Parish Of Cockroaches." McHugh, Vincent.—B. 1935: 241-245.
"Parker's Back." O'Connor, Flannery.—B. 1966: 235-254.
"The Parrot." Duranty, Walter.—P. 1928: 1-21.
"Part Of the Act." Alexander, Sidney.—B. 1948: 1-19.
"The Parting Genius." Crew, Helen Coale.—B. 1920: 83-89.
"A Partnership With Death." Fisher, Vardis.—B. 1943: 105-114.
"The Party." Esslinger-Carr, Pat M.—B. 1974: 45-51.
"A Party In Miami Beach." Singer, Isaac Bashevis.—B. 1979: 84-96.
"The Party Next Door." Brace, Ernest.—B. 1935: 11-27.
"A Passenger To Bali." St. Joseph, Ellis.—B. 1937: 285-315.
"Passing Through." Coates, Robert M.—B. 1939: 52-59.
"Passion?" Baumbach, Jonathan.—P. 1979: 173-186.
"Passion For History." Minot, Stephen.—B. 1977: 210-221; P. 1977: 105-117.
"The Passion For Silver's Arm." Wilner, Herbert.—P. 1958: 249-272.
"The Passion Of Marco Z——." Leaton, Anne.—P. 1979: 117-124.
"The Past." Glasgow, Ellen.—B. 1921: 168-193.
"Past the Island, Drifting." Shreve, Anita.—P. 1976: 220-229.
"Pastor Dowe At Tacaté." Bowles, Paul.—B. 1950: 80-101; P. 1949: 58-78.
"Pastorale." Engberg, Susan.—P. 1978: 87-105.
"The Path Of Glory." Pulver, Mary Brecht.—B. 1917: 412-440.
"Paths Unto the Lord." Clearman, Mary.—B. 1975: 59-68.
"Patients." Strong, Jonathan.—P. 1970: 83-91.
"The Patriot." Polk, William.—B. 1930: 162-170.
"The Pawnshop." Sexton, John S.—B. 1927: 255-258.
"The Peach Stone." Horgan, Paul.—B. 1943: 166-186.
"Pecos Bill and the Willful Coyote." White, William C.—P. 1943: 295-309.

Index Of Titles

"The Peculiar Treasure Of Kings." Douglas, Marjory Stoneman.—P. 1928: 22-48.

"The Pedersen Kid." Gass, William H.—B. 1962: 108-166.

"Peggety's Parcel Of Shortcomings." Hersey, John.—P. 1951: 130-139.

"The Pelican's Shadow." Rawlings, Marjorie Kinnan.—P. 1940: 239-248.

"Penance." Singmaster, Elsie.—B. 1916: 282-293.

"The Pension." Mamet, Louis.—B. 1934: 247-256.

"The People On the Roller Coaster." Hardwick, Elizabeth.—P. 1945: 125-136.

"The People Vs. Abe Lathan, Colored." Caldwell, Erskine.—B. 1940: 20-29; P. 1939: 133-144.

"The People With the Charm." Deasy, Mary.—P. 1962: 137-152.

"Pepicelli." Buechler, James.—P. 1956: 41-59.

"The Perils Of Flight." White, Ellington.—B. 1961: 368-384.

"Perpetural Care." Ballentyne, Sheila.—P. 1977: 87-104.

"Persephone." LeSueur, Meridel.—B. 1927: 202-212.

"A Personal Issue." Bessie, Alvah C.—P. 1936: 41-52.

"Pet Milk." Dybek, Stuart.—P. 1986: 12-16.

"Peter Projects." Brady, Mariel.—B. 1925: 112-129.

"Petrified Man." Welty, Eudora.—P. 1939: 257-275.

"The Petrified Woman." Gordon, Carolyn.—P. 1948: 72-84.

"Phantom Adventure." Dell, Floyd.—B. 1924: 39-52; P. 1923: 46-58.

"Philadelphia Express." Weidman, Jerome.—B. 1943: 391-399.

"Photographs." Bromell, Henry.—P. 1973: 243-251.

"The Phototropic Woman." Thomas, Annabel.—P. 1981: 239-246.

"Piano." Saroyan, William.—B. 1939: 221-224.

"The Piano Tuner." Meinke, Peter.—B. 1985: 139-149.

"The Picnic." Pendergast, Constance.—B. 1953: 239-256.

"The Picnickers." West, Jessamyn.—B. 1963: 380-399; P. 1963: 139-158.

"Pico Never Forgets." Malkin, Richard.—P. 1948: 157-172.

"'The Picture That Wouldn't Fit In the Stove.'" Bradshaw, George.—B. 1958: 84-95.

"Pictures Of Feidelman." Malamud, Bernard.—B. 1969: 129-146.

"A Piece Of Bread." Patton, Frances Gray.—P. 1945: 183-192.

"The Pigeon." Gustafson, Ralph.—B. 1950: 191-200.

"Pigeon Feathers." Updike, John.—B. 1962: 400-419.

"Pigeon Flight." Appel, Benjamn.—P. 1934: 55-62.

"Pigeons En Casserole." Breuer, Bessie.—P. 1943: 91-103.

"The Pitcher." Dubus, Andre.—P. 1980: 373-388.

"A Place Not On the Map." Blake, George.—B. 1967: 13-14.

"Places We Lost." Hedin, Mary.—B. 1966: 95-112.

"Plaisir D'Amour." Schwartz, Lynne Sharon.—B. 1979: 115-130.

"The Plan." Sulkin, Sidney.—B. 1948: 305-320; P. 1948: 236-249.

"Play Like I'm Sheriff." Cady, Jack.—B. 1969: 9-20.

"Pleadings." Corrington, John William.—B. 1977: 66-101.

"The Pleasure Of Her Company." Smiley, Jane.—P. 1982: 62-79.

"The Pleasures Of Solitude." Cheever, John.—B. 1943: 41-46.

Index Of Titles

"The Pleasures Of Travel." Wilcox, Wendell.—P. 1944: 225-233.
"Pluto Is the Furthest Place." Rothberg, Abraham.—B. 1966: 255-268.
"The Poet." Halper, Albert.—B. 1937: 95-104.
"The Poet." Van Dine, Warren L.—B. 1924: 228-239.
"Point Of Conversion." Flythe, Starkey, Jr.—P. 1972: 83-93.
"Poisoner In Motley." Brennan, Louis.—B. 1932: 34-43.
"Polonaise." Rothberg, Abraham.—B. 1975: 212-253.
"The Ponoes." Meinke, Peter.—P. 1983: 216-226.
"Pontifex." Berkman, Sylvia."—P. 1963: 95-107.
"Pontius Pilate." Hagge, John.—B. 1976: 116-132.
"Poor Boy." Lloyd, Lynda.—P. 1983: 285-300.
"Poor Everybody." McLaughlin, Robert.—B. 1945: 123-132.
"Poor Monsieur Panalitus." Boyle, Kay.—P. 1940: 59-69.
"Porcelain Cups." Cabell, James Branch.—P. 1919: 210-227.
"Porkchops With Whiskey and Ice Cream." McGregor, Matthew
    W.—B. 1969: 147-164.
"Porque No Tiene, Porque Le Falta." Stone, Robert.—B. 1970: 318-343.
"The Portable Phonograph." Clark, Walter Van Tilburg.—B. 1942:
    67-74; P. 42: 105-113.
"Portrait." Lewis, Ethel G.—B. 1951: 210-217.
"Portrait Of a Woman." Arnold, Len.—P. 1933: 113-116.
"Portrait Of My Son As a Young Man." Middleton, Elizabeth H.—B.
    1955: 202-208.
"A Postal Creed." Brooks, Ben.—P. 1982: 52-61.
"A Postscript To Divorce." Morris, Gouverneur.—B. 1924: 155-166.
"The Pot Of Gold." Cheever, John.—P. 1951: 61-77.
"Potato Picking." McAlmon, Robert.—B. 1929: 159-168.
"The Power." Konecky, Edith.—B. 1964: 173-190.
"Power Of Horizon." Herald, Leon Srabian.—B. 1929: 123-129.
"The Power Of Language Is Such That Even a Single Word Taken
    Truly To Heart Can Change Everything." Greenberg, Alvin.—B.
    1982: 182-192.
"Powerhouse." Bradbury, Ray.—P. 1948: 26-34.
"The Practice Of an Art." Robinson, Leonard Wallace.—B. 1965:
    271-282.
"Prairies." Eakin, Boyle.—B. 1942: 93-104.
"Prayer For the Dying." Johnson, Willis.—P. 1984: 170-185.
"Preach On the Dusty Roads." Shaw, Irwin.—B. 1943: 292-300.
"The Preacher and Margery Scott." Moseley, William.—B. 1968:
    235-246.
"Prelude." Halper, Albert.—B. 1939: 94-108.
"Prelude." Smith, Edgar Valentine.—P. 1923: 1-18.
"The Presbyterian Choir Singers." Saroyan, William.—B. 1940:
    333-343.
"The Presence Of Grace." Powers, J. F.—P. 1955: 226-247.
"The Present." Buchwald, Emilie Bix.—P. 1959: 129-135.
"The President Of the Argentine." Cheever, John.—P. 1977: 297-303.
"Presque Isle." Oates, Joyce Carol.—B. 1981: 255-270.
"A Pretty Cute Little Stunt." Milburn, George.—B. 1931: 234-242.

"Pride." DeFord, Miriam Allen.—P. 19334: 103-109.
"The Priest's Wife." L'Heureux, John.—P. 1980: 359-372.
"Prince Of Darkness." Powers, J. F.—B. 1947: 293-335.
"The Prison." Malamud, Bernard.—B. 1951: 253-258.
"The Prison." Petrakis, Harry Mark.—P. 1966: 113-120.
"A Private Landscape." Pritchard, Melissa Brown.—P. 1984: 127-133.
"The Prize." Cassill, R. V.—P. 1956: 60-75.
"Prize Tomatoes." Rosner, Anne F.—B. 1982: 260-286.
"Pro Arte." Seager, Allan.—B. 1938: 265-276; P. 1937: 199-210.
"Professional Aid." Loomis, Alfred F.—P. 1931: 195-210.
"Professional Pride." Sanborn, Ruth Burr.—P. 1929: 287-305.
"The Professor and the Poet." Mudrick, Marvin.—B. 1955: 209-218.
"The Professor and the Puli." Morse, Robert.—B. 1948: 222-235; P. 1948: 173-185.
"Professor Boynton Rereads History." Mirrielees, Edith R.—P. 1924: 113-125.
"Professor Todd's Used Car." Robbins, L. H.—P. 1920: 210-222.
"Professorio Collegio." Shaber, David.—P. 1962: 121-136.
"The Professor's Houses." LeGuin, Ursula K.—B. 1983: 155-160.
"The Professor's Punch." Benét, Stephen Vincent.—P. 1935: 71-84.
"Progress." Welles, Harriet.—P. 1924: 238-256.
"Prohibition." Wescott, Glenway.—P. 1928: 255-268.
"The Promise." Steinbeck, John.—P. 1938: 85-105.
"The Promise." Stewart, Ramona.—B. 1950: 378-389.
"The Promise." Vorse, Mary Heaton.—B. 1923: 394-413.
"The Promise Of Heat." Ayer, Ethan.—B. 1967: 1-12.
"The Prophecy." Miller, Arthur.—B. 1962: 257-296.
"The Proud and Virtuous." Betts, Doris.—B. 1957: 19-31.
"Proud Monster—Sketches." MacMillan, Ian.—B. 1982: 287-298.
"The Proud Walkers." Still, James.—P. 1941: 289-304.
"The Psychologist." Thielen, Benedict.—B. 1941: 319-331.
"Psychopolis." McEwan, Ian.—B. 1978: 192-211.
"Public Address System." West, Jessamyn.—P. 1949: 288-305.
"The Pump." Brand, Millen.—P. 1939: 105-118.
"The Pump." Humphrey, William.—B. 1964: 153-160.
"The Purchase." Hardwick, Elizabeth.—B. 1960: 143-164.
"The Pures." Gordon, William J. J.—B. 1963: 175-184.
"Put Yourself In My Shoes." Garver, Raymond.—P. 1974: 215-228.
"Putting & Gardening." Van Wert, William F.—P. 1983: 227-245.

"The Quail." Yngve, Rolf.—B. 1979: 97-101.
"The Quality Of Light In Maine." Pfeil, Fred.—P. 1979: 101-116.
"The Quarrel." Ward, Leo L.—B. 1932: 264-272.
"The Quarry." Norris, Helen.—P. 1985: 51-62.
"The Quarterback Speaks To His God." Wilner, Herbert.—B. 1979: 184-205.
"Query." Dudley, Henry Walbridge.—B. 1926: 90-97.
"A Questionnaire For Rudolph Gordon." Matthews, Jack.—B. 1977: 205-209.

Index Of Titles

"The Quick and the Dead." Krause, Ervin.—P. 1961: 191-208.
"The Quiet Chimneys." Eastlake, William.—B. 1956: 123-133.
"Quitter." Roane, Marianne.—P. 1944: 176-182.

"Race At Morning." Faulkner, William.—P. 1956: 178-193.
"Rachel and Her Children." Newman, Frances.—P. 1924: 45-52.
"The Rags Of Time." Targan, Barry.—B. 1980: 330-355.
"Ragtime." Doctorow, E. L.—P. 1975: 169-184.
"Rain In the Heart." Taylor, Peter.—B. 1945: 283-302.
"Rainbow Pete." Hallet, Richard Matthews.—B. 1917: 307-325.
"Ramona By the Sea." McCorkle, Susannah.—P. 1975: 119-141.
"The Rat Is a Mouse." Ellson, Hal.—B. 1939: 82-93.
"Raven's Wing." Oates, Joyce Carol.—P. 1985: 183-191.
"Raziya." Weston, Christine.—P. 1944: 214-224.
"A Real American Fellow." Rayner, George Thorp.—B. 1938: 228-236.
"The Real Meaning Of the Faust Legend." Greenberg, Alvin.—B.
    1973: 119-131.
"The Real Viennese Schmaltz." Schulberg, Budd Wilson.—B. 1942:
    259-268.
"A Reasonable Facsimile." Stafford, Ann.—B. 1958: 259-280; P. 1959:
    105-128.
"Rebellion." Harnden, Ruth.—P. 1954: 151-159.
"The Record." DeJong, David Cornel.—P. 1947: 162-168.
"A Red Coat For Night." Komroff, Manuel.—B. 1935: 124-134.
"The Red Dress." Shirley, Sylvia.—B. 1947: 401-415.
"The Red Hat." Callaghan, Morley.—B. 1932: 70-75.
"The Red Mountain." Payne, Robert.—B. 1954: 252-267.
"Redbone." Carver, Ada Jack.—P. 1925: 149-169.
"Redemption." Gardner, John.—B. 1978: 248-261.
"Reginald Pomfret Skelton." Yellen, Samuel.—B. 1956: 336-350.
"Reina." Dreiser, Theodore.—B. 1923: 183-215.
"Remarks: None." Haines, William Wister.—B. 1935: 191-209.
"The Rememberer." Whitbread, Thomas.—P. 1962: 259-274.
"The Remission." Gallant, Mavis.—B. 1980: 80-118.
"The Rending." Oppenheim, James.—B. 1920: 187-197.
"The Rented Room." Johnson, Josephine W.—B. 1944: 141-163.
"Renters." Suckow, Ruth.—B. 1923: 362-384.
"Requa I." Olsen, Tillie.—B. 1971: 237-265.
"Request For Sherwood Anderson." Brookhouser, Frank.—P. 1946:
    85-90.
"The Resemblance Between a Violin Case and a Coffin." Williams,
    Tennessee.—B. 1951: 338-350.
"Rest Camp On Maui." Burdick, Eugene L.—P. 1947: 9-21.
"Rest Cure." Boyle, Kay.—B. 1931: 47-54.
"The Resting Place." LaFarge, Oliver.—B. 1955: 147-158.
"Resurgam." Zara, Louis.—B. 1940: 476-480.
"Resurrection." Lish, Gordon.—P. 1986: 105-109.
"The Resurrection and the Life." Jitro, William.—B. 1922: 232-241.
"Resurrection Of a Life." Saroyan, William.—B. 1935: 265-274.

"Retreat." Benson, Sally.—P. 1941: 93-102.
"A Return." Stiles, George.—B. 1944: 358-377.
"The Return." Anderson, Sherwood.—B. 1925: 21-38; P. 1925: 77-93.
"Return By Faith." Broderick, Francis L.—B. 1947: 1-16.
"The Return Of Service." Baumbach, Jonathan.—B. 1978: 354-362.
"The Returning." DePaola, Daniel.—B. 1965: 45-56.
"Reunion." Schumacher, Julie.—B. 1983: 201-209.
"Reunion." Vanderhaeghe, Guy.—B. 1983: 255-268.
"Revelation." O'Connor, Flannery.—P. 1965: 1-20.
"The Revenge Of Hannah Kemhuff." Walker, Alice.—B. 1974: 318-332.
"Revive Us Again." Norris, Gloria.—P. 1984: 37-49.
"Rhodes Scholar." Read, Allen.—B. 1931: 253-257.
"The Rich Brother." Wolff, Tobias.—B. 1986: 289-306.
"Rich Men." Stuart, Jesse.—B. 1940: 422-432.
"The Richard Nixon Freischütz Rag." Davenport, Guy.—P. 1976: 66-74.
"A Ride On the Short Dog." Still, James.—B. 1952: 298-304.
"Rider." Kerr, Baine.—B. 1977: 188-204.
"The Right Honorable the Strawberries." Wister, Owen.—B. 1927: 1-39.
"Ripped Off." Adams, Alice.—P. 1972: 177-185.
"The Rise Of the Proletariat." McClure, J. G.—P. 1963: 159-181.
"Risk." Dickinson, Charles.—P. 1984: 50-65.
"A River Combine—Professional." Spears, Raymond S.—P. 1924: 190-204.
"River Witch." Bradford, Roark.—P. 1928: 115-133.
"The Road Out of Axotle." Southern, Terry.—P. 1963: 120-138.
"Road To the Isles." West, Jessamyn.—B. 1949: 305-314.
"Robinson Crusoe Liebowitz." Michaels, Leonard.—P. 1971: 321-329.
"Robot." Davenport, Guy.—B. 1973: 67-98; P. 1974: 186-214.
"The Rock." Yentzen, Vurrell.—B. 1954: 396-409.
"The Roman Bath." Wheelwright, John J.—B. 1920: 312-319.
"The Romantic Sailor." Stevens, James.—B. 1928: 262-266.
"Roof Sitter." Eisenberg, Frances.—B. 1940: 37-52.
"Room In the World." Zugsmith, Leane.—B. 1937: 388-394.
"The Roomer." Williams, Joy.—P. 1966: 171-179.
"Rosa." Ozick, Cynthia.—B. 1984: 184-222; P. 1984:1-36.
"The Rosebush." Kuehn, Susan.—P. 1947: 169-180.
"Roses." Edwards, Margaret.—B. 1985: 67-83.
"Roses, Rhododrendon." Adams, Alice.—B. 1976: 1-14; P. 1976: 52-65.
"The Rotifer." Gavell, Mary Ladd.—B. 1968: 125-136.
"The Rotter." Springer, Fleta Campbell.—B. 1920: 236-265.
"Rough Strife." Schwartz, Lynn Sharon.—B. 1978: 262-281; P. 1979: 255-274.
"The Ruin Of Soul." Robinson, Leonard Wallace.—P. 1950: 233-243.
"Run, Run Away, Brother." Smith, John Campbell.—B. 1957: 305-319.
"Run, Run, Run, Run. . . ." Liebling, A. J.—B. 1946: 255-276.
"The Runners." Tabor, James.—P. 1981: 52-58.

Index Of Titles

"A Russian Idyll." Prokosch, Frederic.—B. 1938: 218-227.

"The S. S. Libertad." Lanux, Eyre De.—B. 1944: 190-196.
"The Sacred Thing." Ryan, Paul.—B. 1934: 282-284.
"A Sacrifice." Singer, Isaac Bashevis.—B. 1965: 283-289.
"Sacrifice Of Isaac." Seide, Michael.—B. 1942: 250-258.
"The Sacrifice Of the Maidens." Roberts, Elizabeth Madox.—P. 1930: 35-44.
"The Sacrificial Altar." Atherton, Gertrude.—B. 1916: 7-36.
"The Saddle." Terrett, Courtnay.—P. 1948: 250-262.
"The Safe Deposit." Singer, Isaac Bashevis.—B. 1980: 312-324.
"The St. Anthony Chorale." Rubin, Louis D., Jr.—B. 1981: 276-292.
"Saint John Of the Hershey Kisses." Cole, Tom.—P. 1970: 149-183.
"Saint Marie." Erdrich, Louise.—P. 1985: 103-115.
"St. Stephen's Green." Boyle, Kay.—P. 1981: 59-66.
"Salesmanship." Chase, Mary Ellen.—P. 1931: 121-127.
"Salutation To Spring." LeSueur, Meridel.—B. 1939: 169-182.
"The Saluting Doll." Hunt, Hamlen.—P. 1937: 111-119.
"Sam Small's Better Half." Knight, Eric.—B. 1942: 156-173.
"The Samovar." Cournos, John.—B. 1923: 170-182.
"The Sampler." Morris, Ira V.—B. 1933: 208-209.
"Samuel Blane." Dyer, Murray.—B. 1943: 56-69.
"Sand." Burnett, Wanda.—B. 1932: 44-53.
"The Sand Castle." Levin, Mary.—P. 1945: 160-171.
"The Santa Ana." Babb, Sanora.—B. 1960: 1-10.
"Sarah." Hamer, Martin J.—B. 1965: 113-123.
"Sarah Cole: A Type Of Love Story." Banks, Russell.—B. 1985: 1-23.
"The Sardillion." Enright, Elizabeth.—P. 1950: 130-137.
"Saturday Is a Poor Man's Port." Weigel, Henrietta.—B. 1957: 320-330.
"Saul Bird Says: Relate! Communicate! Liberate!" Oates, Joyce Carol.—P. 1972: 16-43.
"The Scale Room." Vukelich, George.—B. 1955: 338-348.
"Scales." Erdrich, Louise.—B. 1983: 141-154.
"The Scarecrow." Fisher, Vardis.—P. 1934: 161-168.
"The Scarlet Woman." Bromfield, Louis.—P. 1927: 25-33.
"The School." Barthelme, Donald.—B. 1975: 8-11.
"The Schreuderspitze." Helprin, Mark.—B. 1978: 72-97; P. 1978: 265-291.
"Scorn and Comfort." LaFarge, Christopher.—B. 1941: 200-220.
"Scotch Sour." Shaber, David.—P. 1973: 216-230.
"The Scout Master." Taylor, Peter.—B. 1946: 425-463.
"The Scream On 57th Street." Calisher, Hortense.—P. 1964: 141-166.
"Sea-Girls." Wheelis, Allen.—P. 1967: 189-202.
"The Search." McHugh, Vincent.—B. 1948: 213-221.
"Search For a Future." Miller, Arthur.—B. 1967: 161-174.
"Search Through the Streets Of the City." Shaw, Irwin.—B. 1942: 269-278.
"The Searchers." Kuehn, Susan.—B. 1952: 212-224.

"Seasmiles." Winslow, Anne Goodwin.—P. 1950: 306-325.

"The Season Of Divorce." Cheever, John.—B. 1951: 89-99.

"The Season Of Miss Maggie Reginald." Pierce, Phoebe.—P. 1949: 198-211.

"Seasons." McClaughlin, Ruth.—B. 1979: 157-166.

"The Seasons." Oates, Joyce Carol.—P. 1985: 254-270.

"The Second Best Girl." Buechler, James.—P. 1967: 93-104.

"Second Circle." Harris, MacDonald.—P. 1959: 165-177.

"The Second Tree From the Corner." White, E. B.—B. 1948: 341-346.

"Second Wife." Kroll, Harry Harrison.—B. 1937: 179-194.

"The Secret At the Crossroads." Mosley, Jefferson.—P. 1924: 126-141.

"The Secret Lives Of Dieters." Klass, Perri.—P. 1983: 301-309.

"A Secret Society." Nemerov, Howard.—B. 1959: 212-227.

"The Secret Weapon Of Joe Smith." Wallace, Robert.—P. 1954: 254-260.

"Secrets." Seabrooke, Deborah.—B. 1985: 206-219.

"See the Moon?" Barthelme, Donald.—P. 1967: 19-29.

"Seed." Bercovici, Konrad.—B. 1923: 81-97.

"The Self-Made Brain Surgeon." Harris, Mark.—B. 1961: 152-167.

"Señor Payroll." Barrett, William E.—B. 1944: 17-20.

"A Sense Of Danger." Deasy, Mary.—B. 1946: 147-164.

"A Sense Of Destination." Kensinger, Faye Riter.—P. 1951: 140-153.

"Sense Of Direction." Casper, Leonard.—B. 1951: 60-72; P. 1951: 46-60.

"The Sense That In the Scene Delights." DeMott, Benjamin.—B. 1954: 48-57.

"Separating." Updike, John.—P. 1976: 296-307.

"The Separation." Rottenberg, Annette T.—P. 1981: 273-288.

"September Sailing." Kittredge, Eleanor Hayden.—B. 1930: 104-123.

"Serenade." Burnett, Whit.—B. 1933: 42-53.

"A Sermon By Doctor Pep." Bellow, Saul.—B. 1950: 59-66.

"Service." Rubin, Michael.—P. 1969: 191-198.

"Seven Blocks Apart." Brush, Katharine.—B. 1928: 31-50.

"Seven Boys Take a Hill." DeJong, David Cornel.—P. 1941: 139-152.

"Seven Candles." Hurst, Fanny.—B. 1923: 277-306.

"The Seven Men Of Rouen." Slocombe, George.—B. 1940: 368-380.

"Seventy Thousand Dollars." Newhouse, Edward.—P. 1950: 196-208.

"Sex Education." Canfield, Dorothy.—B. 1947: 17-30; P. 1946: 91-102.

"Shades Of George Sand!" Taylor, Ellen DuPois.—P. 1927: 239-260.

"Shadow Of a Girl." Ashton, E. B.—B. 1941: 1-13.

"The Shadow Of an Arm." Phillips, Thomas Hal.—P. 1951: 246-255.

"Shadow Of Evil." Aswell, James.—B. 1950: 5-32.

"Shadowed." Synon, Mary.—P. 1923: 193-210.

"Shadows On the Water." Fetler, Andrew.—P. 1977: 66-86.

"Shadrach." Styron, William.—B. 1979: 56-78.

"The Shame Dance." Steele, Wilbur Daniel.—B. 1921: 337-361.

"The Shame Of Gold." Finger, Charles J.—B. 1922: 100-114.

"Shanghai Scene." Buck, Pearl S.—P. 1934: 65-70.

"Shards." Jauss, David.—P. 1983: 189-202.

"The Shawl." Ozick, Cynthia.—B. 1981: 271-275; P. 1981: 15-19.

Index Of Titles

"She Always Wanted Shoes." Ludlow, Don.—B. 1938: 171-176.
"She Did Not Cry At All." Brookhouser, Frank.—P. 1948: 49-61.
"'She Shall Have Music.'" Strong, Austin.—P. 1943: 253-262.
"She Should Have Died Hereafter." Hochstein, Rolaine.—P. 1985: 271-281.
"She Walks In Beauty." Foley, Martha.—B. 1934: 118-125.
"She Walks In Beauty." Hurst, Fanny.—B. 1921: 253-287.
"She Was Right Once." Tarkington, Booth.—P. 1932: 245-268.
"Sheener." Williams, Ben Ames.—B. 1920: 348-358.
"Shelby." Towne, Charles Hanson.—B. 1921: 386-400.
"Shelter the Pilgrim." Licht, Fred.—B. 1982: 75-92.
"Shepherd Of the Lord." Neagoe, Peter.—B. 1932: 198-215.
"Sherrel." Burnett, Whit.—B. 1932: 54-61.
"Sherry." Howard, Maureen.—B. 1965: 125-165; P. 1966: 17-56.
"Shiloh." Mason, Bobbie Ann.—B. 1981: 171-184.
"Ship Island." Spencer, Elizabeth.—P. 1966: 87-112.
"A Ship To Tarshish." Zukerman, William.—B. 1945: 362-378.
"Shirt Talk." Prashker, Ivan.—B. 1971: 266-274.
"The Shirts Off Their Backs." Shultz, William Henry.—P. 1955: 248-261.
"Shock Treatment." Stark, Irwin.—B. 1947: 433-439.
"Shoe the Horse and Shoe the Mare." Meighan, Astrid.—B. 1944: 265-272.
"Shoes." Wood, Frances Gilchrist.—B. 1924: 248-257.
"The Shorn Lamb." Stafford, Jean.—B. 1954: 293-305; P. 1954: 216-227.
"A Short Walk Into Afternoon." Hurlbut, Kaatje.—B. 1979: 44-55.
"Shower Of Ashes." White, Robin.—P. 1960: 70-85.
"The Shroud." McCleary, Dorothy.—B. 1936: 221-236.
"Shut a Final Door." Capote, Truman.—P. 1948: 1-14.
"Shy Bearers." Goldberg, Lester.—P. 1979: 74-85.
"A Sick Call." Callaghan, Morley.—B. 1933: 60-67.
"The Siege." Tucci, Niccolò.—B. 1947: 461-475.
"Siege Of Love." Joffe, Eugene.—B. 1934: 198-209.
"The Signal Tower." Camp, Wadsworth.—B. 1920: 66-82.
"The Silent Day." Greene, Mary Francis.—P. 1948: 85-96.
"Silent Grow the Guns." Kantor, MacKinlay.—P. 1935: 103-121.
"The Silent Infare." Gordon, Armistead C.—B. 1916: 133-148.
"Silent Whistle." Brace, Ernest.—P. 1936: 67-87.
"Silkie." Oates, Joyce Carol.—B. 1973: 228-237.
"The Silver Bullet." McPherson, James Alan.—B. 1973: 206-220; P. 1973: 80-95.
"A Silver Dish." Bellow, Saul.—B. 1979: 1-27; P. 1980: 11-39.
"The Silver Knight." DeFord, Miriam Allen.—P. 1930: 131-142.
"The Silver Sword." Steele, Wilbur Daniel.—P. 1929: 323-339.
"Silver Virgin." Thielen, Benedict.—P. 1939: 237-254.
"A Simple Act Of Piety." Abdullah, Achmed.—B. 1918: 3-23.
"Simple Arithmetic." Moriconi, Virginia.—B. 1964: 227-240.
"Simple Aveu." Hale, Nancy.—B. 1933: 157-160.
"A Simple Case." Dawkins, Cecil.—B. 1963: 92-108.

"Singing Eagles." Jacobs, Marguerite.—P. 1926: 153-172.
"The Singing Lesson." West, Jessamyn.—B. 1946: 525-539.
"The Singing Well." Norris, Helen.—P. 1987: 208-231.
"Singing Woman." Carver, Ada Jack.—P. 1927: 97-108.
"Single Lady." Lavin, Mary.—P. 1949: 181-197.
"Sinners." Norris, Kathleen.—P. 1929: 233-250.
"Sister." Wolff, Tobias.—P. 1985: 199-205.
"The Sisterhood." Halley, Anne.—P. 1976: 252-260.
"Six Dollars." Steele, Wilbur Daniel.—B. 1925: 228-252.
"Six Months Is No Long Time." Wilson, Leon.—P. 1949: 306-323.
"Sixteen." Daly, Maureen.—P. 1938: 163-168.
"The Sixth Shot." Derieux, Samuel A.—P. 1922: 113-123.
"The Skater." Williams, Joy.—B. 1985: 273-282.
"Skaters On Wood." Epstein, Leslie.—B. 1978: 1-25.
"The Skeleton and the Easter Lily." Breuer, Bessie.—P. 1947: 89-97.
"A Sketching Trip." Welty, Eudora.—P. 1946: 272-293.
"Skin Angels." Neely, Jessica.—B. 1986: 207-218.
"The Skylark." Mazor, Julian.—P. 1971: 94-136.
"Sled." Adams, Thomas E.—P. 1962: 217-225.
"Sleet Storm." Lambertson, Louise.—B. 1933: 173-186.
"The Slightest Distance." Bromell, Henry.—B. 1973: 6-22.
"A Slow Boat To China." Hale, Nancy.—P. 1958: 167-177.
"Slow Journey." Shirley, Sylvia.—P. 1951: 275-288.
"Slow Poison." Miller, Alice Duer.—P. 1920: 148-159.
"Slow-Motion." Schwartz, Steven.—P. 1983: 256-269.
"A Small, Good Thing." Carver, Raymond.—P. 1983: 1-25.
"Small Island Republics." Apple, Max.—B. 1981: 29-43.
"Small Miracle." Dolokhov, Adele.—B. 1949: 72-80.
"Small Sounds and Tilting Shadows." Rascoe, Judith.—P. 1972: 44-64.
"The Smallest Part." Gold, Herbert.—P. 1979: 203-212.
"Smile For the Man, Dear." Herman, Justin.—B. 1941: 154-160.
"Smoke." Faulkner, William.—B. 1932: 108-133.
"The Snake." Krause, Ervin D.—P. 1963: 17-22.
"Snake Doctor." Cobb, Ervin S.—P. 1922: 1-22.
"The Snooker Shark." Harrison, William.—B. 1968: 149-160.
"Snow." Adams, Alice.—P. 1981: 94-104.
"Snow." Phillips, Jayne Anne.—P. 1980: 209-223.
"The Snow Girl." Shelton, William R.—P. 1948: 208-220.
"The Snow Goose." Gallico, Paul.—P. 1941: 173-194.
"The Snow Owl." Brown, Morris.—B. 1956: 18-29.
"Snow-On-the-Mountain." DeJong, David Cornel.—P. 1942: 127-136.
"The Snows Of Kilimanjaro." Hemingway, Ernest.—B. 1937: 105-126.
"So I'm Not Lady Chatterly So Better I Should Know It Now." "Sara"
    [pseud.].—P. 1964: 213-225.
"So Large a Thing As Seven." Still, James.—P. 1938: 267-276.
"So Tall the Corn." DeJong, David Cornel.—B. 1932: 90-101.
"So-Long, Oldtimer." Ware, Edmund.—B. 1928: 285-296.
"Society." Olive, Jeannie.—B. 1961: 245-254.
"The Sofa." Whitlock, Brand.—P. 1925: 283-296.

"The Sojourner." McCullers, Carson.—P. 1951:192-201.
"Soldier Harmon." Callaghan, Morley.—B. 1929: 48-59.
"Soldier Of the Republic." Fineman, Morton.—P. 1944: 83-90.
"Solitaire." Springer, Fleta Campbell.—B. 1918: 232-257.
"Some Grist For Mervyn's Mill." Richler, Mordecai.—B. 1963: 246-268.
"Some Manhattan In New England." LaSalle, Peter.—B. 1979: 102-114.
"Some People Are Just Plumb Crazy." Kober, Arthur.—B. 1941: 195-199.
"The Somebody." Santiago, Danny.—B. 1971: 291-297.
"Something Jolly." McCleary, Dorothy.—B. 1940: 194-213.
"Something Just For Me." Lanning, George.—P. 1964: 167-189.
"Something That Happened." Phillips, Jayne Anne.—B. 1979: 324-329.
"Something To Explain." Turner, Thomas C.—P. 1959: 73-104.
"Sometimes You Break Even." Ullman, Victor.—P. 1946: 31-47.
"Somewhere Out Of Nowhere." McCord, Jean.—B. 1958: 168-178.
"Son." Updike, John.—B. 1974: 306-311.
"The Song." Downey, Harris.—B. 1957: 128-137.
"Song Of the Simidor." Radcliffe, Donald.—B. 1967: 211-238.
"Sonny's Blues." Baldwin, James.—B. 1958: 21-53.
"The Sons Of Martha." McKenna, Richard.—B. 1968: 215-234.
"The Sorrows Of Captain Schreiber." Stern, Richard G.—P. 1954: 228-241.
"A Sound In the Night." Herschberger, Ruth.—B. 1949: 135-148.
"Sound Of a Drunken Drummer." Blattner, H. W.—B. 1963: 15-56.
"The Sound Of Waves." Choy, Wayson S.—B. 1962: 16-31.
"The Sound Of Young Laughter." Dikeman, May.—B. 1963: 125-139.
"The Sound That Frost Makes." Barber, Solon R.—B. 1931: 24-26.
"Southern Highway 51." Wexley, John.—P. 1934: 237-242.
"Souvenir Of Arizona." Thielen, Benedict.—B. 1935: 298-305.
"The Spaniard." Pereda, Prudencio De.—B. 1938: 208-217; P. 1937: 187-196.
"Sparrows." Ziller, Eugene.—P. 1960: 266-282.
"Sparrow's Last Jump." Grennard, Elliott.—B. 1948: 124-138; P. 1948: 35-48.
"Speakeasy." Brush, Katharine.—P. 1929: 123-142.
"Speaking Of Courage." O'Brien, Tim.—P. 1978: 159-168.
"Speck's Idea." Gallant, Mavis.—B. 1980: 119-158.
"Spelling." Munro, Alice.—B. 1979: 150-156.
"The Spirit In Me." Hoffman, William.—B. 1975: 111-123.
"Splendid With Swords." Williams, Wythe.—P. 1925: 40-72.
"Sportsmen." McGuane, Thomas.—B. 1986: 150-154.
"A Spot In History." Hall, James B.—B. 1953: 154-164.
"The Spring Flight." Irwin, Inez Haynes.—P. 1924: 1-24.
"Spring Story." LeSueur, Meridel.—B. 1932: 138-152.
"The Stagecoach." Beems, Griffith.—P. 1944: 29-41.
"Standby." Grinnell, Sarah.—P. 1943: 155-163.

"The Star Blanket." Schoonover, Shirley W.—P. 1962: 99-120.

"Star Food." Canin, Ethan.—B. 1986: 48-65.

"Starlight." Thurm, Marian.—B. 1983: 236-248.

"Staus." Rishcl, Mary Ann Malinchak.—B. 1978: 363-380.

"A Stay By the River." Engberg, Susan.—P. 1977: 279-296.

"Stealing Cars." Weesner, Theodore.—B. 1972: 347-372.

"The Steinway Quintet." Epstein, Leslie.—B. 1977: 111-160.

"Stella Crozier." Tarkington, Booth.—P. 1926: 245-268.

"The Stick-In-the-Muds." Hughes, Rupert.—B. 1920: 148-168.

"Sticks and Stones." Michaels, Leonard.—P. 1966: 75-86.

"Stigmata." Oates, Joyce Carol.—P. 1964: 30-48.

"Still Of Some Use." Updike, John.—B. 1981: 312-316.

"Still, Still So." Van Doren, Mark.—B. 1953: 332-343.

"The Stone." Goodman, Henry.—B. 1919: 167-177.

"The Stone Boy." Berriault, Gina.—P. 1958: 99-110.

"The Stone Lovers." Harter, Evelyn.—P. 1971: 137-147.

"A Stop On the Way To Texas." Dorrance, Ward.—B. 1954: 58-71.

"The Storm." Stuart, Jesse.—B. 1942: 303-312.

"Storm Still." Brower, Brock.—P. 1968: 168-194.

"A Story For Teddy." Swados, Harvey.—B. 1964: 299-324.

"The Story Hearer." Paley, Grace.—P. 1984: 233-240.

"A Story In an Almost Classical Mode." Brodkey, Harold.—P. 1975: 13-60.

"The Story Of a Scar." McPherson, James Alan.—P. 1975: 283-296.

"A Story Of Love, Etc." Curley, Daniel.—B. 1964: 85-93.

"The Story Of the Stranger." Cournos, John.—B. 1932: 80-89.

"The Story Vinton Heard At Mallorie." Moseley, Katharine Prescott.—B. 1918: 191-199.

"Story Without End." Johnson, Josephine W.—B. 1946: 214-223.

"Strange-Dreaming Charlie, Cow-Eyed Charlie." Batki, John.—P. 1972: 1-15.

"The Strange-Looking Man." Johnson, Fanny Kemble.—B. 1917: 361-364.

"Stranger Things." Cram, Mildred.—P. 1921: 127-155.

"Strike Up a Stirring Music." Fleming, Berry.—B. 1944: 117-124; P. 1944: 91-99.

"Strip-tease." Weller, George.—B. 1941: 341-355.

"Struttin' With Some Barbecue." Duke, Osborn.—B. 1953: 112-126.

"The Stupendous Fortune." Portugal, Ruth.—B. 1948: 236-248.

"The Stutz and the Tub." Whittemore, Reed.—P. 1954: 287-293.

"Sublime Child." Berriault, Gina.—P. 1960: 108-118.

"Subpoena." Barthelme, Donald.—P. 1972: 265-268.

"Subway System." Shattuck, Katharine.—P. 1945: 234-241.

"Sucker." McCullers, Carson.—B. 1964: 217-226; P. 1965: 189-197.

"The Sudden Trees." Francis, H. E.—B. 1985: 96-115.

"Suffer Little Children." Bragdon, Clifford.—B. 1930: 6-20.

"Suite 2049." Benson, Sally.—P. 1936: 25-31.

"The Suitor." Woiwode, L.—B. 1971: 347-359.

"A Sum In Addition." March, William.—P. 1936: 35-38.

Index Of Titles

"A Summer Day." Stafford, Jean.—P. 1949: 262-275.
"Summer Dust." Gordon, Caroline.—B. 1930: 74-86.
"Summer Evening." Boyle, Kay.—P. 1950: 89-101.
"The Summer Game." Heller, Steve.—P. 1979: 86-100.
"A Summer In Puerto Rico." Clark, Eleanor.—B. 1974: 16-44.
"The Summer Of the Beautiful White Horse." Saroyan, William.—P. 1938: 255-263.
"The Summer People." Jackson, Shirley.—B. 1951: 144-156.
"A Summer Shower." Clemons, Walter.—P. 1958: 145-154.
"A Summer's Long Dream." Hale, Nancy.—B. 1957: 155-170.
"The Sun and the Rain." Wolfe, Thomas.—B. 1935: 313-318.
"The Sun Chaser." Marks, Jeannette.—B. 1916: 226-261.
"Sunday Liberty." Stuart, Alison.—P. 1944: 205-213.
"Sunday Lunch." Hale, Nancy.—P. 1966: 161-170.
"Sunday Morning." McCleary, Dorothy.—B. 1935: 228-240.
"Sunday Morning On Twentieth Street." Maltz, Albert.—B. 1941: 245-254.
"Sunday—1913." Hale, Nancy.—P. 1942: 171-191.
"Sunday's Children." Potter, Nancy A. J.—P. 1965: 93-101.
"Suns That Our Hearts Harden." Brown, Carlton.—B. 1935: 28-40.
"Supers." Booth, Frederick.—B. 1916: 52-57.
"Supperburger." Strong, Jonathan.—P. 1967: 31-50.
"The Supremacy Of the Hunza." Greenberg, Joanne.—B. 1972: 75-92.
"Sur." LeGuin, Ursula K.—B. 1983: 161-177.
"The Surgeon and the Nun." Horgan, Paul.—B. 1937: 142-159.
"The Surveyor." Roth, Henry.—B. 1967: 239-256.
"Surviving Adverse Seasons." Targan, Barry.—B. 1976: 274-313.
"The Survivors." Singmaster, Elsie.—B. 1915: 226-234.
"The Swamper." Edmonds, Walter D.—B. 1928: 125-149.
"The Swastika On Our Door." Adams, Alice.—P. 1973: 107-124.
"Sweet Talk." Vaughn, Stephanie.—P. 1980: 309-319.
"Swimmer In the Secret Sea." Kotzwinkle, William.—P. 1975: 350-380.
"Symphonesque." Fauset, Arthur Huff.—B. 1926: 98-113; P. 1926: 109-124.
"The System Was Doomed." Levin, Meyer.—B. 1941: 221-230.

"T. B." Hurst, Fannie.—B. 1915: 84-117.
"The Tabby Cat." Rader, Paul.—B. 1951: 286-294.
"Tabloid." Bromfield, Louis.—B. 1931: 55-69.
"Tact." Beer, Thomas.—P. 1922: 71-90.
"Take Her Up Tenderly." Norris, Hoke.—B. 1950: 328-336.
"Take the Stand, Please." Crowell, Chester T.—B. 1926: 56-70.
"Taking a Chance On Jack." Raymond, Ilene.—P. 1985: 229-237.
"Taking Care." Horne, Lewis.—P. 1987: 235-250.
"A Tale From the Grave." Morris, Ira V., Jr.—B. 1926: 220-236.
"A Tale Of Inheritance." Goyen, William.—B. 1961: 131-151.
"Talking Horse." Malamud, Bernard.—P. 1973: 35-54.
"The Talking Stick." Sorenson, Virginia.—P. 1948: 221-235.

Index Of Titles

"Tarzan Meets the Department Head." Caldwell, Price.—B. 1977: 15-23.

"The Tattoo." Oates, Joyce Carol.—P. 1978: 129-147.

"The Tea Bowl Of Ninsei Nomura." Shipley, Margaret.—B. 1969: 265-274.

"The Tea Time of Stouthearted Ladies." Stafford, Jean.—B. 1965: 313-324.

"Teacher." Gration, Gwen.—P. 1968: 116-128.

"Teachers." Katterjohn, Elsie.—P. 1936: 253-264.

"A Telephone Call." Parker, Dorothy.—B. 1928: 222-227.

"Tell Him I Waited." Fineman, Morton.—B. 1942: 105-115.

"Tell Me a Riddle." Olsen, Tillie.—B. 1961: 255-290; P. 1961: 21-57.

"Tell Me How Long the Train's Been Gone." Baldwin, James.—B. 1968: 1-28.

"Telling." Paley, Grace.—B. 1986: 241-257.

"Telling the Bees." Sinetos, L. Hluchan.—B. 1978: 292-302.

"The Temperate Zone." Enright, Elizabeth.—B. 1951: 115-120.

"The Tenant." Hudson, Helen.—B. 1968: 187-200.

"Terminal Procedure." Battin, M. Pabst.—B. 1976: 15-33.

"The Terror In the Streets." Lowry, Robert.—B. 1948: 189-199.

"The Test." Gill, Brendan.—B. 1945: 82-89.

"Thanks For Nothing." Richmond, Roaldus.—B. 1936: 251-263.

"That Blowzy Goddess Fame." Komroff, Manuel.—B. 1936: 197-202.

"That Evening Sun Go Down." Faulkner, William.—B. 1931: 104-121.

"That Fine Place We Had Last Year." Lull, Roderick.—B. 1940: 155-169.

"That Frozen Hour." DeJong, David Cornel.—B. 1942: 75-92.

"That Golden Crane." Cox, James Trammell.—P. 1963: 195-215.

"That Greek Dog." Kantor, MacKinlay.—B. 1942: 141-155.

"'That In Aleppo Once. . . .'" Nabokov, Vladimir.—B. 1944: 285-294.

"That Lovely Green Boat." Berge, Bill.—B. 1952: 1-17.

"That Will Be Fine." Faulkner, William.—B. 1936: 87-105.

"That Woman." Hale, Nancy.—P. 1940: 119-143.

"That's My Brother." Hope, Marjorie.—P. 1940: 100-108.

"That's My Johnny-Boy." Clay, George R.—B. 1948: 57-72.

"That's the Man!" Post, Mary Brinker.—B. 1948: 249-265.

"That's What Happened To Me." Fessier, Michael.—B. 1936: 106-112.

"The Theft." Hudson, Helen.—P. 1976: 141-152.

"Theft." Oates, Joyce Carol.—B. 1982: 311-358.

"Theft." Porter, Katherine Anne.—B. 1930: 171-176.

"Their Losses." Taylor, Peter.—P. 1950: 273-286.

"Their Name Is Macaroni." Boyle, Kay.—P. 1942: 91-102.

"Then Christs Fought Hard." Krunich, Milutin.—B. 1926: 171-184.

"Then We Were Three." Shaw, Irwin.—P. 1957: 199-221.

"Theo's Girl." Willard, Nancy.—P. 1970: 219-235.

"There." Taylor, Peter.—B. 1965: 345-370; P. 1965: 125-148.

"'There's Money In Poetry.'" Bercovici, Konrad.—B. 1929: 38-47.

"They Grind Exceeding Small." Williams, Ben Ames.—P. 1919: 42-55.

"A Thing Of Beauty." Lieberman, Elias.—B. 1919: 305-311.

"The Thing They Loved." "Rutledge, Marice" [pseud.].—P. 1920: 223-247.

"The Things." Gardner, John.—P. 1974: 105-116.

"Things Changed." Sunwall, Betty.—P. 1957: 222-235.

"Things To Be Thrown Away." Penner, Jonathan.—B. 1984: 238-242.

"The Third Count." Fetler, Andrew.—P. 1984: 139-160.

"The Third Guest." Traven, B.—B. 1954: 328-362.

"This Healthy Life." Baum, Vicki.—B. 1943: 1-9.

"This Heavy Load." March, William.—B. 1934: 257-266.

"This Is a Love Story." Zugsmith, Leane.—B. 1945: 356-361.

"This Morning, This Evening, So Soon." Baldwin, James.—B. 1961: 1-40.

"This Town and Salamanca." Seager, Allan.—B. 1935: 275-284.

"Thomas Hardy's Meat." Weidman, Jerome.—P. 1937: 283-291.

"Thompson." Zorn, George A.—P. 1964: 190-212.

"Thoreau In California." Ludwig, Jack.—P. 1961: 209-245.

"Thorofare." Minot, Susan.—B. 1984: 150-160.

"Those Are As Brothers." Hale, Nancy.—B. 1942: 129-140; P. 1941: 197-209.

"The Thousand-Yard Stare." Martin, Hansford.—P. 1945: 172-182.

"The Three Aspects." LaFarge, Christopher.—P. 1948: 148-156.

"Three Lumps Of Sugar." Hare, Amory.—B. 1927: 118-122.

"Three Players Of a Summer Game." Williams, Tennessee.—B. 1953: 363-383.

"The Three Swimmers and the Educated Grocer." Saroyan, William.—B. 1941: 269-279; P. 1940: 257-268.

"The Three Telegrams." Storm, Ethel.—B. 1920: 293-311.

"Three Thousand Dollars." Lipsky, David.—B. 1986: 136-149.

"Three Washington Stories." Just, Ward.—B. 1972: 153-179.

"The Threesome." Ansell, Helen Essary.—P. 1963: 182-194.

"Threnody For Stelios." Gray, Peter.—B. 1943: 135-143.

"The Threshing Ring." Ward, Leo L.—B. 1931: 283-297.

"The Thrice Bereft Widow Of Hung Gow." Dobie, Charles Caldwell.—P. 1926: 91-108.

"Thrift." Faulkner, William.—P. 1931: 153-169.

"The Thunderstorm." Thielen, Benedict.—B. 1939: 283-291.

"Tib's Eve." Currie, Ellen.—P. 1959: 136-149.

"The Tide and Isaac Bates." Minot, Stephen.—B. 1974: 167-178.

"Tide Pools." Adams, Alice.—P. 1987: 65-80.

"The Tie That Binds." Pattullo, George.—P. 1924: 142-154.

"The Tiger." Buechner, Frederick.—P. 1955: 53-61.

"Time and Ebb." Nabokov, Vladimir.—B. 1946: 292-301.

"Time's End." Gibbons, Robert.—B. 1943: 122-134.

"Tinkle and Family Take a Ride." Kelm, Karlton.—B. 1936: 191-196.

"Tip On a Dead Jockey." Shaw, Irwin.—B. 1955: 249-281.

"Titty's Dead and Tatty Weeps." MacDougall, Ursula.—B. 1937: 200-206.

"To a Tenor Dying Old." Carter, John Stewart.—B. 1964: 27-84.

"To Be an Athlete." Corfman, Eunice Luccock.—P. 1969: 147-167.

"To Endure." Granat, Robert.—P. 1960: 183-190.

"'To Hell the Rabbis.'" Maddow, Ben.—B. 1962: 235-245.

"To See You Again." Adams, Alice.—P. 1982: 301-311.

"To the Bitter End." Hallet, Richard Matthews.—B. 1919: 178-199.

"To the Invader." Hale, Nancy.—P. 1933: 63-71.

"To the Least. . . ." Exall, Henry.—B. 1941: 59-73.

"To the Mountains." Horgan, Paul.—B. 1939: 109-138.

"To the North." Hale, Nancy.—P. 1937: 77-98.

"To the Open Water." Ford, Jesse Hill.—P. 1966: 225-233.

"To the Wilderness I Wander." Butler, Frank.—B. 1957: 39-69.

"To Those Who Wait." Moll, Elick.—B. 1938: 198-207; P. 1937: 21-31.

"Toadstools Are Poison." Bishop, John Peale.—B. 1933: 21-29.

"The Toast To Forty-Five." Pelley, William Dudley.—B. 1918: 200-222.

"The Today Tomorrow." Montague, Margaret Prescott.—B. 1923: 307-321.

"Today Will Be a Quiet Day." Hempel, Amy.—B. 1986: 113-119.

"The Token." Hergesheimer, Joseph.—B. 1922: 203-231.

"Tom." Lavin, Mary.—B. 1974: 95-111.

"Tom Rivers." Gordon, Caroline.—B. 1934: 133-151.

"Tonight At Nine Thirty-Six." Gillespie, Alfred.—B. 1970: 115-137.

"Too Young To Have a Gun." Lowrey, P. H.—P. 1954: 167-179.

"A Tooth For Paul Revere." Benét, Stephen Vincent.—B. 1938: 59-73.

"Torrent Of Darkness." Field, S. S.—B. 1936: 113-133.

"Total Stranger." Cozzens, James Gould.—P. 1936: 3-21.

"Towers Of Fame." Folsom, Elizabeth Irons.—P. 1923: 38-45.

"The Town Mouse." Becker, Stephen.—B. 1953: 41-52.

"Tradition." Nemerov, Howard.—P. 1956: 221-236.

"The Tragedy In Jancie Brierman's Life." Sharp, Dolph.—B. 1948: 274-293.

"Transactions In a Foreign Currency." Eisenberg, Deborah.—P. 1986: 130-151.

"The Transient." Elkin, Stanley.—B. 1965: 57-91.

"The Translation." Oates, Joyce Carol.—B. 1978: 26-45.

"Travel Stories." Bromell, Henry.—P. 1979: 35-56.

"The Traveler." Stegner, Wallace.—B. 1952: 289-297.

"Travelin Man." Matthiessen, Peter.—P. 1958: 293-309.

"Traveling Salesman." Thomas, Elisabeth Wilkins.—B. 1936: 282-292.

"Travelling." Peterson, Mary.—P. 1979: 299-308.

"Travelogue." Lardner, Ring W.—B. 1926: 185-196.

"The Treasure." Lumpkin, Grace.—P. 1940: 169-177.

"Treat You Clever." Chapman, Mariston.—P. 1929: 145-161.

"A Tree. A Rock. A Cloud." McCullers, Carson.—P. 1943: 223-231.

"Treeshy." Carver, Ada Jack.—P. 1926: 47-68.

"Trepleff." Harris, MacDonald.—B. 1967: 85-100.

"Trespasser." Johnson, Curt.—P. 1973: 231-242.

"The Trial In Tom Belcher's Store." Derieux, Samuel A.—P. 1919: 192-209.

"Triall By Armes." Hergesheimer, Joseph.—B. 1927: 123-141.

"The Tribute." Kniffin, Harry Anable.—P. 1921: 229-233.

Index Of Titles

"Trip In a Summer Dress." Sanford, Annette.—B. 1979: 206-213.
"A Trip To Czardis." Granberry, Edwin.—P. 1932: 39-46.
"Triple Jumps." Cooke, Charles.—B. 1935: 125-134.
"Triumph Of Justice." Shaw, Irwin.—B. 1941: 280-292.
"Troop Withdrawal—The Initial Step." Parker, Thomas.—P. 1971: 148-167.
"The Trouble." Powers, J. F.—P. 1945: 202-214.
"The Trouble Of Marcie Flint." Cheever, John.—P. 1959: 289-305.
"The Trouble With Being Good." Busch, Frederick.—B. 1977: 1-14.
"Troy Street." Hemenway, Robert.—P. 1974: 138-154.
"True Believer." Jenison, Madge.—B. 1939: 139-158.
"The Trumpeter Swan." Enright, Elizabeth.—P. 1949: 150-161.
"The Trunk." Horgan, Paul.—P. 1936: 245-250.
"Truth Or Consequences." Adams, Alice.—P. 1980: 345-357.
"Turista." Guérard, Albert J.—B. 1947: 125-140.
"Turkey Hunt." Hannum, Alberta Pierson.—B. 1938: 146-152.
"Turkey Red." Wood, Frances Gilchrist.—B. 1920: 359-373; P. 1919: 105-119.
"Turn About." Faulkner, William.—P. 1932: 165-192.
"Turn Ever So Quickly." Andersen, U. S.—B. 1963: 1-14.
"Twenty Below, At the End Of a Lane." Molloy, Ruth Branning.—B. 1956: 249-263.
"Twilight In Southern California." Fuchs, Daniel.—P. 1955: 173-189.
"Twilight Of the God." Vorse, Mary Heaton.—P. 1922: 250-260.
"Twin Bed Bridge." Hecht, Florence M.—P. 1971: 1-27.
"The Two Deaths Of Kaspar Rausch." Storm, Hans Otto.—B. 1940: 387-421.
"Two For a Cent." Fitzgerald, F. Scott.—B. 1922: 115-131.
"Two Heroes." Brecht, Harold W.—P. 1925: 130-148.
"Two Men Free." Burnett, Whit.—B. 1930: 21-33.
"Two Red-Haired Women." Marquis, Don.—P. 1929: 205-229.
"Two Rivers." Stegner, Wallace.—P. 1942: 33-48.
"Two Scenes." Bowles, Jane.—B. 1978: 310-315.
"Two Soldiers." Faulkner, William.—P. 1942: 139-158.
"Two Women and Hog-Back Ridge." Van Den Bark, Melvin.—B. 1924: 211-227.
"Two Words Are a Story." Hall, Elizabeth.—B. 1936: 169-183.
"Tyranny." DeJenkins, Lyll Becerra.—B. 1975: 69-79.

"Unbelievable Characters." Nemerov, Howard.—B. 1960: 245-261.
"The Unborn Ghosts." Cardozo, Nancy.—B. 1952: 71-85.
"Uncle George and Uncle Stefan." Meinke, Peter.—B. 1986: 70-79.
"The Undefeated." Hemingway, Ernest.—B. 1926: 127-155.
"Under a Wine-Glass." LaMotte, Ellen N.—B. 1919: 297-304.
"Under the Dome." Frank, Waldo.—B. 1921: 130-141.
"Under the Ginkgo Trees." Heth, Edward Harris.—B. 1947: 208-220.
"Under the Ridge." Hemingway, Ernest.—B. 1940: 109-122.
"Under the Rose." Pynchon, Thomas.—P. 1962: 49-78.
"Under the Sky." Bowles, Paul.—B. 1949: 48-54.

Index Of Titles

"Understand What I Mean?" Gerry, Bill.—B. 1945: 71-81; P. 1945: 105-115.

"The Undertow." Davis, Wesley Ford.—B. 1956: 76-89.

"Undeveloped Photographs." Schell, Jessie.—P. 1978: 169-185.

"The Unfaithful." Cook, Whitfield.—P. 1943: 143-152.

"The Unhappy Hunting Grounds." Eastlake, William.—B. 1957: 138-154.

"Unknown Feathers." Benedict, Dianne.—B. 1984: 19-34.

"An Unknown Warrior." Boogher, Susan M.—B. 1922: 42-48.

"Unmailed, Unwritten Letters." Oates, Joyce Carol.—P. 1970: 253-274.

"The Unpopular Passenger." Bingham, Robert.—P. 1955: 62-67.

"Unshapely Things." Hackett, Francis.—P. 1925: 183-191.

"Untitled Story." Villa, José Garcia.—B. 1932: 253-263.

"Up From Slavery." Larson, Charles R.—P. 1971: 300-320.

"Up Home." Wallace, Warren.—P. 1987: 251-273.

"Up the Road a Piece." Harris, Ruth McCoy.—B. 1947: 171-188.

"Upon the Sweeping Flood." Oates, Joyce Carol.—B. 1964: 241-256.

"The Upper and the Lower Millstone." Henson, Robert.—P. 1978: 41-66.

"The Urge." Allen, Maryland.—P. 1921: 45-65.

"Uriah's Son." Benét, Stephen Vincent.—P. 1924: 53-70.

"Useless." Ryerson, Florence, and Colin Clements.—P. 1931: 255-275.

"Usurpation (Other People's Stories)." Ozick, Cynthia.—P. 1975: 61-98.

"The Vacation." Biddle, Livingston, Jr.—B. 1949: 19-38.

"The Vacation." Porter, Joe Ashby.—B. 1972: 290-308.

"Vacia." Macdonald, Agnes.—B. 1949: 193-204.

"The Valet Of the Splendide." Bemelmans, Ludwig.—B. 1942: 19-27.

"The Valiant Woman." Powers, J. F.—P. 1947: 194-203.

"The Valley Of the Shadow." Brown, T. K., III.—B. 1946: 74-86.

"The Value Of the Dollar." Gordon, Ethel Edison.—B. 1951: 128-138.

"The Vault." Mabry, T. D.—B. 1949: 179-192.

"Vega." Cheever, John.—P. 1950: 102-118.

"Vengeance Is Mine." Jordan, Virgil.—B. 1915: 145-152.

"The Venus." Williams, William Carlos.—B. 1929: 256-264.

"Venus, Cupid, Folly and Time." Taylor, Peter.—B. 1959: 311-339; P. 1959: 15-45.

"Verlie I Say Unto You." Adams, Alice.—P. 1975: 99-110.

"Verona: A Young Woman Speaks." Brodkey, Harold.—B. 1978: 65-71; P. 1978: 238-244.

"Very Sharp For Jagging." Clay, Richard.—P. 1954: 67-91.

"The Vestibule." Hurlbut, Kaatje.—B. 1961: 168-182.

"The Veterans Reflect." Shaw, Irwin.—B. 1944: 345-357.

"Via Negativa." Salter, James.—P. 1974: 117-125.

"The Vicar-General and the Wide Night." Downey, Harris.—B. 1966: 35-57.

"The Victim Of His Vision." Chittenden, Gerald.—P. 1921: 84-112.

"Victrola." Morris, Wright.—B. 1983: 191-200; P. 1983: 80-89.

Index Of Titles

"Vienna Roast." Brecht, Harold W.—B. 1927: 59-71.
"A View Of the Woods." O'Connor, Flannery.—B. 1958: 192-212; P. 1959: 234-256.
"The Village." Pitzen, Jim.—P. 1987: 132-143.
"The Vindication Of Dr. Nestor." Myers, E. Lucas.—B. 1962: 297-323.
"Vinelands's Burning." Justice, Donald.—P. 1954: 160-166.
"The Vineyard At Schloss Ramsburg." Upson, William Hazlett.—B. 1930: 177-200.
"Vision In the Sea." Caldwell, Ronald.—B. 1939: 16-24.
"A Vision Of the World." Cheever, John.—B. 1963: 83-91.
"The Visit." Coatsworth, Elizabeth.—P. 1936: 107-109.
"The Visit." Logan, Andy.—P. 1941: 49-57.
"The Visit." Spencer, Elizabeth.—B. 1965: 299-311.
"The Visit Of the Master." Johnson, Arthur.—B. 1918: 131-148.
"The Visitation." Pansing, Nancy Pelletier.—B. 1969: 213-232.
"Visiting the Point." Molyneux, Thomas W.—P. 1979: 133-149.
"Visitor From Philadelphia." Clayton, John Bell.—B. 1948: 73-77.
"The Voice Of the Turtle." Draper, Edythe Squier.—B. 1930: 46-53.
"The Voyage Out." Callaghan, Morley.—B. 1937: 23-28.

"The Wager." Glenn, Isa Urquhart.—P. 1923: 75-91.
"The Waiting." Agee, James.—B. 1958: 1-20.
"Waiting At Dachau." Price, Reynolds.—P. 1971: 67-93.
"Waiting For Astronauts." Chaikin, Nancy.—B. 1975: 47-58.
"Waiting For Jim." Randal, Vera.—B. 1964: 285-297.
"The Waiting Years." Roof, Katharine Metcalf.—B. 1915: 197-218.
"The Wake." Byrne, Donn.—B. 1915: 35-45.
"A Walk With Raschid." Jacobsen, Josephine.—P. 1973: 201-215.
"Walking, Walking." Flythe, Starkey.—B. 1985: 84-95.
"Walking Wounded." Gerald, John Bart.—B. 1969: 37-48.
"Walking Wounded." Shaw, Irwin.—P. 1944: 1-18.
"A Wallow Of the Sea." Vorse, Mary Heaton.—B. 1921: 401-417.
"The Waltz Dream." Reid, Barbara.—P. 1981: 217-238.
"The Wanton Troopers." Steele, Max.—P. 1955: 262-277.
"War Front: Louisiana." Gordon, Ethel Edison.—P. 1945: 116-124.
"The War In the Air." Cassill, R. V.—P. 1954: 51-66.
"A War Marriage." Rowell, Donna.—B. 1945: 205-221.
"The Warlock." Stafford, Jean.—P. 1957: 83-106.
"Warm River." Caldwell, Erskine.—B. 1932: 62-69.
"The Warrior Princess Ozimba." Price, Reynolds.—P. 1962: 251-257.
"Wash." Faulkner, William.—P. 1934: 143-157.
"Wash Far Away." Berryman, John.—P. 1976: 230-251.
"The Watchman." Van Doren, Mark.—P. 1949: 17-29.
"Water." Santee, Ross.—P. 1935: 205-208.
"Water Never Hurt a Man." Edmonds, Walter D.—B. 1931: 95-103.
"The Water-Hole." Burt, Maxwell Struthers.—B. 1915: 15-34.
"Waves Of Darkness." Meyer, Cord, Jr.—P. 1946: 48-64.
"Waxing Wroth." Kurtz, M. R.—P. 1967: 147-158.
"The Way Death Comes." Pereda, Prudencio De.—B. 1940: 285-295.

"Way For a Sailor." Adams, Bill.—B. 1923: 3-29.
"The Way Of the Transgressor." Coates, Grace Stone.—B. 1930: 39-45.
"The Way the Luck Runs." Wolfert, Ira.—B. 1939: 336-352.
"The Way We Went." Knight, Wallace E.—B. 1973: 180-194.
"The Weaver Who Clad the Summer." Lyon, Harris Merton.—B. 1915: 153-171.
"The Wedding: Beacon Hill." Stafford, Jean.—B. 1945: 257-271.
"The Wedding Week." Brown, Rosellen.—B. 1979: 79-83.
"The Wedding-Jest." Cabell, James Branch.—B. 1919: 108-122.
"A Week Of Roses." Wesely, Donald.—B. 1953: 344-352.
"Weekend At Grimsby." Gellhorn, Martha.—B. 1952: 160-180.
"Welcome Home." Parsons, Elizabeth.—P. 1948: 186-193.
"We're All Guests." Clay, George R.—B. 1956: 30-63.
"The Whale and the Grasshopper." O'Brien, Seumas.—B. 1915: 189-195.
"What a Darling Little Boy!" Knight, Ruth Adams.—P. 1944: 116-123.
"What a Thing, To Keep a Wolf In a Cage!" Calisher, Hortense.—P. 1958: 47-62.
"What a World, Said the Bicycle Rider." Saroyan, William.—B. 1963: 269-279.
"What Do You Mean—Americans?" Steele, Wilbur Daniel.—P. 1924: 205-224.
"What Do You See, Dear Enid?" Flandrau, Grace.—B. 1943: 115-121.
"What Feels Like the World." Bausch, Richard.—P. 1987: 144-159.
"What Hurts Is That I Was in a Hurry." Cherkasski, Vladimir.—B. 1938: 100-109.
"What I Wish (Oh I Wish) I Had Said." Cavanaugh, Arthur.—P. 1965: 233-247.
"What Is a Miracle?" Komroff, Manuel.—B. 1939: 159-168.
"What Is It?" Carver, Raymond.—P. 1973: 147-155.
"What Kind Of a Man Cuts His Finger Off?" Hochstein, Rolaine.—P. 1974: 155-166.
"What Was Truly Mine." Flandrau, Grace.—B. 1933: 133-139.
"What We Don't Know Hurts Us." Schorer, Mark.—B. 1947: 350-365; P. 1947: 204-217.
"What We Have Missed." Hardwick, Elizabeth.—P. 1946: 123-132.
"What's In a Corner." Horton, Philip.—B. 1952: 204-211.
"Wheat Closed Higher, Cotton Was Mixed." Epstein, Seymour.—B. 1962: 81-95.
"Wheels." Greenwald, Tupper.—B. 1926: 120-126.
"When Old Age Shall This Generation Waste." Cassill, R. V.—P. 1957: 245-261.
"'When Spring Brings Back. . . .'" Shenton, Edward.—P. 1935: 219-226.
"When the Lord Calls." Norris, Gloria.—P. 1983: 157-174.
"Where Are You Going, Where Have You Been?" Oates, Joyce Carol.—B. 1967: 193-210; P. 1968: 296-313.
"Where Did Yesterday Go?" Angoff, Charles.—B. 1950: 1-4.
"Where I'm Calling From" Carver, Raymond.—B. 1983: 68-83.

"Where It Happens." Hopper, James.—B. 1927: 158-168.
"The Whipping." Noland, Felix.—B. 1953: 227-238.
"Whip-Poor-Willie." Stuart, Jesse.—P. 1937: 225-240.
"Whistle and the Heroes." Wilner, Herbert.—P. 1954: 294-307.
"White Anglo-Saxon Protestant." Hazel, Robert.—B. 1967: 101-134.
"The White Battalion." Wood, Frances Gilchrist.—B. 1918: 325-332.
"The White Boat." Alexander, Sidney.—B. 1944: 1-16.
"White Boy." Goodman, Ivy.—P. 1982: 186-195.
"The White Bull." King, Mary.—B. 1941: 174-194.
"The White Camel." Wright, Eugene.—B. 1939: 353-373.
"The White Circle." Clayton, John Bell.—P. 1947: 1-8.
"White For the Living." Smith, Margarita G.—P. 1943: 245-250.
"The White Horses Of Vienna." Boyle, Kay.—P. 1935: 3-20.
"The White Hound." Dorrance, Ward.—B. 1949: 81-93; P. 1949: 30-42.
"White Man's Town." Wimberly, Lowry Charles.—B. 1931: 303-314.
"The White Pigeon." Paulding, Gouverneur.—B. 1930: 158-161.
"Who Is Harry Kellerman and Why is He Saying Those Terrible
    Things About Me?" Gardner, Herb.—B. 1968: 79-100.
"Who Lived and Died Believing." Hale, Nancy.—B. 1943: 144-165; P.
    1943: 181-200.
"Who Too Was a Soldier." Smith, John Campbell.—P. 1951: 289-298.
"Who Was Jesse's Friend and Protector?" Taylor, Peter.—B. 1960:
    334-353.
"The Whole World Is Outside." Komroff, Manuel.—B. 1938: 153-159.
"The Whole World Knows." Welty, Eudora.—B. 1948: 321-340; P. 1947:
    257-275.
"Whose Dog——?" Gregg, Frances.—B. 1915: 77-79.
"Why I Quit the Gowanus Liberation Front." Brown, Rosellen.—P.
    1976: 261-276.
"Why Were You Sent Out Here?" Hersey, John.—B. 1948: 148-156.
"The Wide Net." Welty, Eudora.—P. 1942: 3-30.
"The Widow, Bereft." Blake, James.—B. 1971: 24-66.
"A Wife Of Nashville." Taylor, Peter.—B. 1950: 407-431.
"Wife-Wooing." Updike, John.—P. 1961: 326-330.
"Wild Earth." Kerr, Sophie.—P. 1921: 193-228.
"The Wild Flower." Babb, Sanora.—B. 1950: 33-41.
"The Wild Horses." Boyle, Kay.—B. 1967: 25-36.
"Wild Nigger." Godschaux, Elma.—B. 1935: 168-181.
"Wild Plums." Coates, Grace Stone.—B. 1929: 86-91.
"Will You Please Be Quiet, Please?" Carver, Raymond.—B. 1967:
    37-66.
"The Willow Walk." Lewis, Sinclair.—B. 1918: 154-190.
"Willum's Vanilla." Babcock, Edwina Stanton.—B. 1919: 34-64.
"The Wind and the Snow Of Winter." Clark, Walter Van Tilburg.—B.
    1946: 110-127; P. 1945: 1-14.
"The Wind Is Blind." Ingles, James Wesley.—P. 1948: 125-135.
"The Windmill Man." McCarthy, Tim.—B. 1978: 282-291.
"The Window." Wilson, Ethel.—B. 1959: 381-394.
"Windwagon Smith." Schramm, Wilbur L.—P. 1941: 51-71.

"Wings For Janie." Rice, Laverne.—P. 1931: 239-251.

"Winkelburg." Hecht, Ben.—B. 1922: 195-202.

"Winter." McCleary, Dorothy.—B. 1934: 224-246.

"The Winter Father." Dubus, Andre.—B. 1981: 129-149.

"Winter Meeting." Appel, Benjamin.—B. 1934: 3-14.

"Winter Night." Boyle, Kay.—P. 1946: 74-84.

"Winter: 1978." Beattie, Ann.—B. 1981: 44-76.

"Winter Term." Bingham, Sallie.—B. 1959: 15-25.

"The Wishbone." Macauley, Robie.—B. 1951: 228-252.

"Wissler Remembers." Stern, Richard.—B. 1981: 293-302.

"The Witch." Gold, Herbert.—P. 1954: 133-141.

"Witch Chicken." Sandburg, Helga.—P. 1959: 178-193.

"Witch Mary." Larsson, Genevieve.—P. 1923: 104-119.

"With All Flags Flying." Tyler, Anne.—P. 1972: 116-126.

"With Ché At Kitty Hawk." Banks, Russell.—P. 1975: 297-315.

"With Ché In New Hampshire." Banks, Russell.—B. 1971: 1-9.

"With Glory and Honour." Chapman, Elisabeth Cobb.—P. 1927: 109-125.

"With No Breeze." Cady, Jack.—B. 1970: 1-19.

"With Some Gaiety and Laughter." Kelly, Frank K.—B. 1936: 184-190.

"Without Hal." Brooks, Roy Patchen.—P. 1940: 73-83.

"The Woman Across the Street." Dikeman, May.—B. 1964: 95-107.

"A Woman Like Dilsie." Thibault, David.—P. 1937: 243-265.

"A Woman Of Her Age." Ludwig, Jack.—P. 1965: 213-231.

"The Woman On the Shore." Childs, Marquis W.—B. 1934: 52-66.

"The Woman Who Thought Like a Man." Newman, Charles.—B. 1977: 222-234.

"The Woman Who Was Loved." Stern, James.—B. 1946: 400-418.

"The Women." Sullivan, Richard.—B. 1943: 345-359.

"The Women In a Roman Courtyard." Hallinan, Nancy.—P. 1980: 41-55.

"The Women On the Wall." Stegner, Wallace.—B. 1947: 440-460.

"The Women Who Walk." Packer, Nancy Huddleston.—P. 1981: 67-80.

"Wondermonger." Rothschild, Michael.—B. 1976: 220-273.

"Wood." Munro, Alice.—B. 1981: 241-254.

"Wood Smoke." Chidester, Ann.—B. 1952: 97-107.

"Words Without Music." Seide, Michael.—B. 1940: 344-356.

"Words Words Words." Elliott, George P.—B. 1960: 29-43.

"Work." Plante, David.—P. 1983: 320-336.

"A Working Day." Coover, Robert.—B. 1981: 77-109.

"The Workmanship Has To Be Wasted." Laing, Alexander.—P. 1942: 219-227.

"Workout On the River." Shattuck, Roger.—B. 1953: 279-294.

"The World Outside." Maier, Howard.—B. 1950: 301-307.

"The World War I Los Angeles Airplane." Brautigan, Richard.—B. 1972: 16-19.

"World's End." Theroux, Paul.—P. 1981: 289-300.

"A Worn Path." Welty, Eudora.—P. 1941: 17-27.

"The Wounded." Putman, Clay.—P. 1950: 220-232.

Index Of Titles

"A Wreath For Miss Totten." Calisher, Hortense.—B. 1952: 61-70.
"The Wreck Job." Detzer, Karl W.—P. 1926: 69-90.
"The Wrists On the Door." Fish, Horace.—B. 1919: 123-146.
"A Writer Interviews a Banker." Mamet, Louis.—P. 1935: 141-149.
"The Writer-Upward." Terhune, Albert Payson.—P. 1922: 234-249.
"The Wrong Man." Klein, Norma.—P. 1974: 175-185.

"Xavier Fereira's Unfinished Book: Chapter One." Strong,
    Jonathan.—B. 1971: 298-315.
"Xmas." Disch, Thomas M.—P. 1979: 309-318.

"Yankee Odyssey." Shuman, John Rogers.—B. 1942: 241-256.
"Yarbwoman." Lane, Rose Wilder.—B. 1927: 181-201.
"The Year Of the Hot Jock." Faust, Irvin.—P. 1986: 208-225.
"The Yellow Beret." Lavin, Mary.—B. 1961; 191-206.
"The Yellow Cat." Steele, Wilbur Daniel.—B. 1915: 235-256.
"Yellowstone Park." McCarthy, Mary.—P. 1957: 292-309.
"Yiddish In America." Ozick, Cynthia.—B. 1970: 236-287.
"Yoneko's Earthquake." Yamamoto, Hisaye.—B. 1952: 361-371.
"The Yoodeler." Stuart, Alison.—P. 1942: 275-297.
"Yore." Nemerov, Howard.—B. 1955: 219-229.
"You Can Get Just So Much Justice." Rice, John Andrew.—P. 1949:
    225-248.
"You Can Wreck It." Elder, Walter.—P. 1947: 124-142.
"You Could Look It Up." Thurber, James.—B. 1942: 355-371.
"You, Johann Sebastian Bach." Maddow, Ben.—P. 1969: 209-236.
"Young Man In an Astrakhan Cap." Morris, Edita.—B. 1943: 256-270.
"The Young Men Go Down." Hervey, Harry.—B. 1924: 110-118.
"The Young Priest." Callaghan, Morley.—B. 1931: 88-94.
"Your General Does Not Sleep." Lussu, Emilio.—B. 1940: 170-193.
"Your Lover Just Called." Updike, John.—P. 1968: 259-266.
"Your Place Is Empty." Tyler, Anne.—B. 1977: 317-337.
"You've Come a Long Way, Mickey Mouse." Jafek, Bev.—B. 1985:
    116-125.

"Zelig." Rosenblatt, Benjamin.—B. 1915: 219-225.

Collections from the Volumes

Fifty Best American Stories 1915-1939. Edited By Edward J. O'Brien. Boston: Houghton Mifflin Company, 1939.

The Best Of the Best American Short Stories 1915-1952. Edited By Martha Foley. Boston: Houghton Mifflin Company, 1952.

Fifty Best American Short Stories 1915-1965. Edited By Martha Foley. Boston: Houghton Mifflin Company, 1965.

First Prize Stories, 1919-1966, From the O. Henry Memorial Awards. Introduction By Harry Hansen. Garden City: Doubleday & Company, 1966.

Fifty Years Of the American Short Story: From the O. Henry Awards 1919-1970. Edited By William Abrahams. Garden City: Doubleday & Company, 1970.

Prize Stories Of the Seventies: From the O. Henry Awards. Edited By William Abrahams. Garden City: Doubleday & Company, 1981.